Sport in Prison

Although prison can present a critical opportunity to engage with offenders through interventions and programming, reoffending rates among those released from prison remain high. Sport can be a means through which to engage with even the most challenging and complex individuals caught up in a cycle of offending and imprisonment, by offering an alternative means of excitement and risk taking to that gained through engaging in offending behaviour, or by providing an alternative social network and access to positive role models.

This is the first book to explore the role of sport in prisons and its subsequent impact on rehabilitation and behavioural change. The book draws on research literature on the beneficial role of sport in community settings and on prison cultures and regimes across disciplines including criminology, psychology, sociology and sport studies, as well as original qualitative and quantitative data gathered from research in prisons. It unpacks the meanings that prisoners and staff attach to sport participation and interventions in order to understand how to promote behavioural change through sport most effectively, while identifying and tackling the key emerging issues and challenges.

Sport in Prison is essential reading for any advanced student, researcher, policy maker or professional working in the criminal justice system with an interest in prisons, offending behaviour, rehabilitation, sport development or the wider social significance of sport.

Rosie Meek is a chartered psychologist and Head of Criminology and Sociology at Royal Holloway University of London, UK. She is a Fulbright Distinguished Scholar and holds honorary visiting appointments at John Jay College of Criminal Justice, New York, US and the Institute of Criminology at the University of Cambridge, UK.

Routledge research in sport, culture and society

'Bridging literature from diverse fields, and combining theoretical insight with an unusually broad range of empirical sources, Rosie Meek has provided a vital analysis of the history, role and potential benefits of sports and physical activity in prisons. *Sport in Prison* is a groundbreaking and well-grounded book and it deserves a wide readership.'

Dr Ben Crewe, University of Cambridge,
Institute of Criminology, UK

'With an abundance of negative information about prison cultures, Sport in Prisons is a refreshing look at how even simple programs such as physical education can make a positive difference for staff and residents of these institutions. Dr. Meek makes a compelling case to invest in sports programs in prisons while also providing critical knowledge about organizational and other barriers to implementing these changes. Given the rampant problems associated with prisons worldwide, this book will most certainly appeal to an international audience.'

Associate Professor Laura S. Abrams, UCLA,
Luskin School of Public Affairs, USA

'There is a dangerous, tabloid-led movement afoot in the UK that seeks to reduce prisoner gym access and involvement in sport. Meek's thoughtful, rigorous analysis of the impacts of such activities on prisoners and prison climates is precisely what is needed to combat such blatant stupidity. It should be widely read by those genuinely interested in a rehabilitation revolution.'

Professor Shadd Maruna, Institute of Criminology
and Criminal Justice, Queen's University Belfast,
N. Ireland

Sport in Prison

Exploring the role of physical activity
in correctional settings

Rosie Meek

LONDON AND NEW YORK

First published 2014
by Routledge
2 Park Square, Milton Park, Abingdon, Oxon OX14 4RN

Simultaneously published in the USA and Canada
by Routledge
711 Third Avenue, New York, NY 10017

Routledge is an imprint of the Taylor & Francis Group, an informa business

British Library Cataloguing-in-Publication Data
A catalogue record for this book is available from the British Library

Library of Congress Cataloging-in-Publication Data
Meek, Rosie.
Sport in prison : exploring the role of physical activity in penal practices / by
    Rosie Meek. — First Edition.
        pages cm. — (Routledge research in sport, culture and society ; 28)
    1. Prisoners—Recreation.   I. Title.
HV8860.M44   2013
365'.668—dc23   2013017706

ISBN: 978-0-415-85761-1 (hbk)
ISBN: 978-0-203-79705-1 (ebk)

Typeset in Times
by Apex CoVantage, LLC

Contents

Foreword

During my time as Chief Inspector of Prisons, I saw many examples of how sport could and should be used, while – like the author of this book – bemoaning the extraordinary inconsistency of Prison Service management and its inability to turn good practice somewhere into common practice everywhere. For example, imaginative use of football in the education of young offenders, who, in mathematics, had to measure and mark out football pitches and, in literacy, write essays about their favourite footballer or enabling prisoners to design and organise 'sporting' visits for physically or mentally handicapped members of the public, were confined to establishments in which someone had the good sense to introduce them.

I therefore welcome this book, and its wake-up call for sport – in its widest sense – to be more readily available and used in the rehabilitation of prisoners. In outlining the advantages I am glad that Rosie Meek has also recognised the problems that prison staffs face in the current climate of reduced resources. But, as she so rightly says, both the target and the weapons are human. Those in charge must think through the purpose of sport, including physical education, in the rehabilitation of prisoners and, having done so, relate its provision to its prison audience. For example, young offenders should be enabled to play team games; those with mental health problems need stimulation to counter the negative effect of being left in their cells all day long, doing nothing; women need suitably designed programmes that may include being taught how to exercise children. I also agree that, because almost every prisoner will return to the community, maximum encouragement must be given to local communities both to seek advantage from what can be provided by prisons, and contribute in any way they can, including the imaginative suggestion of encouraging sportsmen in residence, along the lines of artists and writers in residence, as role models as well as teachers.

I am very glad that Dr. Meek mentions the Arts Alliance in the final chapter of her timely and meticulously researched book because of the similarity of the roles of the arts and sport in prison. Arthur Koestler, himself once a prisoner in Nazi Germany, recognising that any work of art, in any medium, was an individual, recognisable and rewardable personal achievement, instituted an annual exhibition of offender art, for which entries are encouraged and professionally judged. He hoped that arts programmes would form part of the regime in every prison because of their vital contribution to developing self-esteem, an essential ingredient if individuals were to be encouraged to engage in specific activities designed to help them to live useful and law-abiding lives. Neither the arts nor sport are ends in themselves but proven means to the end of protecting the public by preventing reoffending.

The Secretary of State for Justice and the Chief Executive of the National Offender Management Service, and their subordinates inside and outside prisons, should be enormously grateful to Dr. Meek for all the work she has put into researching and explaining the underused contribution of sport in the rehabilitation of offenders. Unfortunately, unless common sense prevails, like the arts, sport will fall foul of the government's obsession with payment by results, which is why neither are ends in themselves as far as the prevention of reoffending is concerned. However both are such valuable means to the achievement of that end, because of what they contribute to the mental and physical well-being – and the all-important self-esteem – of individuals, that they must not be disregarded for all the wrong reasons. Now that all the right reasons have been set out so clearly in this book, I hope that those at whom it is aimed will show their appreciation to its author, by listening to her advice, commissioning the suggested research and vastly increasing access to the benefits that sport brings to the rehabilitation process, and so the protection of the public.

Lord Ramsbotham, May 2013
HM Chief Inspector of Prisons 1995–2001

Acknowledgements

Producing this book would not have been possible without contributions from a number of people. Thanks are due in particular to Gwen Lewis, who provided indispensable research assistance, but also to Melissa for her unfaltering encouragement, and to Simon Whitmore and Josh Wells at Routledge for their patience and guidance. I am grateful to my students past and present who have volunteered to help with the research and have been enthusiastic about my findings. Thank you to those who have motivated, distracted and supported me throughout this process – in particular Alison, Charlotte, Dawn, Klara and James, and my brothers Leon, Robin, Hereward and Max. This book originated from a piece of evaluative research I carried out several years ago and I am grateful to those involved in that initial project for supporting my research, both then and now, in particular James Mapstone and Justin Coleman at 2nd Chance, and the staff at HMP & YOI Portland, particularly Andy Bastick, Alex Browne, Barry Clark, Neil Davies, Kevin Jess, Martyn Peel, Sean Phelps, Mike Porter and Julian Stout. Special thanks to Russ Trent. Thank you to colleagues in academia and criminal justice who have helped me shape my ideas through discussion and suggestions. I am indebted to the prison gym staff throughout England and Wales who participated in the research, especially those who hosted visits and took time to explain their work and experiences. Most of all, thank you to the men, women and children in prison who engaged with the research process.

The author is grateful to the British Psychological Society, Emerald and Sage for permission to use extracts from the following previously published articles:

The role of sport in reducing reoffending among young men in prison: Assessing the evidence base. *Forensic Update*, 107, 12–18 (2012).

The role of sport in promoting prisoner health. *International Journal of Prisoner Health*, 8, 3/4, 117–131 (2012).

The impact of a sports initiative for young men in prison: staff and participant perspectives. *Journal of Sport and Social Issues* (in press).

Abbreviations

Black and Minority Ethnic (BME)
Department for Education and Skills (DfES)
Department of Health (DoH)
Enhanced Thinking Skills (ETS)
Head of Learning and Skills (HOLS)
Her Majesty's Inspectorate of Prisons (HMIP)
Incentives and Earned Privileges (IEP)
Independent Monitoring Board (IMB)
Integrated Drug Treatment Programme (IDTP)
National Offender Management Service (NOMS)
Offender Behaviour Programmes (OBP)
Offender Learning and Skills Service (OLASS)
Offender Management Unit (OMU)
Physical Education Instructor (PEI)
Primary Care Trust (PCT)
Prison Service Instruction (PSI)
Prison Service Order (PSO)
Prison Service Sports Association (PSSA)
Release on Temporary Licence (RoTL)
Senior Management Team (SMT)
Thinking Skills Programme (TSP)
Young Offender Institution (YOI)
Youth Justice Board (YJB)
Youth Offending Team (YOT)

1 Introduction

This book attempts to draw together and make further contributions to two established and separate bodies of literature devoted to (a) the beneficial role of sport in community settings and (b) investigations of prison cultures and regimes. By focusing on the role of sport and physical activity in prison, it blends a disparate body of literature from the fields of criminology and criminal justice, psychology, sociology and sports studies, supplemented with a substantial body of original qualitative and quantitative data. The result seeks to be a detailed and thorough resource with equal appeal to policy makers and practitioners (including representatives from sporting organisations, prison governors, officers and other criminal justice practitioners) as well as academics, researchers and advanced students.

Why explore the role of sport and physical activity in prison?

The unprecedented levels of political and public interest currently being enjoyed by sport and physical activity may have been boosted in no small part by the overwhelming success of the London 2012 Olympics, the aftermath of which has initiated renewed awareness of the power of sport to promote social, psychological and physical well-being, but a substantial body of academic literature has long been devoted to the role of sport in promoting social cohesion and psychological well-being. To date, however, the focus on the positive effects of sport has almost exclusively been in community settings and much of it centred solely on young people (see Cameron & MacDougall, 2000; Coalter, 2009; Morris, Sallybanks, Willis & Makkai, 2003; Nichols, 2007; Nichols & Taylor, 1996; Taylor, Crow, Irvine & Nichols, 1999; Tsuchiya, 1996). Research specifically concerning the role of sport in prisons and with offending populations remains sparse, despite the obvious lessons that may be drawn from the more established practices in community settings and the additional opportunities and uses for sport in the context of incarceration and rehabilitation. Research undertaken for this book has confirmed that practitioners, policy makers and fellow academics recognise a pressing need to identify and explore the key emerging issues, challenges and debates surrounding sport in prison. To unpack the meanings that prisoners and staff attach to participation in sport and physical activity will inevitably help us to develop a better understanding of how to make best use of such initiatives and how to promote behavioural change through sport most effectively. So far though, no text has drawn together this rapidly developing body of international literature nor explored the processes underpinning sport's benefits and its potential consequent impact on rehabilitative processes.

It is perhaps telling that my own interest in this area began with a small scale evaluation of a sports-based initiative which developed well beyond the two year period of the programme itself and sparked in me an eagerness to explore and expand the evidence base for the actual and potential role of sport in prison. The sociological and psychological examination of sport may be well-developed broader disciplines, but whereas in criminology, sociology and forensic psychology the study of prisons, penology, prisoners and prison staff is thriving, when first commencing my research in this area I was struck by the lack of academic attention paid to what many recognise as a cornerstone of the prison environment – the prison gym and its associated facilities.

Amongst the general population, the benefits of regular physical activity to psychological and physical health are well understood and participation in physical activity is recognised as an important contributor to well-being and quality of life for people of all ages. Those who are more physically active tend to live longer, healthier lives, an outcome of increased functional and cognitive capacity, reduced anxiety and depression, the prevention of obesity and the diminished likelihood of developing chronic diseases. Social and psychological benefits include improved opportunities for social contact and the promotion of social inclusion and community cohesion. Increasing or maintaining physical activity, particularly among those who are sedentary, is therefore a major goal of health and fitness professionals, psychological services and health care providers, and as communities that house those with an increased likelihood of significant health needs, prisons represent an especially important target population. Indeed, recognition of the role of physical activity in promoting prisoner well-being is reflected in the Prison Service Physical Education operating manual which states that:

> PE plays an important part in a prison regime by providing high quality purposeful activity and engagement with prisoners; in addition PE can make a major contribution to the physical, mental and social well-being of prisoners. (HM Prison Service, 2009, p. 4)

A small but substantial body of international literature has made a case for the primary benefits of prison-based sport and physical activity in terms of improved physical health (Elger, 2009; Nelson, Specian, Tracy & DeMello, 2006), mental health (Buckaloo, Krug & Nelson, 2009; Cashin, Potter & Butler, 2008; Libbus, Genovese & Poole, 1994; Verdot, Champely, Clement & Massarelli, 2010; Woodall, 2010), and to a lesser extent, in coping with prison life and facilitating social control (Martos-Garcia, Devis-Devis & Sparkes, 2009a; Murtaza & Uddin, 2011; Wagner, McBride & Crouse, 1999). Contemporary policy regarding the use of sport with offenders – in line with social policy more widely – has increasingly advocated the use of sport and physical activity as a vehicle for achieving non-sport policy objectives (Bloyce & Smith, 2010), and several rationales have been proposed to explain the therapeutic potential of sport for offenders and how it may contribute to efforts to reduce crime. Although sport may previously have received limited critical recognition because of its associations with 'play', there is a growing awareness of its wider potential psychological, as well as social, impact. For instance, sport may offer an alternative means of excitement and risk taking to that gained through engaging in offending behaviour (Pfefferbaum & Wood, 1994; Zuckerman, 1991) or provide an alternative social network, access to positive role models and a way of receiving positive feedback for nondeviant behaviour, as explained by social learning processes (Bandura, 1977). Participating in sport may offer an alternative means for a positive identity (Busseri, Costain, Campbell, Rose-Krasnor & Evans, 2011; Horne, Tomlinson, Whannel & Woodward, 2012; Kehily, 2007; Ravizza, 2011; Schafer, 1969), and promote well-being by enhancing personal growth in relation to self-esteem, self-concept, locus of control, empathy, tolerance, cooperation and self-discipline, problem solving, decision making, teamwork and conflict resolution (Coalter, 2005; Ekeland, Heian & Hagn, 2005; Nichols, 1997; Ravizza & Motonak, 2011; West & Crompton, 2001). Sport may offer a form of social control (Hirschi, 1969), for example by strengthening attachments to positive role models, increasing commitment to and involvement in law abiding behaviour, and offering a belief system aligned to social rules. Lastly, and in line with routine activity theory (Felson, 1997), participation in sport may simply reduce opportunities to engage in criminal activities.

There is, clearly, a strong body of evidence suggesting that, aside from the well-established psychological and social benefits, the provision of physical activity represents a simple intervention which can ameliorate the negative health effects of a sedentary lifestyle in prison. Despite an expectation that prisoners should spend a significant period of time engaged in 'meaningful activity' each day, prisoners consistently report highly sedentary lifestyles in custody, with extended periods of time spent within their cells. Various reviews and reports published by the Inspectorate of Prisons in England and Wales have indicated that, contrary to policy expectations, many prisoners do not spend the recommended one hour a day or more in the open air, and a substantial proportion of the prison population are consistently found to be locked up with nothing to do during the week. Although widespread changes to introduce the working prison agenda may have an impact on this, the situation remains that men and women in prison are typically less likely than those in the community to participate in sufficient physical activity.[1] Sedentary behaviour has consequently been identified as a high-risk health behaviour in prisons which contributes to an increased risk of obesity, hypertension, diabetes, cardiovascular disease and mortality (Jebb & Moore, 1999; Math, Murthy, Parthasanthy, Kumar & Mudhusudhan, 2011; Plugge, Foster, Yudkin & Douglas, 2009) thus placing a considerable cost burden on health care providers both in custody and the community.

However, it is also widely acknowledged that although prison can present a critical opportunity to engage with offenders through interventions and programming, reoffending rates among those released from prison remain consistently high: around half of those released from prison reoffend within a year, and this figure increases for younger offenders and those serving short sentences (Ministry of Justice, 2012e). Previous research has identified a clear need for specialist delivery and carefully planned methods of motivating offenders to make positive life changes during their time in prison custody, and it is not surprising that there is an assumption – albeit a largely untested one – that sport can present a valuable and unique opportunity to engage with even the most challenging and complex individuals caught up in a cycle of offending and imprisonment.

Methodology

The research that contributed to this book aimed to be sufficiently detailed to capture the particular experiences of prisoners and prison staff from specific institutions and representatives from associated organisations but general enough to be applied nationally and internationally. Permission was sought and granted by the Ministry of Justice to gather data from prisons throughout England and Wales, followed by approval from governors or research coordinators at each of the individual establishments that participated.

Recognising the value of combining different methodological approaches in order to generate a robust research design, to capture fully the details of a particular topic, and to establish the most valuable theoretical contribution, a variety of quantitative and qualitative techniques were employed. Primary data were also collected from a number of sources, specifically:

1   A series of interviews and focus groups were carried out with a total of 152 prisoners and newly released ex-prisoners (107 males and 45 females), with over half of these interviewed two or more times, either whilst in custody ($n = 54$), or both in custody and after release ($n = 24$).

2   A national structured interview/survey of the managers of prison gyms ($n = 52$) capturing qualitative and quantitative data from establishments of different categories (security level, type of prisoner accommodated) and representing public sector ($n = 47$) and privately run ($n = 5$) prisons throughout England and Wales. All prisons operating in England and Wales during the period of data collection were invited to participate, resulting in responses from over a third of all establishments.

Supplementing the gym manager surveys, in-depth research visits ($n = 21$) were carried out at gym departments operating across the prison estate in England and Wales in order to observe practice, interview staff and prisoners, and identify good practice case studies. These case studies punctuate the chapters that follow and aim to capture the way that individual establishments have drawn upon sport and physical activity in order to find innovative and effective ways of responding to the challenges present within prison establishments and criminal justice systems.

Table 1.1 Survey responses from gym managers across the prison estate

Type of establishment	% of the prison estate	Number of establishments who responded
Juvenile*	5%	2
Young Offenders Institute (YOI) / YOI & Adult*	13%	4
Category B*	10%	5
Category C*	23%	13
Category D (Open)	7%	6
Local	22%	12
Female*	11%	4
High Security (Category A)	6%	4
Immigration Removal Centre (IRC)	3%	2
Total	100%	52

* Including responses from privately run establishments (operated by G4S, Serco and Sodexo)

3 Individual semi-structured interviews were carried out with relevant stakeholders (n = 46) including those involved in overseeing and implementing sport in prison, prison governors and senior managers, prison and probation staff, employers in the sport and fitness industry and representatives from the voluntary sector and sporting organisations.
4 Questions relating to participation in sport and physical activity were integrated into a wider survey of young adult male prisoners (n = 67) and women prisoners (n = 190).

Primary data were supplemented with a secondary analysis of key policy documents, Ombudsman reports and Prison Service Instructions, as well as official prisoner participation figures obtained using requests under the 2000 Freedom of Information Act,[2] which is emerging as a valuable but rarely used social science research approach (Murray, in press). Extensive use was also made of HM Inspectorate of Prisons (HMIP) reports, given that these are published for every prison establishment in England and Wales and contain detailed information on all aspects of the regime, thus allowing for comparisons over time and across different establishments. In total, the contents of 185 HMIP reports were analysed. Although a useful data source, analyses of these inspectorate reports should be considered in light of methodological limitations, chiefly that the level of detail and focus in each report is dependent on the type of inspection being carried out (i.e. full/short/follow up), the specific previous recommendations raised by the Inspectorate for each establishment and the length of time since the previous inspection. It is also recognised that there will be instances where the most recently published Inspectorate report available for an establishment is outdated (some were up to six years old at the point of analysis) and will not necessarily accurately reflect the most current practice and provision. Nevertheless, whilst acknowledging that provision and practice in establishments changes rapidly and as a consequence cannot be captured with absolute accuracy, as an analytical tool scrutiny of inspection reports provides a comprehensive insight into the importance placed on sport and physical education in assessment of the performance of prisons.

How this book is organised

This work represents an attempt to present, from an independent academic standpoint, a comprehensive overview of the research evidence accumulated over a period of several years of researching prisons, prisoners, prison staff and community organisations which work with prisoners, and the role that sport and physical activity has to play for each of these. As a psychologist I am especially interested not just in observing and theorising the prison gym itself but in identifying, revealing and debating the narratives of those who work in and engage with prison-based sport and physical activity and the rhetoric of those decision makers who prescribe the ways in which prisons make use of physical activity. The book therefore comprises a detailed international literature review, supplemented with extensive primary and secondary qualitative and quantitative data. The fieldwork for this project was carried out between 2008 and 2012 in England and Wales, but international observations and implications are included where relevant and possible.

Chapter 2 introduces some of the historical developments of the role of sport and physical activity in prisons and demonstrates how, just as we see the contrasting notions of punishment, containment and rehabilitation separately constructed and contested in characterisations of the primary purposes of imprisonment, there are also substantial differences in the competing concepts of exercise, leisure and physical education or activity and their roles in prison regimes and penal practices. Alongside the continued increase in the numbers of people detained in prison, recent years have seen significant changes in the management and staffing of prisons generally and prison gyms in particular, substantial efforts to reduce the running costs of prisons and an increased commitment to efforts to reduce reoffending, all with implications for the delivery of sport and physical education in prison settings. In summarising the evidence base for the role of physical activity in meeting broader non-sport policy objectives, the perceived impact of sport on physical, social and psychological outcomes is introduced alongside the academic rationales for such perspectives and a discussion of prison masculinities. The chapter concludes with a summary of the most relevant national and international legislation informing the provision of sport and physical activity in prison, examples of organisations seeking to use sport to promote social change, and global applications of the use of sport in prison.

Chapter 3 explores the way in which, although various regulations stipulate that prisoners should be able to participate in minimum standards of physical activity and exercise, wide variation is apparent in England and Wales, not just across the prison estate but also between different establishments of the same type. Official data in the form of Prisoner Participation Levels is presented, confirming that juvenile establishments have the highest levels of prisoner participation in contrast to female establishments where participation represents the lowest within the secure estate. These official figures are supplemented with observations from hundreds of Inspectorate reports and the findings of the national survey of prison gym managers, exploring how and why the prevalence and different uses of sport and physical activity are apparent across the prison estate. Extending the survey focus on the perceived benefits of and challenges associated with delivering sport in prison, in-depth interviews with members of prison gym staff and senior managers serve to explain varied participation in sport, referring to the factors which contribute to organisational-level support, variation in resource and types of regime and the challenges associated with promoting physical activity among a varied and diverse prisoner population.

The concept of a diverse prisoner population is returned to in Chapter 4 where issues of equality and inclusivity are explored, with a particular focus on the challenges associated with promoting physical activity among 'non-sporty' prisoners without replicating or increasing existing inequalities. Extending this, consideration of the particular needs of vulnerable prisoners (specifically those unwilling or unable to engage in the wider prison regime or at risk of victimisation or self-harm) leads to a discussion of the role of sport in reducing anxieties, improving mental health and promoting therapeutic interactions. Specific attention is paid to particular groups of offenders, including those with physical and learning disabilities, older prisoners, individuals convicted of sex offences and those held in high-secure facilities, followed by a discussion of minority ethnic groups and foreign national prisoners, describing their over-representation in the prison system and making links with existing research into participation in sport according to ethnicity. Lastly, recognising that the 10 Immigration Removal Centres currently operating in England and Wales make up part of our prison system, the chapter concludes by considering the particular needs of detainees and the unique role of sport and physical activity in meeting those needs.

Chapter 5 explores how and why female prisoners are significantly less likely to participate in sport and physical activity than male prisoners or females in noncustodial settings. Summarising the research evidence supporting the gender-specific benefits of participation, a strong case is made for the role of sport in meeting the particularly complex and unique needs of female prisoners. Survey responses from 190 female prisoners and individual interviews with 45 women demonstrate the recognised importance of using physical activity to respond to the enhanced levels of unmet physical and mental health needs of female prisoners and in promoting education and employment opportunities but also highlight the perceived barriers to participating in prison sport for women and girls.

Chapter 6 explains that in the context of contemporary youth justice policy, the tension between the competing goals of welfare and justice can be exacerbated in sports-based interventions and although sport has become widely used as a social cohesion or inclusion strategy in community settings (with the majority of such initiatives targeting children and young people in particular) such focus has not necessarily translated to the secure estate, despite the fact that the importance placed on sport as a 'moral good' for children and young people has become ingrained in political rhetoric. Assumptions that participation in sport can divert young people from criminal behaviour may be partially explained by a recognition that adolescence and emerging adulthood are characterised by identity exploration and that sport can provide a meaningful and positive sense of self, as well as offering an opportunity to improve social, interpersonal and life skills while providing a positive use of leisure time (although some of these assumptions are subsequently challenged in Chapter 13). Methodological shortcomings in the evaluation of sports initiatives which seek to inhibit youth offending may prevent a conclusive claim of their effectiveness but given that sport and physical education remain comparatively prominent features of youth incarceration (participation figures for juveniles and young adults are among the highest across the secure estate), a case is made for using sport as a rehabilitative, therapeutic, health promotion or educational tool. Use of, and provision for, sport in such ways remains varied, with existing evidence (in the form of Inspectorate reports) and newly gathered data from staff working in young offender establishments confirming that sporting opportunities depend heavily on local resources and preferences, which in turn are largely predicted by the design of an individual prison and the facilities afforded to it. The chapter concludes with a summary of why exploring innovative and effective ways of working with young prisoners is especially important, highlighting the ways in which sport can and does respond to the need to achieve a broad range of positive outcomes for young people in custody as well as after their return to the community.

Extending the focus in Chapter 6 on sport's contribution to a range of positive outcomes in youth justice settings, Chapter 7 looks specifically at evidence for the role of sport in efforts to reduce reoffending and promote desistance from crime. Given the high reconviction rates among those who have completed a custodial sentence, interventions and initiatives targeting those in prison have become a prominent feature of the government's 'rehabilitation revolution'. Utilising sport as a way of responding to the factors that are known to contribute to reoffending (such as attitudes to crime, education and employment opportunities, and mental and physical health) would therefore be expected to play a part in efforts to reduce reoffending. Likewise, aligning sports initiatives with factors associated with the promotion of desistance from crime – such as developing a commitment to a prosocial identity as an alternative to that of offender, reducing stigma and developing the necessary social and cultural capital to enable ex-prisoners to 'go straight' – were predicted to have a meaningful impact, with staff observations and prisoner interviews corroborating this. In meeting these resettlement and desistance aims and aspirations, the particular importance of community partnerships is a theme developed throughout the chapter, illustrating the importance of involving external organisations at a number of levels, including the critical element of providing meaningful and effective through-the-gate support for those preparing to leave prison custody and the role that sport may play in this.

Chapter 8 extends the focus of the previous two chapters by presenting a quantitative and qualitative evaluation of a series of football and rugby initiatives developed to identify and respond to the resettlement needs of young men in prison. Drawing on interviews with delivery staff and participants, as well as presenting reconviction analyses and data from a broad spectrum of psychometric measures taken before and after participation, the evaluation explores the impact of the initiative on a range of dimensions. The chapter culminates in a discussion of the implications of the findings for the future use of prison-based sports interventions in general, and in particular in efforts to reduce reoffending by providing meaningful intervention and support for those in prison and in the transition from custody to community.

Chapters 9 and 10 maintain a focus on the use of sport in meeting resettlement needs, with an in-depth exploration of, firstly, education and employment opportunities and secondly health promotion in prison and the unique role of physical activity in contributing to these primary concerns. Both chapters outline policy and practice and use prisoner and staff interview and questionnaire data to examine how and why sport and physical activity have come to be drawn on as such a valuable resource in meeting non-sport policy objectives.

Chapter 11 takes a broader view of the role of sport in prisons, exploring ways in which physical activity plays a pivotal role in promoting order and control throughout prison establishments, in reducing violence and in enabling prisoners to adapt to and cope with incarceration. Data from staff and prisoners illustrates the increased importance placed on sport in prison settings and the reasons behind and implications for this prominence are discussed alongside consideration of the ways in which engaging in sport can provide unique opportunities to promote citizenship among prisoners.

Having devoted previous chapters predominantly to the benefits and potential role of sport and physical activity in responding to a range of broader objectives in the running of prisons and the management of offenders, Chapter 12 serves to challenge some of the assumptions inherent in debates around the role of sport and physical activity, not just in prison settings but in its wider uses. In particular it explains how the relationship between participation in sport and offending is more complex and indirect than might be assumed. Alongside findings supporting the rationale that participation in sport can reduce offending in a number of ways, evidence is also presented of some unintended negative consequences of participation in different types of sport. Likewise, the notion that sport's cathartic effect in reducing aggression and improving social control is based on robust evidence is contrasted with the counterargument that engaging in some types of sport or being over-committed to a 'sport ethic' may lead to an increase in the perceived legitimacy of aggressive behaviour, lower levels of moral functioning and heightened risk of body image anxieties and self-presentation concerns (which may lead in turn to the illicit use of performance enhancing substances). The chapter concludes by considering ways in which, unless managed carefully, sport may replicate and create social inequalities and conflict and introduce new power dynamics and opportunities for bullying and intimidation, as well as presenting additional challenges in avoiding the risk of undermining security concerns in the provision of physical activity.

Recognising that prison gym staff remain an under-researched population, Chapter 13 sets out some of the operational and organisational issues associated with staffing the prison gym. It explores the processes and dynamics at work in interactions between staff with responsibilities for Physical Education (PE) and those in their care, as well as the importance of physical activity for staff themselves and how it may contribute to their well-being and the resulting improved performance of individual prisons.

Finally, Chapter 14 draws together the key themes and findings of the book, setting out the policy and practice implications and identified areas of future research.

Some notes on terms and definitions

Any research in criminal justice settings will inevitably draw on a broad range of established terms, with each tending to have subtly different meanings attached to them, some more contentious than others. Unless indicated otherwise, the terms used in this text adhere broadly to Department of Health (2004) definitions for physical activity, exercise and sport, as follows:

> *Physical Activity*: Any force exerted by skeletal muscle that results in energy expenditure above resting level.
> *Exercise*: Physical activity that is volitional, planned, structured, repetitive, and aimed at improving or maintaining any aspect of fitness or health.
> *Sport*: Socially and culturally relative but generally involves structured competitive situations governed by rules.

Within prison settings, the term *physical education* is typically used in preference to and in contrast with the term physical activity, since the former is perceived to reflect better the training and expertise of *physical education instructors* (PEIs) and the types of activities they design and deliver. While recognising the importance of this distinction at an organisational level, the terms are used interchangeably in this text, as are 'PEIs' and 'gym staff'.

An important additional acknowledgement to make regarding definitions concerns the terms used to describe the primary subject matter of this text – sport and physical activity. Although the residential wings of prisons will typically be equipped with games for use during periods of 'free association' (normally including pool tables but also occasionally table tennis or table football), and although it is recognised that these games and facilities serve an important function in the provision of recreation and socialisation on prison landings, for the purposes of this research the main emphasis is on organised and supervised sport and exercise, and for that reason the prison gym, its users and the members of staff responsible for its operating were the primary focus.[3] Although I am aware of and draw upon established (yet broad) definitions of sport, physical education, activity, and exercise, I also embrace a phenomenological approach, welcoming the subjective understandings of what constitutes sport or relevant physical activity from the perspectives of my research participants rather than imposing upon them my own working definitions. Reflecting this, some participants would refer to activities such as yoga, walking and games in their discussions whereas others would operationalise more concrete definitions of organised sport. Rather than problematising such diverse working concepts, I suggest that they emphasise the plurality of prison sport and physical activity – while also highlighting the need to work towards a shared understanding of the concepts used in this field of study.

Although aware of the subtle differences between different meanings and the need to devote academic time and discussion to consideration of alternative descriptors (for example where the term *offender* may serve to make most salient the act of offending, or the offence committed, it could be argued that the term *prisoner* is less value-laden and simply reflects the incarcerated state of an individual), the terms prisoner and *ex-prisoners* are primarily used throughout this text but also interchangeably with the terms *inmate* and offender.

In considering the use of different terms, aside from the terms prisoner, offender and inmate, references to those who have previously served a prison sentence are potentially even more contentious, as reflected in the following quote:

> I feel 'ex-offender' is a permanent label based purely on the worst thing you have ever done and I find it deeply offensive . . . a change of language is critical if we are to tackle the life sentence of stigma attached to even a minor criminal record. (Ryder, 2013)

In *Becoming an Ex*, a sociological exploration of exits from significant roles, Ebaugh (1988) identifies common stages of the role exit process, from disillusionment with a particular identity to searching for alternative roles to the turning points that trigger the final creation of an identity as an 'ex'. In agreement with Ryder (2013), Ebaugh's argument suggests that incorporating ex into a descriptor for oneself renders an individual less able to leave behind a previous identity. Partially reflecting this, campaign and advocacy organisations such as UNLOCK (www.unlock.org.uk) have reported that they are moving towards greater use of the term *people with convictions* as well as *reformed offenders*.

Prison and prisoner categories in England and Wales: An overview

Prisoner categories are based on a combination of the type of crime committed, the length of sentence, the likelihood of escape and the danger to the public if the prisoner did escape. The four categories are:

Category A prisoners are those whose escape would be highly dangerous to the public or national security.

Category B prisoners are those who do not require maximum security but for whom escape needs to be made very difficult.

Category C prisoners are those who cannot be trusted in open conditions but who are unlikely to try to escape.

Category D prisoners are those who can be reasonably trusted not to try to escape and are given the privilege of an open prison.

High-security prisons hold Category A and B prisoners. Category A prisoners are managed by a process of dispersal, and these prisons also hold a proportion of Category B prisoners for whom they provide a similar regime to a Category B prison. The Category B prisoners held in a high-security prison are not necessarily any more dangerous or difficult to manage than those in Category B prisons.

Category B and *Category C* prisons hold sentenced prisoners of their respective categories, including life sentenced prisoners. The regime focuses on programmes that address offending behaviour and provide education, vocational training and purposeful work for prisoners who will normally spend several years in one prison.

Because of their smaller numbers, *female prisons* are not divided into the same number of categories although there are variations in security levels.

Local prisons serve the courts in the area. Historically their main function was to hold unconvicted and unsentenced prisoners and, once a prisoner had been sentenced, to allocate them on to a Category B, C or D prison as appropriate to serve their sentence. However, pressure on places means that many shorter term prisoners serve their entire sentence in a local prison, while longer term prisoners also complete some offending behaviour and training programmes there before moving on to lower security conditions. All local prisons operate to Category B security standards.

Open prisons have lower levels of physical security and only hold Category D prisoners. Many prisoners in open prisons will be allowed to go out of the prison during the day in order to take part in voluntary or paid work in the community in preparation for their approaching release.

Young adult offenders are aged between 18–21 years and are held in *young offender institutions*.

Juveniles are aged 10–17 years (although some young people remain in juvenile custody upon reaching 18, particularly when their release date is imminent) and are held in a distinct secure estate made up predominantly of young offender institutions, with a smaller number of younger juveniles held in *secure training centres* and *secure children's homes*. Statutory responsibility for juveniles has been with the Youth Justice Board since 2000.

Immigration Removal Centres hold illegal immigrants. Three of those operating in England and Wales are currently operated by the Prison Service.

Notes

1   For example, the majority (87%) of women in British prisons have been identified as being insufficiently active to benefit their health (Plugge, Foster, Yudkin & Douglas, 2009).
2   Access to information via Freedom of Information requests can be made to any public authorities. The response has to be made within 20 working days of the receipt of the request, but access to information can be refused if, for example, if it is deemed not to be in the public interest or if the cost of accessing the information would be above the set 'appropriate limit'.
3   This doesn't necessarily mean that recreational games don't have the potential to contribute to broader policy agendas. Indeed, a new partnership between Brighton Table Tennis Club and Her Majesty's Prison (HMP) Lewes will enable young prisoners to train as industry-recognised coaches and engage in volunteering after release (Active Sussex, 2013).

2 Towards a conceptualisation of the role of sport in prison

Along with health, culture, education and work opportunities, access to sport and exercise is now widely recognised as a fundamental right of all prisoners. However, this is not necessarily a global or consistent perspective, and it could be argued that the perceived function of sport and exercise in prison has varied and evolved in line with associated fluctuations in policy and societal perceptions of the primary purpose of imprisonment. Historically, penal political rhetoric in Britain has moved from the notion of prison serving to punish and deter towards a recognition of the need to contain humanely, and only from the late 20th century onwards has there been a focus on rehabilitating offenders through the provision of purposeful activity with the ultimate aim of reducing reoffending. Just as we see the contrasting notions of punishment, containment, and rehabilitation being separately constructed and contested in characterisations of the primary purposes of imprisonment, there are also substantial differences in the competing concepts of *leisure* (and its associations with free time, autonomy and enjoyment) and *play* (being characterised as freely chosen, personally directed and intrinsically motivated) and the contrasting *exercise* (recognised as structured, repetitive and aimed at improving or maintaining fitness or health) and *physical instruction* (embodied by military style drills and underpinned through a focus on being physically exhausting). It is no accident that these competing notions of the role of physical activity in prison also represent the three primary competing discourses regarding the purposes of incarceration – punishment, containment and rehabilitation – that continue to be balanced and negotiated within policy and by those responsible for the running of prisons. An inevitable result of combining these two layers of diverging assumptions in contemporary understandings of sport in prison is that exercise may be characterised as a way of containing or physically managing prisoners as much as it is increasingly recognised for its rehabilitative function.

Delivering sport in prison: The organisational context

As well as a rapidly changing penal political context and a continued increase in the numbers of people detained in prison, recent years have seen significant changes in the running and management of prisons. Attempts to increase efficiency have led to substantial efforts to drive down the running costs of prisons, including a rapid process of privatisation of the prison estate in England and Wales, which now has among the highest proportion of privately run prisons worldwide. In 1992 under the then Conservative government, HMP The Wolds was the first prison to be privatised in England and Wales,[1] and in the 20-year period that followed 12 prisons were contracted out to private providers. Plans were announced in early 2013 for the privatisation of four further prisons, the closure of six publicly run prisons, and the construction of a number of large 'titan prisons' in which to detain over 2,000 offenders each, with four further closures announced later in the same year. At the same time, within publicly run prisons austerity measures are increasingly leading to the outsourcing of nonoperational elements of incarceration which, in the context of prison gym and sports and exercise provision, represents an aspect of the prison where subcontracting could be seen as offering a cost saving, a move which would represent a clear shift from the historic increase in specialist training of custodial staff in physical education.

Coupled with a staff restructuring process in 2013 which sees PE fall under the remit of custodial managers who may not necessarily have expertise in the domain, and the development of Payment by Results initiatives (see Ministry of Justice, 2010a) that have led to an increased focus on measurable outcomes, PE staff are clearly in a position of particular vulnerability in terms of job security and role and the allocation of resources. Not only are PE staff anxious about the security of their role, but stakeholder interviews also revealed a concern from senior figures regarding the risks of outsourcing a role recognised as requiring considerable expertise to external providers:

> There isn't the same kind of provision in the community. PE officers have to be able to organise and supervise offenders who display challenging behaviour. They teach PE, deliver vocational courses, coach a range of different sports, provide remedial treatment programmes for prisoners, mentor and influence prisoners in the unique custodial setting. You can't find this skill set currently in community provision. (Senior Manager)

Perhaps in response to some of these recognised threats, there is widespread evidence of increased attempts to integrate sport and physical activities into the wider prison regime, for example through the development of sports-based learning and employment opportunities, health promotion and efforts to rehabilitate.

From just 30 individuals in 1955, PE staffing increased progressively to a total of 714 in 1989 and 743 in 2013. Numbers of PE staff may have remained relatively stable over the past 25 years, but the prison population has increased dramatically during this time, from just under 50,000 in 1988 (Home Office, 1988) to 84,000 in 2013 (Ministry of Justice, 2013b). Training of Prison Service PE staff was originally delivered through an intensive 23-week programme but between 1997 and 2011 this was progressively reduced to 13 weeks in duration. Alongside the PE instructors who make up the majority of those prison staff with responsibility for sport and physical activity, a smaller number of sports and games officers[2] (who do not hold the same level of qualifications as PEIs, nor attract the additional financial allowance) are sufficiently trained in physical education to be able to act as instructors and take classes. PE provision in prisons in England and Wales is currently monitored and guided by three specialist PE area managers who oversee departmental PE managers at an establishment level. Beyond the prison service of England and Wales, it is notable that in a European context physical education and sports instructors are recognised by the European Committee for the Prevention of Torture and Inhuman or Degrading Treatment or Punishment (2006) in rule 89(1) alongside teachers, social workers and psychologists as representing the specialist staff necessary in a prison.

Significant historical developments of physical activity in the prison service

1898: Half an hour per day drill for fit prisoners up to 25 years of age

1926: Physical training compulsory for all fit male prisoners up to 40 years of age

1937: All trainee Prison Officers graded for physical training and allowance paid for expertise in the use of gym apparatus

1947: Compulsory daily physical training for girls, boys and men under 30 years of age

1955: A total of 30 members of PE staff. Weight lifting introduced to Prison Service establishments

1959: Circuit training officially approved for use in prisons

1968: Regional Physical Education advisors appointed

1976: The first three female PEIs are trained

1987: As a result of recommendations for additional PE staff within the service, numbers rise to 474

1989: Numbers of PE staff rise to 714

2013: The number of PEIs across the Prison Service stands at 743, 7.5% of whom are female (across the Prison Service, 26% of officers and operational support staff are female: National Offender Management Service, 2012b)

Source: Prison Service College of PE

Synonymous with penal reform more widely, although physical activity may traditionally have been most closely aligned with the punitive element of incarceration, it is increasingly recognised as contributing to a rehabilitation agenda within prisons, as reflected in prison rules and operational guidelines. For example, current Prison Service directives state that physical activities should have a structured approach which may support prisoners in tackling their offending behaviour, impact upon individual's attitudes and behaviour, enable prisoners to gain vocational qualifications, link effectively with resettlement policy and community provision and even encourage the purposeful use of leisure time after release (Ministry of Justice, 2011b). However, there is substantial local variation in the degree to which these objectives are implemented, and despite calls for a rigorous evaluation of *what works* in sport and physical activity in prison settings

(HM Prison Service, 2002) there has until now been no in-depth exploration of how sports-based initiatives can facilitate well-being and behavioural change in prisons, despite an abundance of anecdotal evidence and a growing number of organisations seeking to use sport to promote social change.

Community organisations and their involvement in prison sport

Although many prisons have established partnerships with local sports clubs, either informally or through the social responsibility agenda of a premiership club or governing body, organisations that engage directly with prisoners through specialist provision are relatively few in number. The Bristol-based Second Chance Project (www.2ndchanceproject.co.uk) uses sport to promote social change among disadvantaged communities, including casework, mentoring and specialist resettlement support with juveniles, young adults and adults in prison and after release, and since 2012 the Cage Rugby (www.cagerugby.org.uk) initiative has delivered in several English prisons, combining physical sessions with classroom-based activities exploring identity and emotion, communication and interview skills. Other organisations have modified their work to engage directly with prisons and prisoners, for example as part of its broader programme of work that aims to use cricket to change the lives of disadvantaged young people, Cricket for Change (www.cricketforchange.org.uk) works directly with young men in several English prisons and has also established the Street Team initiative, which trains young ex-prisoners as coaching staff and mentors in community settings.

More broadly, the United Kingdom is recognised as having a thriving network of voluntary and community organisations directly concerned with sport and social inclusion. To illustrate this, a keyword search of registered charities included in the Charity Commission's register (Charity Commission, 2013) carried out in March 2013 revealed a total of 869 charities in England and Wales identifying sport as one of their objects (as described in their governing document) and 1,709 charities in England and Wales that specified sport as one of their activities (as described by their trustees).[3] Specific sporting organisations that are not primarily concerned with prison-based initiatives but who nonetheless evidently have the infrastructure and potential to incorporate prison-based work into their wider remits of promoting sport in disadvantaged communities include Access Sport (www.accesssport.org.uk), Active Communities Network (www.activecommunities.org.uk), Beyond Sport (www.beyondsport.org), Laureus Sport for Good (www.laureus.com), Positive Futures (www.posfutures.org.uk), Sport England (www.sportengland.org), Street Games (www.streetgames.org), Wooden Spoon (www.woodenspoon.com) and the Youth Sport Trust (www.youthsporttrust.org), to name just a few. A number of national criminal justice organisations also have a sporting element, including the Prince's Trust (www.princes-trust.org.uk), NACRO (www.nacro.org.uk) and Catch 22 (www.catch-22.org.uk). Meanwhile, the Football Foundation (www.footballfoundation.org.uk), which is funded by the Premier League and the Football Association, and governing bodies such as Premiership Rugby (www.premiershiprugby.com) and the RFU (www.rfu.com) have funded and supported a number of prison-based initiatives.

At an international level, Euro Sport Health (www.eurosporthealth.eu), the International Platform on Sport and Development (www.sportanddev.org), and United through Sport (www.unitedthroughsport.org) promote the role that sport plays in education, development, public health and social inclusion. And lastly, established by the Council of Europe, the Enlarged Partial Agreement on Sport (www.coe.int/epas) aims to promote sport, emphasise its positive values and establish international standards. It has also announced 2014 as the year of 'sport in prison'.

Sporting masculinities in prison

A significant shortcoming of criminological research is that although crime is far more frequently committed by men, who in turn make up over 95% of the prison population, academic consideration of crime rarely examines issues of gender and masculinity. In one of the few notable exceptions to the tendency to ignore issues of masculinities within criminology generally, and prisons more specifically, Jewkes (2005) highlights the manner in which prison creates and reinforces a type of masculinity characterised by aggression and violence, concluding that this legitimatised form of masculinity is adopted as a coping strategy within prisons. Similarly, in his analysis of diverse and contested masculinities, Messerschmidt (1993) explains youth crime as a means of 'doing masculinity' in the absence of other resources, whereas Beesley and McGuire (2009) explain violent offending in the context of gender role identity and Sim (1994) focuses on the interaction between power, violence and masculinity in prison.

Although sport is rarely specifically mentioned within these debates of masculinity and criminal identities, perhaps it should be. Indeed, unlike other institutions, sport seems to enjoy a disproportionate significance in prisons. This may be partially explained by the hypermasculine environment of a prison (Toch, 1998) and because there is a dominant form of masculinity in sport – and in organised sport in particular – which has managed to remain relatively unchallenged in contrast to other versions of masculinity in the wider society (Wellard, 2009). However, the observation that masculinities and sport are entwined is not a new one. Eminent philosopher and sociologist Pierre Bourdieu devoted considerable attention to discussions of sport and physical culture (Bourdieu, 1978, 1999) and his conceptual work has subsequently attracted the interest of scholars of the sociology of sport, physical activity and physical education (see, for example, Brown, 2005; Clement, 1995; Kay & Laberge, 2002; Light & Kirk, 2000; Tomlinson, 2004). A likely reason for this attention will be the way in which the sporting body exemplifies many of Bourdieu's conceptual ideas around how the body acts as a mediating entity, linking individuals to the broader sociospatial processes of power, reproduction and change. Brown (2005) points out that Bourdieu consistently used the metaphor of 'the feel for the game' in articulating how the body binds together his central theoretical constructs of habitus, capital and field, and in his 1998 text, Bourdieu refers to *illusio* as 'the fact of being caught up in and by the game' (p. 76).

As Whitehead and Barrett (2001) propose, 'since masculinity is something that one does rather than something that one has, it would be appropriate to say that men 'do' masculinity in a variety of ways and in a variety of settings, depending on the resources available to them' (p. 18). Theorists have considered the ways in which sporting masculinities are played out in the institutionalised settings of the playground (Swain, 2000), the physical education class (Penney, 2002) or the sports field (Salisbury & Jackson, 1996), but not within the prison, although it could be argued that 'doing' sport has long been recognised as an obvious way of rehearsing or asserting masculinity in the constricted environment of the prison, where the practice of other forms of 'hegemonic masculinity' (culturally norma-tive ideals of male behaviour, such as heterosexual activity and demonstrations of power and dominance) are less easily exercised.

Although beyond the scope of this text to explore sporting masculinities in the same detail as has been afforded in gender study texts, these theoretical under-standings should help to contextualise some of the subsequent findings. Readers keen to develop a more comprehensive understanding of issues associated with sporting masculinities are directed to Ian Wellard's (2009) *Sport, Masculinity and the Body*, and Pierre Bourdieu's (1998) *Practical Reason: On the Theory of Action*, while readers curious about academic debates of masculinities and crime would do well to commence their reading with Tim Newburn and Betsy Stanko's (1994) edited volume *Just Boys Doing Business?* which brings together a range of criminological essays on men, masculinities and crime.

International perspectives on sport in prison

Prison-based sport and physical activity may be classified in different jurisdictions under the responsibility of recreation, health or education, but provision and access is generally considered part of the basic principles of prison laws and policies of many countries (van Zyl & Snacken, 2002). Prison practice in England and Wales is determined by well-defined Prison Service orders and instructions and practice around the world is also subject to national and international regulations on sport and physical activity, although adherence to these standards varies. Key legisla-tion includes that from the United Nations Commission for Human Rights (2006), where the standard minimum rules for the treatment of prisoners prescribe that:

> Every prisoner who is not employed in outdoor work shall have at least one hour of suitable exercise in the open air daily if weather permits . . . Young prisoners, and others of suitable age and physique, shall receive physical and recreational training during the period of exercise. (21.1-2)

Likewise, Principle XIII of the Inter-American Commission on Human Rights (2008) stipulates that:

> Persons deprived of liberty shall have the right to take part in cultural, sport-ing, and social activities, and shall have opportunities for healthy and con-structive recreation.

In a European context, the European Committee for the Prevention of Torture and Inhuman or Degrading Treatment or Punishment (2006) recognises the importance of exercise and recreation with a set of rules, including 27(6), which states that:

> Recreational opportunities, which include sport, games, cultural activities, hobbies and other leisure pursuits, shall be provided and, as far as possible, prisoners shall be allowed to organise them.

In order to explore further the meanings and practices of sport in prison across Europe, the recently establishment European Commission project *Prisoners on the Move: Move into Sport, Move through Sport* has brought together various professionals involved in prison sport from five European countries, resulting in a report promoting the social inclusive, health and rehabilitative functions of sport in prisons (Prisoners on the Move, 2012). In their survey of 341 individuals responsible for sport activities in 153 prisons from five European Union countries (Belgium, Denmark, Romania, Spain and the Netherlands), Devis-Devis, Peiro-Velart and Martos-Garcia (2012) identified 61 different supervised and unsupervised activities offered in the prisons, the most common being football, body building, table tennis, badminton, basketball and volleyball. These activities were regarded by staff as therapeutic, educational, occupational and recreational; they were also associated with opportunities for temporary release to participate in community sport events and visits to the prison by community organisations, although this varied dramatically in different countries. For example, those working in Spanish and Romanian prisons reported substantially more community sports activities than those from Belgium, Denmark and the Netherlands. Apart from in Spanish prisons, levels of engagement in accredited sports programmes were low, but there was a broad consensus in the perceived role of sport in prison across the five countries surveyed. When asked to report the primary aim of sport and physical activities offered in their establishments, the majority of the surveyed prison staff referred to the role of sport in improving prisoner health and instilling positive social values.

Conclusions from the European Commission study included the need for more professional specialisation in physical activity and sport, the extension of physical activity and sport beyond a recreational role to one more embedded in formal education, further promotion of social values through physical activities, using sport to facilitate future inclusion after release, increases in community participation (both inside and outside of the prison) and a requirement to improve the quality of facilities and the professional development of staff involved.

International examples of sporting initiatives in prisons

As has been observed in British practice (see the subsequent chapter), establishments operating under the same legislation may prioritise sport in different ways. Unsurprisingly, and reflecting a relatively progressive prison system,

Scandinavian prison systems emphasise the importance of physical activity; for example the Sønder Omme State Prison in Denmark offers prisoners golf and spinning as well as links with local swimming and cycling clubs. In the United States, by contrast, the primary concern that inmates may use their strength as a weapon against correctional officers tends to overshadow and undermine recognition of the potential benefits of sport and physical activity, as highlighted by Amtmann (2001) who argues that, given that the prison system has to pay for inmate health care during their incarceration, sport should be prioritised not least for its associated health benefits and the resulting financial savings. In reality though, mirroring the 'punitive turn' (Muncie, 2008) observed in the United Kingdom, the 1970s saw U.S. policy and public attitudes shift from a largely rehabilitative focus to a more punitive one which emphasised punishment as the primary purpose of imprisonment and saw an explosive growth in the prison population (which remains higher today than that of any other developed country). As the 1980s and 1990s saw a general decline in U.S. public support for prison inmate rehabilitation programmes and activities and an increased emphasis on punishment, the development of the 'no-frills' U.S. prison movement and enacted legislation has led to the reduction of recreational facilities, including a call to ban weightlifting, and specifically free weights, in federal prisons. Responding to the weightlifting ban, the National Correctional Recreation Association, the U.S. professional organisation concerned with prison sport issued an official statement in 1995 declaring weightlifting programmes an integral aspect of rehabilitation services within prison settings, a stance supported by U.S. research demonstrating the benefits of weightlifting in the context of improved physical health (Tucker, 1983) and mental health (Folkins & Sime, 1981; Mehrabian & Bekken, 1986). Although access to sports and fitness equipment may be less plentiful in U.S. prisons, this hasn't prevented the development of a thriving specialist literature on 'felon fitness' (Teufel & Kroger, 2011) or 'convict conditioning' (Wade, 2009), published texts where prisoners report their self-devised exercise programmes based on body-weight exercises, further promoting the rhetoric of physical fitness as a way of protecting oneself from physical intimidation and/or as a way of passing time during incarceration.

Sport and physical activities are comparatively well embedded into policies and practices concerned with imprisonment in the United Kingdom, with an established history of the promotion of physical fitness as an integral element of the regimes, structures and staffing of British prisons. Although this text focuses predominantly on examples from and data collected in England and Wales, there is a robust international evidence base which reflects global recognition of the role of sport and physical activity in prisons and in meeting wider policy objectives, particularly in health promotion and efforts to reduce reoffending. Though less widespread and formalised than might be expected in a British context, there are still numerous examples of the innovative and successful use of prison sports in global settings. As well as the inevitable verification of sport being prioritised in countries considered to have more liberal penal systems, such as in Scandinavian settings (Gentleman, 2012), there is also evidence of sport having powerful effects in more brutal prison systems, for example the Project Hope football intervention in Drakenstein Prison, one of the largest and most overcrowded jails in South Africa, where dramatic reductions in reoffending have been attributed to the development of positive role models and meaningful alternatives to gang culture through sport (Chalat, 2012).

Prisoners in many countries have access to physical activity in custody, although the types of activity vary immensely, from the minimal use of a basic exercise yard still prevalent in some U.S. prisons to more elaborate facilities, such as the Danish prison with its own golf course, and the Canadian prisons equipped with ice hockey rinks (Caplan, 1996). Depending on the individual establishment, and national policy, sports initiatives have been used to reach a range of different objectives. In 1988, in collaboration with the Italian Justice Minister, the Italian Union of Sport for All introduced a sports-based initiative across prisons in Italy which focused on sport as a mechanism for improving skills, behaviour and resettlement opportunities. The project reported positive outcomes in terms of the promotion of social development and improved physical and mental health among prisoners, attributed in part to the ability of sport to relieve boredom and isolation in custody. Elsewhere in the world, specific interventions have been found to contribute to improved health and well-being and opportunities for rehabilitation, for example in male prisons in Cameroon (Digennaro, 2010) and in male and female prisons in Australia (Sherry, 2010, 2012).

Rugby interventions within prisons: Global examples

Internationally, rugby has been regarded as a sport which can have particular value in addressing a range of objectives within penal institutions. In a maximum security prison for adults in Buenos Aires, Argentinian inmates came together to start a rugby team which was utilised by the prison to promote good behaviour by limiting participation to those with good behavioural records and employment within the prison. The rugby team was supported by professional coaching from the Buenos Aires Rugby Association, and matches outside the prison were arranged in an effort to promote mental and physical health (Deges, 2010).

Similarly, in a Georgian young offenders institute a UNICEF (United Nations International Children's Emergency Fund) project which aimed to boost children's health, improve academic performance and help reduce crime has used rugby as a tool to promote the health of young prisoners and to support the development of values and skills such as respect, discipline, friendship and teamwork. As well as improving health and well-being in custody, the project aimed to support young offenders in their community reintegration by linking with local rugby clubs upon release (UNICEF, 2011). Rehabilitative rugby interventions are also evident in Fijian prisons – rugby coaching and refereeing clinics have been delivered within Nasinu prison as a way of offering young offenders opportunities to develop skills and gain qualifications, with the ultimate aim of aiding rehabilitation (Fiji Corrections Service, 2011).

In Venezuela, on the other hand, rugby has also been used as part of a wider diversionary programme. The Alcatraz project involves young men being offered the option by police either to engage in an educational programme involving agricultural work, psychological counselling and rugby, or to be sentenced to custody through the courts. Project organisers have reported that the project has had particular value in terms of diverting young people from crime, and in reducing pervasive gang related offending in the region (Morsbach, 2011).

The principles underpinning many of these international examples are largely consistent with the objectives of U.K. initiatives discussed in more detail elsewhere in this book, whereby sport is used to promote well-being and rehabilitation among prisoners, with the ultimate aim of reducing reoffending. In Brazil, although the impact on subsequent offending is unknown, an unusual example of the use of physical exercise in prison can be found in Santa Rita do Sapucaí where prisoners cycle on stationary bicycles connected to power generators which provide green energy to power street lights in the local vicinity. Participating prisoners are awarded a day off their sentence for every 16 hours of pedalling completed. Denying that the initiative is a form of free labour, the prison authorities claim that it has been successful in incentivising physical health (Bevins, 2012).

Such diverse global examples serve to illustrate how sport in prison has been and can be used for a range of purposes, but they also highlight the need for a robust evidence base for best practice principles, given how far reaching yet disparate these different prison-based initiatives can be. The next chapter returns to the United Kingdom but maintains a comparative focus by exploring the different types of sport and physical activities delivered in prisons across England and Wales.

Notes

1   Although in the 2013 announcements it was declared that this establishment would return to being publicly run when the G4S contract expired later that year.
2   Approximately 95% of those working in prison PE departments are PEIs, with only 5% being sports and games officers (National Audit Office, 2006) who in turn are more likely to be located on the prison landing than in the prison gym.
3   These figures were reduced to 203 and 176 when applied to organisations operating throughout England and Wales (i.e. not specific to a particular region).

3 Setting the scene

Participation in sport and physical activity across the prison estate

Taking part in physical education activities may no longer be mandatory, but prisoners are still encouraged to be physically active (National Audit Office, 2006), and a number of parliamentary publications refer explicitly to engagement – or lack of engagement – in sporting activities in the context of promoting purposeful activity in prisons (Conservative Party, 2011; Home Affairs Select Committee, 2004). Operational regulations may specify minimum entitlements for exercise and recreation (whereby, in England and Wales, all prisoners have the opportunity to participate in a minimum of one hour – or two hours on average for those under 21 – of physical education per week) but initial research interviews with prisoners and staff focusing on sport and physical activity highlighted the disparity of provision across the estate. Individuals who had experience of several different prisons (either as prisoner or staff member) were able to reel off names of establishments where sporting facilities or opportunities were especially good or poor, prioritised or neglected. Official inspections also provide a general gauge for how well a particular prison is meeting statutory requirements, but within this there is wide variation even between prisons of the same size and category.

Using official data to establish participation levels

In spite of some ambitious objectives and the routine delivery of physical education in prisons, there has until recently been no exploration of whether participation is equitable across diverse offender populations or the extent to which current practices are congruent with existing policy. Although prominent themes were identified in PE manager responses from across the estate, in order to assess variations across types of secure establishments, average monthly *prisoner participation level* (PPL) data were obtained for 2010–2011 for 107 English and Welsh public sector prisons from the Ministry of Justice through a Freedom of Information request.[1] PPLs represent the total number of individual prisoners within an establishment who have participated in physical activities during a set time frame (figures are typically collated monthly), expressed as a percentage of the total population for that prison, and they therefore provide a useful indicator of participation in physical activity across the estate. Statistical analysis of prisoner

Table 3.1 Number of prisons considered according to establishment type and average/ range of prisoner participation levels (PPL) in physical activity

Type of establishment	Number of prisons considered	Average monthly PPL (%)	Minimum PPL (%)	Maximum PPL (%)
Juvenile	5	90	63	100
Young Offenders Institute	10	67	50	83
Split YOI & Adult	3	55	50	63
Category B & C	37	60	44	82
Category D Open Prisons	9	63	52	76
Local Prisons	25	50	28	68
High Security	9	60	45	86
Female Estate	7	48	29	89
Immigration Removal Centre	2	72	71	74
Total	$n = 107$	56%		

Note: Establishments where reception criteria incorporated two or more categories were placed according to their principal population.

participation levels showed that these differed significantly according to type of prison, $F(8, 98) = 8.39$, $p < .001$, with substantial variation between establishments within the same category.

As expected, given that PE is scheduled as part of the core curriculum within juvenile facilities, average participation levels were highest within the juvenile estate. Participation figures within the young adult estate varied across establishments, ranging from 50% to 83%, but on average were among the highest after juvenile establishments, which perhaps reflects the fact that sports participation is typically higher among younger populations in non-prison settings (Sport England, 2012). In terms of the adult male population, average PPLs within local prisons were significantly lower than those elsewhere within the Category B or the Category C estate. The diverse range, and the transient nature, of prisoners held within local prisons and the high proportions of remand prisoners whose sentence length is yet uncertain will inevitably present a particular challenge for prison gym staff in motivating prisoners to engage in and sustain participation, which in turn makes it difficult to ensure that PE provision meets all prisoner needs and that participation opportunities are maximised. Despite large variations in PPLs within the high-security estate, average participation levels did not differ significantly from the rest of the adult male estate, suggesting that although elevated security concerns may inhibit participation, physical activity remains an important aspect of the regime of high-security establishments. However, as has been previously noted in a thematic inspection of close supervision and high-security segregation (HM Chief Inspector of Prisons, 1999) and reviews of healthy choices across the estate (Condon, Hek & Harris, 2008), the quality of exercise in high-secure establishments has been found to vary dramatically from a bleak exercise yard to a broad range of specialist facilities.

In immigration removal centres, average PPL was consistently high, despite language barriers presenting particular difficulties for those delivering PE within such establishments. At 48%, the female estate had the lowest average PPL of all prison types but was also characterised by the greatest variation across establishments, ranging between 29% and 89%. Participation figures within the female estate may reflect the well documented lower levels of sports participation among females more generally (Sport England, 2012). However, reports published by HM Inspectorate of Prisons also indicate that establishments holding female prisoners are much less likely to have outdoor sporting facilities, so participation may also be limited by provision.

Across the estate, although access to sufficient PE is considered readily available in Inspectorate reports, concerns about low participation rates have been partially explained by physical activity being perceived as voluntary or due to clashes with other regime activities such as work or education. The National Audit Office (2006) have identified low uptake rates in some establishments as being directly influenced by the range of activities and facilities available, the emphasis on particular activities within certain departments (for example, team sports or noncompetitive activities), equity of access, and staff availability.

National survey findings

In seeking to explore further the prevalence and different uses of sport and physical activity across the prison estate, in 2012 we distributed a survey to every prison gym manager in England and Wales. In total, 52 completed surveys were returned within the required time period, representing a good response rate of well over a third of all establishments from across the prison estate. The survey generated qualitative and quantitative data from a representative group of prisons, reflecting each establishment type by security level and type of prisoner accommodated. Unlike the PPL data generated through a Freedom of Information request, the national survey also included responses from five privately run prisons.[2] The survey sought detailed information on the sporting resources and provision offered and solicited more subjective accounts of the perceived opportunities, challenges and threats associated with delivering sport and physical activity within prison settings.

The gym manager survey was designed to elicit a range of information about the structure and organisation, resources and facilities of each gym, and it included opportunities for gym staff to respond to a series of qualitative responses about their experiences and opinions of prison-based sport and physical activity. A paper version of the survey was initially sent by mail to the manager of each prison gym, with a subsequent email reminder circulated by a national PE advisor with an electronic version of the survey attached.

Sporting facilities and activities available in custody

Aside from published participation rates, no information was previously available to summarise the types of sporting activities promoted within prison settings. Because of this, the survey sought to establish the quality and quantity of facilities offered in prison gyms throughout England and Wales. As well as the common facilities of a gym, sports hall and Astroturf or grass pitch, 60% (*n* = 31) of establishments reported having a range of additional facilities beyond the gym, including fitness suites on wings, dedicated classrooms, tennis courts, cricket pitches, basketball courts, climbing walls, assault courses, healthy lifestyle centre/rehabilitation suites, physiotherapy rooms, weights rooms, spin cycling suites, swimming pool and outdoor gym equipment.

No statistically significant differences were identified in the type of facilities available according to the type of prison establishment, with the exception of grass pitches, χ^2 (8) = 25.39, *p* < .01, where provision varied significantly across the estate: all responding Category D prisons reporting having a grass pitch, as did 69% of Category C establishments and 50% of YOIs and Immigration Removal Centres (IRCs). Only one Category B and local prison, and none of the female or high-security establishments, reported having use of a pitch.

All establishments surveyed reported offering standard gym-based activities (typically complete with weights and cardiovascular machines), but as well as the most commonly offered sporting activities (football, volleyball, basketball, cricket, running and rugby) two thirds of establishments also reported offering more diverse activities, which included racquet sports, indoor cycling, swimming, circuit training and aerobics, hockey, walking, dodge ball, climbing, yoga, bowls,

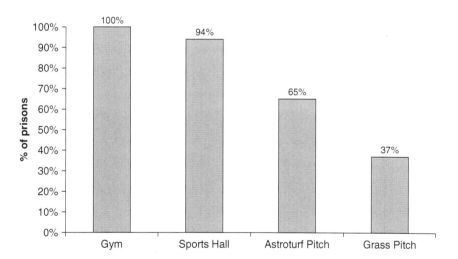

Figure 3.1 Frequency of most common sports facilities in prisons.

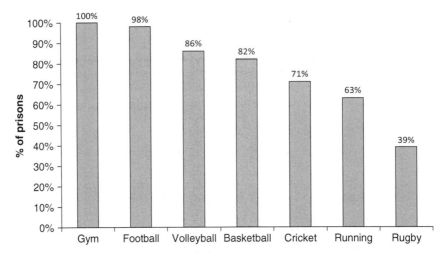

Figure 3.2 The most common sporting activities offered in prison establishments.

dance, trampolining, gymnastics, Pilates, power lifting, Tai Chi, boxing, minor games and outdoor pursuits.[3]

No significant statistical differences in the type of sports offered were identified according to type of establishment, with the exception of rugby, χ^2 (8) = 17.31, $p < .05$, which was offered in all responding juvenile and YOI establishments and yet in over half (54%) of Category C establishments and fewer than a quarter of all other types of establishments.

Almost a third ($n = 17$) of responding prisons reported delivering activities in partnership with external providers. Community partners were typically utilised in the delivery of professional coaching, for example for football and rugby, or to deliver specialist classes such as yoga or dance. A statistically significant difference in whether or not external partners were used to deliver activities was identified according to type of establishment, χ^2 (8) = 19.26, $p < .05$, in that all responding juvenile establishments and YOIs reported using them, compared with 40% of Category B establishments, 27% of local establishments and 23% of Category C establishments. No female or high-security prisons or IRCs reported using external partners.

Over half ($n = 27$) of responding establishments reported that they had prisoner sports teams, most commonly for football, but also for a further seven sports. Whether or not prisons had prisoner teams did not differ significantly according to the type of establishment, suggesting that the security status of a prison did not have an impact on whether or not prisoner teams were created within each prison.

Just over half ($n = 27$) of responding prisons reported that they had involvement with external sports teams, leagues or organisations. Most commonly, this arrangement consisted of visiting community/university sports teams or organisations (for example community groups of disabled individuals or representatives

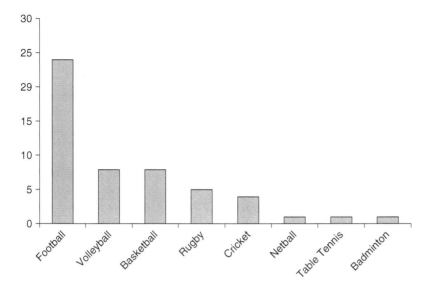

Figure 3.3 Frequency of types of prisoner sports teams.

from sporting bodies) coming into the prison in order to participate in activities or to facilitate coaching opportunities, but there was also evidence of external organisations coming into the prison to make use of the facilities – including the case of a swimming pool which was staffed by prisoners trained as lifeguards. Furthermore, almost a third ($n = 17$) of responding establishments reported that prisoners had participated in sporting activities in the community (while Released on Temporary Licence) within the previous year. These community-based activities most commonly consisted of playing in matches on behalf of external local teams, representing football (half of such activity), rugby, volleyball and basketball, as well as activities for the Duke of Edinburgh award. Other community-based sporting activities included work placements in the fitness industry, for example within leisure centres and sports clubs. The number of prisoners participating in community activities ranged greatly across prisons from two to over 100 within a year.

A significant difference was identified in whether or not prisoners participated in sports-based activities in the community according to type of establishment, $\chi^2 (7) = 18.72, p < .05$. Whereas all responding juvenile and YOI establishments reported this kind of participation, it occurred in only five out of the 12 local establishments, three out of the 13 Category C establishments, two out of the six Category D establishments, one out of the four female establishments and in none of Category B, high-security or IRC establishments.

All 52 responding prisons reported that they employed prisoners in orderly roles within their PE departments. The number of prisoners thus employed within PE departments at any one time ranged from one to 23, with a mean average of seven ($SD = 4.7$). The majority (86%; $n = 44$) of establishments reported that they offered accredited sports-based qualifications, but the number of different courses offered within each establishment varied widely and ranged from 1 to 22 ($M = 6$, $SD = 5.5$).

The perceived benefits of delivering sport in prisons

Staff perceptions of the benefits of offering sport and physical activity in prison were identified in terms of the observed positive impact on prisoners and within the establishments more generally. The most frequently cited benefits – particularly from team sports – were the opportunities to develop prisoners' communication, team work and leadership skills. Improving prisoners' physical health was identified as the second most prominent benefit by staff, followed by the bolstering of self-esteem and confidence and the direct targeting of offending behaviour, for example by reducing impulsivity and aggression through participation in sport. The promotion of education and employment opportunities was closely followed by recognition of the improvements to the wider prison environment and regime as a result of the introduction of sporting initiatives as a way of promoting social control within establishments and contributing to a more positive atmosphere. Encouraging prisoners to develop new prosocial interests was also identified as a primary value of sport, linked to the potential to encourage constructive use of leisure time, both in custody and in the community. Following the promotion of positive values and improved mental health, significant numbers of staff also referred to the role of sport and physical activity in facilitating improved relations between staff and prisoners as well as among prisoners.

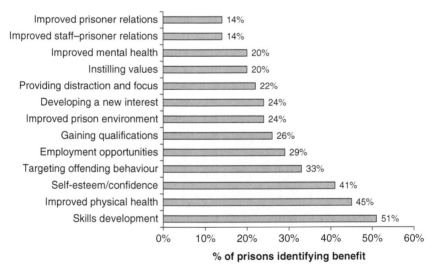

Figure 3.4 Staff-identified benefits associated with delivering sport and physical activity in prisons.

The perceived challenges and threats to sport provision in prison

The challenges that prison gym staff identified when delivering sporting activities in custody primarily related to security concerns, risks and the practical difficulties associated with delivery in a custodial setting. The most common challenge identified in relation to delivering to offender populations concerned the elevated risk of having to manage challenging behaviour such as aggression during sporting activities – although staff also reported how this could be managed and moderated through appropriate delivery techniques, careful planning of activities and risk assessment of prisoners, for example by ensuring that members of conflicting gangs were not taking part in the same initiative. That being said, when carefully managed there is evidence of potential for the successful use of sport to bring together disparate groups and to reduce inter-group conflicts (see Lawson, 2005). As well as managing gang issues, staff also noted that aggressive or intimidating behaviour posed a potential challenge when vulnerable prisoners and those in the wider prison population came into contact during participation in sport and physical activity. Low literacy levels and prisoners being released or transferred were further commonly cited obstacles to successfully delivering sports based programmes and qualifications, whilst attention and commitment issues were noted as a wider challenge to engaging prisoners in sporting activities.

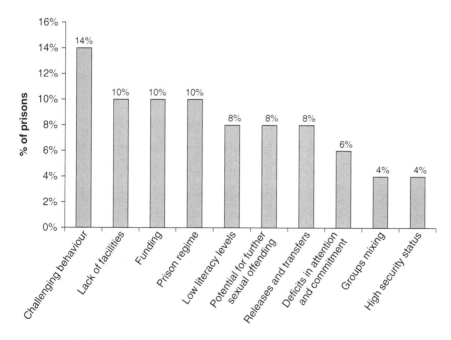

Figure 3.5 Staff-identified challenges associated with delivering sport and physical activity in prisons.

Supplementing the staff survey with interview findings

In keeping with the national survey findings, the subsequent in-depth staff interviews revealed that the key challenges of delivering sport and physical activity in prison could be categorised as relating to organisational factors (institutional support, resources, and regime), issues connected to prisoners themselves (reluctance to engage in sport, limited experience, literacy issues, difficulties maintaining involvement and low self-esteem), and the associated challenges of engaging with specific types of offenders (for example sex offenders, older prisoners, transient populations and high-security prisoners). While discussions surrounding the promotion of the engagement of different populations of prisoners will follow in subsequent chapters, the remainder of this chapter will explore organisational factors.

Although the core provision for and treatment of those held in prison custody is guided by national policies, it should be recognised that an institution's attitudes towards sport provision is also strongly influenced by individual governors. Despite a move towards a centralised commissioning framework, prison governors are still expected to maintain a degree of independence in specifying services for their establishments, which can lead to a considerable degree of variation in service provision, depending on an individual's agenda (Meek, Gojkovic & Mills, 2010). As with other aspects of the prison regime, the governor of each establishment has a certain amount of autonomy regarding the allocation of resources (financial and staffing) to sport and physical activity. However, a governor will typically be in post at an establishment for an average of just over two years (Hansard, 2009) before moving on to another prison or role and being replaced by a new figure who may be anxious to leave their mark by making changes within the institution. As the following quote from a prison gym manager demonstrates, staff are also acutely aware of the differing views that governors can have and the impact of this on prison gyms:

> We're fortunate in as much as we've got a good governor who is pro-sport, who sees the value of it and sees it as a way to change lives and wants to see that happen. But the trouble is, of course, if the governor changes. Not every governor is the same. Some think highly of PE, some don't think highly of PE, some think it's something that they should just have a chance to take part in at weekends and evenings and should just be a leisure activity.

It is therefore not surprising that the research found that attitudes towards, support for and the resourcing of sport and physical activity varies dramatically between institutions, even those of the same security status holding comparable populations, with provision evidently improving or deteriorating in the same prison over time. A straightforward illustration is the example of some prison governors reporting a strong stance that free weights should not be available in their establishment whereas in other similar prisons such activity may be actively encouraged. Policies are also changing in terms of the sporting opportunities granted in prisons: for example, until recently public prisons were not authorised to offer boxing, but this has now been approved as a way of engaging nonviolent offenders (Hansard, 2013).

Factors which contribute to organisational-level support for sport and physical activity

Members of prison senior management teams who have previously occupied more junior roles as PE officers within the Prison Service, who are active within the Prison Service Sports Association, or who hold a personal belief that sport can be an effective way of promoting positive behaviour and reducing reoffending were found to be more likely to support sport and physical activity, for instance in prioritising activities within the regime or in allocating financial and/or staffing resources. Interviews with staff reveal a keen awareness of the competing priorities between gym staff and senior management, often exacerbated in the context of pressures to reduce staffing and delivery costs and a lack of awareness of the importance of sport and physical activity:

> In the prison regime, there's a lack of understanding as to what PE can offer. (Staff, Local)

> The benefit of engaging prisoners in sport and physical education in prisons is exactly the same as engaging pupils in schools and colleges. Unfortunately the vast majority of senior managers either do not understand the concept or do not subscribe to it. (Staff, Local)

Stakeholder interviews confirmed the perceived influence of individual members of staff in senior positions on the type of provision offered:

> Local managers with little or no interest in or understanding of PE can inhibit even basic provision, let alone innovation. (Senior Manager)

However, even in establishments that were generally supportive of sport and physical activity and the work of gym staff, this would not always translate into prioritising integration of the gym with other aspects of the prison:

> Gym staff get pulled off due to staff shortages to cover the landings, about 50% of the classes three days a week are lost due to this. (Staff, Female)

Likewise, it was widely acknowledged that pressures on the wider regime of the prison would impinge on efforts to promote positive activities in the gym, particularly as prisons are increasingly operating under a more structured working week regime:

> It's difficult to fit it in with the regime, facilitating activities around work. (Staff, Category C)

> We have to deal with the challenge of regimes and changing to a work based prison in line with government incentives. (Staff, Local)

> Gym competes with association in free time and then with work or other courses and appointments during the day. (Staff, Female)

Responses to the national survey of gym managers mirrored the interview findings, whereby the prison regime was regularly identified as presenting a challenge in delivering sport in a custodial setting – for example in scheduling activities around prisoners' work and other elements of the regime. A lack of facilities was identified by some establishments as limiting the range and type of provision that they could offer and a number of establishments attributed this directly to funding cuts – in terms of funding for qualifications as well as reductions in staffing levels:

> The only risk we have is in financing the courses. Numbers and delivery are not an issue. (Staff, Category C)

Other identified challenges were more specific to the type of establishment, for example for high-security establishments their security status presents a challenge in terms of the range of activities they can realistically offer, the movement of prisoners to activities and in their capacity to establish links with external organisations.

Facilities and resources across the prison estate

Prison design and layout varies considerably, whereby although some establishments cover large rural sites with ample outdoor spaces, others occupy relatively small urban premises. It is hardly surprising, therefore, that staff referred to the lack of indoor and outdoor facilities as being a key determining factor in the activities they could offer:

> As a Cat B local with no outside facilities it has never been an option to accommodate external sports teams. (Staff, Local)

> We simply don't have room in the establishment to extend our already small department. (Staff, Category B)

Just as prison establishments themselves vary dramatically in their physical size, the facilities available to PE departments range from a small general purpose gym to a variety of indoor and outdoor facilities. Reported numbers of gym staff also varied dramatically, ranging from two to 15, with a mean average of seven members of PE staff in each prison. Although analysis did not control for other factors contributing to staffing levels, for example the size of the prison, the number of PE staff differed significantly according to type of establishment, $F(8) = 3.15$, $p < .01$, with YOIs having the highest average number of gym staff ($M = 11$), followed by high-security establishments ($M = 9$), Juvenile establishments ($M = 8$), Category C and local prisons ($M = 7$), Category B prisons ($M = 6$), IRCs ($M = 5$), female establishments ($M = 4$) and open prisons ($M = 3$).

Widespread reductions to prison staff across the estate were reported to have had a particular impact of prison gyms, with establishments having to manage with fewer members of staff:

> The challenge is fitting it all in as we are now two members of staff and we were three. We can't complete all the work. (Staff, Category C)

> Reduction in staffing within the PE department – there are not enough staff to be able to run activities. (Staff, Local)

Conclusion

Participation in sport and physical activity within prison clearly varies dramatically according to age and gender, mirroring trends found in the general population. Despite levels of participation also varying according to security level and an establishment's remit, these differences are less stark than one might anticipate, suggesting relative equity of access when comparing establishment types. However, variation between prisons of the same type remains substantial, suggesting that access to physical education can be dependent on the operational priorities of different establishments. Corresponding with variable levels of participation, practical delivery of sport across the secure estate is especially divergent and alignment with wider policy agendas is variable, although this is to be expected considering the needs and security issues associated with different prisoner populations. Reports from the Prisons Inspectorate suggest that although education provision is good across the estate, the holistic integration of wider prison objectives into PE provision is not yet widespread and there is evidently a need for greater dissemination of such examples of good practice across the estate. Subsequent chapters will explore this in the context of specific and diverse populations and in relation to specific issues such as health promotion, violence reduction and efforts to reduce reoffending.

Notes

1   Although 10% of prisons in England and Wales are privately run, data from these prisons is not available since private establishments are not included in Freedom of Information requests.
2   Analyses of responses from public prisons in comparison to private prisons did not reveal any statistical significance.
3   Definitions of what constituted sport and physical activity were purposefully omitted from the questionnaire, leaving gym mangers free to determine what activities to include in their responses (i.e. yoga or dance).

4 Promoting sport and physical activity in diverse prisoner populations

> There must be equality of access to PE programmes and resources to meet the requirements of all prisoners, through identifying and giving full considerations to meet specific needs of their gender, religion, age, disability, race and sexual orientation. All those involved in delivering PE will recognise the diverse needs and abilities of those who use its services and give everyone an equal chance to develop and fulfil their potential. (Ministry of Justice, 2011b, p. 6)

Despite this commitment from the Ministry of Justice, and as well as the fact that the same guidance also recognises the need to respond to the diverse needs of prisoner populations ('the balance and content of the PE programme . . . must include a varied range of physical education activity to meet the diverse needs of the prisoner population,' p. 7) the participation figures and facilities discussed in Chapter 3 demonstrate that across the prison estate, different incarcerated populations remain more or less likely to participate in and benefit from physical activity and sporting initiatives. However, limited data are available to assess participation in and access to sport and physical education within prison according to these diversity strands. What we do know is that prisons hold a diverse range of populations, presenting particular challenges in the provision of sport and physical activity.

Until now there has been very little exploration of the use of physical activity among diverse prisoner populations, but the broader non-criminological literature has recognised the importance of studying equalities and inclusion in sport and physical education (see Stidder & Hayes, 2012) and confirmed that there are a number of specific groups of people who face an increased risk of experiencing intimidation in and exclusion from mainstream sporting activities. Where research in non-prison settings has identified particular sporting inequalities for ethnic minorities (Jones, 2002; Krouwel, Boonstra, Duyvendak & Veldboer, 2006), those with disabilities (Catton, 2007; French & Hainsworth, 2001), and nonheterosexuals (Griffin, 1992; Wellard, 2002), other psychological barriers to participation in sport, including a lack of confidence, exercise anxiety and body image concerns (Allender, Cowburn & Foster, 2006) have also been detected. Recognising this, an aim of the research detailed in this chapter was to explore the extent to which such sporting exclusions and barriers are replicated, heightened or minimised in prison settings.

Recent years have seen significant attempts to monitor and address service provision and prisoners' experiences according to characteristics and population type (Ministry of Justice, 2012c), reflecting Section 95 of the Criminal Justice Act 1991 which stipulates that information must be published 'for the purpose of facilitating the performance of those engaged in the administration of justice to avoid discriminating against any persons on the ground of race or sex or any other improper ground'. The Equality Prison Service Instruction (Ministry of Justice, 2011a) identifies race, gender, disability, religion, sexual orientation and age as 'protected characteristics of offenders' – populations within the prison estate for whom 'fair service' needs to be ensured. In contributing to broader Ministry of Justice equalities objectives, a commitment to identifying ('and where appropriate addressing') disparities in outcomes for different groups of offenders has been published (National Offender Management Service, 2012b, p. 23).

Although prisoners represent a particularly diverse population, compared to those in their care prison staff represent a relatively nondiverse population. There is little ethnic diversity among prison staff, with an overall average of 6% of Black and minority ethnic (BME) staff in public prisons, ranging from just 1.5% in the North East, to 24% in the Greater London region (Ministry of Justice, 2012c). Prison staff are also significantly more likely to be male,[1] but this is especially so in the gym where, according to unofficial figures from the Prison Service PE college, only 7.5% of current PE staff are women.

When asked to reflect upon patterns of participation or any particular challenges arising from engaging different populations in sport and physical activity, the majority of prison gym staff interviewees reported that participation was equitable across discrete groups of the prison population, although younger prisoners were consistently identified as a group who were more likely to engage in sport in prison, and it was recognised that provision needed to accommodate and include the different populations held within prisons:

> Some prisoners, individuals or groups, may want to influence and dominate sports provision at the expense of others. And with a population with an increasing range of requirements due to age, obesity, mental health, substance misuse and disability, the need for a balanced provision increases. (Senior Manager)

When asked about engagement of diverse prisoner populations in sport and physical activity, staff referred to specific examples of the ways in which practice had been developed so that participation was made equitable so that groups that had been identified as less likely to engage were catered for with tailored activities. However, when asked to describe the types of offenders who were least likely to engage in sport in custody, older prisoners were identified most frequently (by a quarter of the gym staff respondents), followed by prisoners who had substance misuse issues, those experiencing mental health problems or low self-esteem, vulnerable prisoners, sex offenders and foreign nationals. A detailed discussion of the role of sport and physical activity for prisoners with substance misuse problems is presented in Chapter 10 dedicated to health promotion, but a focus on the unique challenges involved in engaging diverse populations in sport and physical activity follows.

Engaging 'non-sporty' prisoners in physical activity

Although it is widely recognised that sport can serve to promote inclusion and participation, it can also – especially if used in a crude or clumsy way – serve to replicate existing inequalities or lead to further exclusions. It is no accident that the main focus of community involvement and research into sport in prison has tended to focus on young male prisoners, given that it is young males who are most likely to participate in sports in wider settings, especially in the context of the mainstream activities of football and use of the gym which have historically been most prominent in prison sport.

Given that evaluations to date have tended to focus on opportunity samples of those who opt to participate in sporting initiatives, there is little accumulated evidence for the impact of participating in sport when motivation or ability levels are low and whether such an impact is positive or detrimental. This raises the question of how constructive or problematic widespread pro-physical activity policies may be for the more vulnerable or excluded populations held within prisons. Although traditionally a place on the football team may have been reserved for only the most gifted athletes within a prison, the importance of seeking inclusive practices that can cater for as wide a population as possible has become more widely recognised, given the diverse support and rehabilitative needs of those groups who might previously have remained invisible in discussions around sport as a moral agent and symptom of change.

In practice, interviews with gym staff revealed a key challenge of engaging those with a limited experience of participating in sport, or a reluctance to try out new activities:

> Many have never done any sport before – skill level and coordination is low. Prisoners fear starting something new. (Staff, YOI)

Staff within prisons were well aware of the challenge of engaging those prisoners who would feel intimidated by or excluded from mainstream sporting environments and some had sought to promote participation by those less likely to engage by considering them specifically in the programming of activities:

> One problem is that some people don't put in for activities because they don't think they're good enough, like the football squad is pretty good – which can put people who haven't played before off. We have addressed this by putting on sports skills courses targeting those who don't play – for example football skills, volleyball skills, basketball skills. We don't label them as sessions for non-participants however as this would result in them being perceived negatively. Guys come down and see others enjoying it and learning skills and it encourages them to get involved. (Staff, Category C)

Participation of vulnerable prisoners

Those held in prison who are unwilling or unable to engage in the wider prison regime and individuals who may be especially vulnerable or at risk of victimisation and/or self-harm represent a small but significant population that can be among the most difficult for staff to engage with. Despite the increased need, finding ways of creating positive outcomes is a particular challenge when working with those who have previously failed to engage with interventions and activities or who present with conduct and problem behaviours.

There is a well-established literature base confirming the importance of physical activity in improving self-image (Ekeland et al., 2005; West & Crompton, 2001) as well as active play in social and psychological development, particularly in promoting resilience and recovering from and adapting to adversity (Lester & Russell, 2008). Woodward's (2012) definition of sport as 'organised play' may be especially important in the context of engaging and supporting vulnerable prisoners, many of whom struggle with, or are prevented from participating in, routine activities within the prison environment. As well as providing a safe environment in which to reduce anxiety, when appropriately used, sport, physical activities and games are increasingly recognised as providing a valuable tool in engaging some of those hardest to connect with in a population that already presents significant challenges.

In the same way that sports-based activities have proven to be an effective way of increasing motivation and promoting engagement among the wider prisoner population, there is clearly a real potential benefit in utilising carefully designed sporting activities in work with more vulnerable populations. In one of the few studies to date to focus on promoting well-being among vulnerable prisoners, Lewis and Heer (2008) identified an innovative scheme for young adult offenders which aimed at improving physical and mental well-being through the use of physical activities to enhance confidence and develop social and emotional coping skills among those vulnerable to self-harm and bullying. Interviews with prison staff revealed a good awareness of the need to target those reluctant to engage in sport and physical activity, and there was evidence of innovative and creative practice from across the estate in supporting those who felt intimidated by or incapable of participation. For example, many establishments offered designated time slots reserved for 'poor copers' and some establishments had well-embedded referral routes whereby health care and mental health teams routinely referred individuals with psychological difficulties to the physical education department in order to receive tailored one-to-one programmes.

Sex offenders

> We hold sex offenders who have an older population age. Many have never used a gym before so we incorporate sessions on the wings to encourage the older prisoners. We hold modified and beginner sessions to enable us to be diverse. (Staff, Category C)

There are in the region of 10,000 convicted sentenced sex offenders in prisons in England and Wales (Berman, 2012), the majority of whom are housed in a separate wing within each prison for their own protection from other prisoners (sex offenders are at heightened risk of assault by other prisoners). The older demographic of sex offender populations, coupled with their vulnerability within the wider population and the likelihood of restrictions in terms of access to sporting environments after release, raise unique considerations and challenges in providing access to physical activity. When reporting on the types of provision they offered, many establishments referred to designated sessions for sex offenders, often with a focus on noncompetitive low-impact activities, and some establishments provided additional physical activities within the vulnerable prisoner units themselves in order to avoid those living on the units having visit more central facilities. In addition to the consideration of prisoners' safety with regard to delivering physical activity to sex offenders, staff also referred to the need to manage, through careful selection processes and limiting the types of opportunities available, the risk of equipping sexual offenders with qualifications which could contribute to further offences once released. For example, staff reported that sex offenders were more likely to be encouraged to take up healthy living qualifications and excluded from undertaking the coaching qualifications that are popular with other categories of prisoners.

Sport for older prisoners

> I can't keep warm when I go out for exercise in the winter, so I tend to stay inside. This means that I not only lack regular walking exercise round the circuit to keep my joints in good order but I get little fresh air for months on end. (Older prisoner, cited by Prison Reform Trust, 2008, p. 8)

Prison populations are getting progressively older, and people over 60 represent the fastest growing age group in custody. 'Older' prisoners are typically recognised as those being aged 50 and over in prison populations, and of the 86,457 in prison on 30 November 2012, 11% of these (9,913) were aged 50 or older (Ministry of Justice, 2012d). Critics have argued that current responses to the increasingly aging prison population are inadequate and that prisons are generally insufficiently equipped to meet the specific needs of older prisoners (Cooney & Braggins, 2010; HM Inspectorate of Prisons, 2008; Prison Reform Trust, 2008).

As part of their investigation into older prisoners, the Prison Reform Trust (2008) conducted a survey of prisons throughout England and Wales and found that although gyms can be physically inaccessible (i.e. reached by stairs) or intimidating for older people; when reporting social activities that were organised specifically for this age group, more than two thirds of the prisons surveyed reported that they ran gym sessions adapted for older people, which were met with enthusiasm and were often the aspect of their work that staff were most proud of. Areas of good practice that were identified in the report included instances of gym staff working in tandem with physical and mental health care professionals and the development of groups specifically targeting older prisoners (for example, a 'nifty over fifty' group).

Of the 16 female survey respondents (see Chapter 5 on women and girls) aged 50 and over, three quarters reported that they 'never' used the gym, attributing their lack of participation to health problems, a lack of appropriate activities or insufficient time or interest. Although gym staff responses mirrored the concerns raised by campaign groups by highlighting the challenge of engaging with older prisoners, there is also widespread evidence of individual establishments responding to the specific needs of older prisoners, often demonstrating particularly innovative or creative practices:

> We have problems with engaging elderly and vulnerable prisoners. Two days a week we respond to their specific needs with carpet bowls, badminton, etcetera. (Staff, High Security)

> We secured some funding from Age UK and can now offer yoga classes for older prisoners. (Staff, Open)

Sport for those with physical and learning disabilities

A recent survey indicated that 36% of the prison population in England and Wales were considered to have a disability (including physical and mental health), compared to 19% of the general population, with an even greater proportion of female prisoners (55%) reporting disabilities, compared to male prisoners (34%). Furthermore, prisoners with disabilities are more likely to experience a poorer quality of prison life throughout the regime (HM Chief Inspector of Prisons, 2009) and are more likely to present with elevated needs, for example substance misuse problems, experiences of abuse and homelessness prior to custody (Cunniffe, Van de Kerckhove Williams, & Hopkins, 2012) thus presenting a further challenge to prisons in addressing the needs of disabled prisoners appropriately. Within community settings, the significant barriers to people with disabilities (both physical and learning) taking part in physical activity have been identified in terms of physical access to activities, appropriate facilities and specialist staff and negative attitudes of staff and other users (French & Hainsworth, 2001; Messent & Cooke, 1998). Such barriers are likely to be equally salient within custody: indeed, a Prison Inspectorate review indicated that prisoners who said they had a disability reported less access to activities and association than those who did not, and many prisons still struggle to provide access to activities for disabled prisoners. Although tailored physical education provision for people with mobility issues and physical impairments is available in some prisons, only 30% of prisoners reporting a disability indicated that they went to the gym at least twice a week, in comparison to 53% of those without a disability (HM Chief Inspector of Prisons, 2009). Visits to establishments revealed small pockets of innovative practice in terms of delivery of sporting activities to this group, for example evidence of the development of links with local sports development units for disabled people and the introduction of and demonstrations about activities such as blind football and wheelchair rugby. These help to cater better for the disabled populations held in custody but are also as an effective way of promoting community links and increasing awareness among the wider prisoner population. Although when asked about their participation in physical activity, prisoner interviewees with disabilities still voiced a concern that they could not participate due to a lack of appropriate provision (for example, 'There's none available to me – I'm disabled'), there were also positive examples of disabled prisoners actively participating in football and rugby teams.

Innovative practice case study: Engaging disabled prisoners in sport

Gym staff at HMP Parc (a large Category B privately run prison under the management of G4S) have worked in partnership with Disability Sport Wales to ensure that disabled prisoners have equitable access to sporting activities. Wheelchair rugby demonstrations have been held within the prison by Bridgend Sports Development Unit who have also supported the PE department to introduce games such as blind football for visually impaired prisoners and Boccia for physically impaired individuals.

Activities for disabled people are also open to able-bodied prisoners with the aim of reducing stigma and increasing levels of awareness and empathy towards people with disabilities.

Staff training has also been provided by Bridgend Sports Development Unit to equip staff with the knowledge and skills to work effectively with disabled prisoners.

Principles of best practice

> Promoting disabled prisoners' engagement in sport by offering appropriate activities.
> Allowing access to disabled activities to able-bodied prisoners to challenge stigma, increase awareness and promote inclusion.
> Providing staff with specialist training for delivering sporting activities to disabled prisoners.

In terms of learning disabilities, a public commitment has been made to ensuring that reasonable adjustments are made for all prisoners with learning disabilities (National Offender Management Service, 2012b, p. 24). Although there is evidence of some good practice, historically this has not been consistent or widespread across the estate (Bradley, 2009; Cooper, 2011), and prisoners with learning disabilities experience poorer access to activities and heightened vulnerability in prison. Furthermore, these individuals often try to conceal their impairment due to embarrassment or fear of ridicule (Talbot, 2011), which can serve to exclude them further from activities, including sport and physical education. Previous research has established that prisoners with learning disabilities would welcome more constructive activities in prison (Talbot, 2008), but other than generic attempts to engage those considered vulnerable, no specific sports provision was evident in the establishments visited, other than the fact that several prisons had arrangements with local organisations supporting people with learning difficulties whose clients visited the PE departments and received support from prisoners to participate in activities. There is clearly an increased risk that prisoners with learning disabilities may be overlooked with regard to their involvement in physical education in custody, particularly considering the poor recognition of learning difficulties in custody, problems with communicating needs, and elevated fears of ridicule or bullying. In encouraging participation of individuals with physical and learning disabilities, peer lead models may offer particular value in terms of drawing on existing peer supporters to encourage those with disabilities to take part.

The role of sport and physical activity in the high-secure estate

The provision and promotion of sport and physical activity is recognised as being a particular challenge in the high-security estate, but one that has been met with some examples of particularly innovative practice by gym staff, even in the highly controlled conditions of closed supervision and high-secure segregation, locations that hold the most dangerous and challenging prisoners in the prison system (HM Chief Inspector of Prisons, 1999). Previous reviews have established that alongside the education department, the workshops and the chapel, the gym is seen as an important feature of high-secure prisons, where the mutual cooperation, hope, care and motivation reported to be absent from the wings were found, as were prison staff relationships of a better quality. However, although providing an important means for prisoners to cope with their extreme experiences of incarceration, gyms in high-secure establishments are also recognised as being high-risk environments, where some of the most serious prisoner-on-prisoner assaults take place (Liebling, Arnold & Straub, 2011).

Interviews with gym managers in high-secure prisons confirmed that although physical education in such settings is inevitably less likely to involve community links than prisons elsewhere, sport and physical activity is still highly integrated within the wider regime. In particular, the research revealed several examples of gym-led activities being utilised as a tool to engage offenders in further educational and offender behaviour programmes as well as in promoting healthy living. As with other establishments across the estate, high-security prisons typically offer a broad range of accredited group offender behaviour programmes that target criminogenic needs and aim of reduce risk and reoffending, but the PE departments in such establishments were found to be especially likely to work closely with other staff in planning and providing tailored courses to prepare prisoners for structured group programmes. Specific activities delivered within the gym were designed to respond to a specific need, according to the areas of development for the group that might have been identified or as required by the programme facilitator, for example in developing communication or teamwork skills. Typically a range of low-intensity activities might be delivered to groups of prisoners prior to commencing offender behaviour programmes, with the aim of encouraging a rapport to be built within the group, to develop skills such as interaction and cooperation and for individuals to get to know each other in a non-threatening environment in order to break down barriers between prisoners before going on to discuss difficult and challenging issues during the subsequent programme. Principles of best practice in this context were found to include effective partnership working with the wider regime, including programmes staff and the Offender Management Unit, a tailored focus on the specific group's needs with clear objectives for activities, and the careful use of structured sporting activities as a means of promoting engagement, motivation and cooperation in preparation for engaging in more challenging group work.

Innovative practice case study: Engaging with Category A prisoners with cardiac problems

High-security prisons detain a significant proportion of older prisoners who often present with physical health problems which would usually exclude them from participation in physical activity in custody. The PE department in one such establishment operates an innovative outreach approach to ensure that prisoners with cardiac problems have the opportunity to participate in appropriate exercise.

A member of the PE staff is BACSPR (British Association for Cardiovascular Prevention and Rehabilitation) qualified, enabling them to assess and deliver rehabilitative exercise programmes to those with cardiovascular problems who have been deemed unfit to use the gym. Such intervention prevents individuals from remaining sedentary, a known risk factor of cardiovascular disease. Outreach one-to-one work is carried out on the wings in order to assess, develop individual exercise programmes and support individuals to follow them.

Staff report the cardiac work as being key to challenging the stereotype of people who don't do PE, thus promoting participation among those who would otherwise be inactive and involving people who would never usually have the option to participate.

Principles of best practice

> Specialist training for gym staff to meet the distinct needs of those with cardiovascular problems.
> Outreach work by PE staff on the wings.
> Targeting those excluded from mainstream PE.

As with those working with sex offenders, staff in high-security establishments reported the need to modify the curriculum and the qualifications offered and reported focusing more on using activities that could be aligned to offender behaviour and therapeutic programmes, rather than necessarily promoting employment opportunities. In contrast to the frustrations that their peers in local prisons would encounter in working with a more transient population, the priorities for PE staff in high-security settings were found to be quite different:

> We have a fairly static population. The priority is treatment so there may be less time for qualifications. (Staff, High Security)

Innovative practice case study: PEI involvement in a therapeutic regime for dangerous and severe personality disordered offenders

Westgate is a purpose built unit forming part of the Dangerous and Severe Personality Disorder (DSPD) service at high-security establishment HMP Frankland. It offers a complex assessment and treatment model with a specific focus on the reduction of risk of future offending within the DSPD population. An extensive complementary regime (including horticulture, education and physical activities) is offered alongside the clinical framework and dedicated Physical Education Instructors (PEIs) within the unit make a number of significant and unique contributions.

All PEI staff are actively involved with various elements of the clinical framework at Westgate, including positions in multidisciplinary assessment teams, a role involving the comprehensive assessment of risk and personality disorder through observation, interview and collateral reviews. PEIs actively engage in each of these three elements and contribute to the identification of treatment needs for this complex and challenging population. PE staff are also facilitators on risk reduction and offence related programmes, including those which target substance misuse, social and interpersonal skills and relationship and intimacy issues. The level of engagement with formal assessment and treatment processes falls significantly outside a traditional PEI job description, yet the PEI team at Westgate has welcomed opportunities to become actively involved in these processes and have developed the required clinical skills accordingly.

Members of PE staff on the unit are trained to facilitate *parallel therapy,* an approach referring to a set of activities designed to reinforce and consolidate treatment objectives and treatment gains through experimental learning. Sessions typically involve a number of clinical processes, including check in, a task/exercise and a group debrief which reflects the relevance of the parallel therapy to the formal treatment aim that it relates to. In addition to parallel therapy, PEIs are trained in, and frequently utilise, team-building skills which require mental and physical participation. The PE department has played a fundamental role within the adaptation of this equipment/exercise directory to fall in line with the treatment objectives of the broader clinical framework, all of which has a risk reduction focus.

PEI contributions to the broader therapeutic regime at Westgate

Behavioural monitoring at Westgate involves a multidimensional approach where risk-related behaviours are monitored across all areas within the unit. The PEI team plays a key part in the observation of risk-paralleling behaviours and skills implementation outside the formal treatment setting (for instance in the gym and sportshall) which proves invaluable to the risk assessment and progression monitoring systems used at Westgate. The PEI team is also actively involved in the establishing and monitoring of targets and coordinating gym-based incentives as a feature of broader risk reduction processes.

The unit is committed to offering purposeful activities that encourage prisoners to work towards achieving positive life goals and provide opportunities to demonstrate the skills learned within formal treatment. The PEIs are responsible for offering a comprehensive programme of physical activities throughout the year, including structured gym sessions, team sports, remedial health referral activities, certificated courses (such as first aid) and games. The majority of the Westgate population, of varying ages and levels of physical ability, is currently actively involved in the programme offered by the PEI team, who have also developed their own certification scheme to acknowledge prisoners' progress within their levels of physical ability.

Despite interviews with gym staff in high-security establishments confirming the perceived importance of using sport and physical activity to focus on psychological work, staff still revealed a commitment to using physical activity to promote education, while recognising the amplified importance of tailoring sporting and educational provision of the specific needs of high-security prisoners:

> We cannot provide qualifications like coaching qualifications that could enable extremely high risk prisoners to work with vulnerable people on release. Many are serving very long sentences therefore the focus is not so much on equipping them with qualifications to attain employment on release. (Staff, High Security)

This also raises the issue of how the role of sport and physical activity may be significantly different for those serving very long sentences, As testified by a gym manager from an establishment predominantly holding prisoners who were nearing the end of long sentences of 10 years and over, working with such populations poses its own challenges:

> This is a fairly static population. They've been in the system a long time and have either done all the courses they want to by now or they're simply not interested. The challenge for us is engaging them and being able to offer something new.

Innovative practice case study: Using sport to promote high-security prisoners' engagement in education

Due to the high risk profile of many of the offenders in high-security establishments, offering sports-based qualifications in domains such as coaching is often not appropriate or practical considering security restrictions. However PE departments offer a range of accredited courses including nutrition performance and healthy eating, understanding stress and stress-management techniques, sports anatomy and physiology and taking part in sport, qualifications that focus on theoretical elements of sporting activities. Prisoners undertaking courses are required to join the library, thus promoting integration with the wider prison regime.

Individuals are offered a clear progression route whereby they can work through a range of sports-based qualifications. PE staff refer to the initial importance of short courses in breaking down barriers to education, encouraging participation among prisoners who may lack learning motivation or confidence or who have experienced negative experiences of education.

Prisoners with educational needs identified on their sentence plans are prioritised, and the PE departments work in partnership with education to support individuals with literacy difficulties. The programme aims to enhance confidence and motivation in order to encourage individuals to progress onto further educational programmes. Staff suggest that taking what might be seen as a low-level qualification in PE can give prisoners the confidence and motivation to go on to further education. By, for example, creating a portfolio, prisoners develop skills which they may not have thought they were capable of.

Physical education staff are also involved in supporting courses delivered by education staff, by facilitating continuity for those who have progressed through PE courses onto further education. One-to-one support and learning plans are created for individuals wishing to undertake PE related courses who are detained in the Close Supervision Centre.

Principles of best practice

> Ensuring engagement in the wider regime by linking participation in physical education to facilities such as the library.
> Integrating PE into sentence planning.
> Providing a clear progression route through a range of courses.
> Ensuring continuity by partnership working between the gym and education department.

Minority ethnic groups and foreign nationals

Mirroring an over-representation at every stage of the criminal justice process (Edgar, 2007), Black and minority ethnic (BME) groups are significantly over-represented in the prison system, representing 13% of the total population of

England and Wales (Office for National Statistics, 2012) but over a quarter of the prison population (Ministry of Justice, 2011c). The foreign national prisoner population is represented by a huge range of nationalities and languages which, alongside cultural and religious diversity, prisons and their staff are expected to recognise and cater for. At the beginning of 2013 the foreign national population in England and Wales stood at just under 11,000 (or 13% of the prison population), having doubled in the last 10 years. Although not necessarily at the same rate, the proportion of young male prisoners from BME backgrounds or identifying as Muslim has also continued to increase, and given evidence that their experiences of prison life tends to be more negative than that of their White counterparts (Cripps, 2010; Summerfield, 2011), this raises particular challenges in the design of sports and other activities. Although participation in sport within the community is typically lower among ethnic minorities, differences also exist across minority groups and sporting activities (Long, Hylton, Spracklen, Ratna & Bailey, 2009). For example, national trends have established that BME groups are less likely to participate in recommended levels of physical activity but that participation in football, swimming and athletics is higher than other activities (Sporting Equals, 2010). However, in their exploration of racism in sport across EU member states, the European Union Agency for Fundamental Rights (2010) established that ethnic minorities were underrepresented and that racism was evident in both amateur and professional sport, with a particular reluctance to recognise such incidents in amateur sports.

Although sports-based interventions for low-income and at-risk BME young people have been promoted by policy makers (House of Commons Home Affairs Committee, 2007a, 2007b), evidence to support such initiatives has been inconclusive. Stark, Kent and Finke (1987) found that athletic involvement among adolescent Black males (but not White males) was correlated with law-abiding behaviour in early adulthood, leading to the conclusion that this may be due to sport being a source of pride and upward mobility in Black communities, thus promoting a commitment to sporting ideology, increased self-esteem and higher aspirations encouraging law-abiding lifestyles. In contrast, Hughes and Coakley (1991) argue that such a strong commitment to a sporting ideology may be detrimental and promote deviance, particularly within low-income ethnic minority communities where participation in sport may offer one of the few sources of potential upward mobility.

The relationship between delinquency, sporting involvement and ethnicity remains contentious (Miller, Melnick, Barnes, Sabo & Farrell, 2007) and the impact of sport in custody upon differing ethnic groups has yet to be fully explored. It has been established, however, that prisoners from BME backgrounds are more likely to attend the gym at least twice a week compared to their White peers (HM Inspectorate of Prisons, 2010), and interviews with prison gym staff confirm that engaging those from BME backgrounds in sport and physical activity is not perceived as a problem, with the main concern of staff being to ensure that a broad range of activities is made available in order to capture the interest of the diverse population of those held in prisons. In terms of team-based sports, football and cricket were recognised as being especially attractive to members of BME groups, with 'taster sessions' proving to be an effective way of encouraging those who had no previous experience of a given sport to try it out.

Given the substantial numbers of people from BME groups in prisons, there may be particular scope to draw on sport as an engagement tool, particularly considering that the participation data and staff testimonies point to high levels of involvement in prison sports among those from BME backgrounds. It would seem that sport has an important role to play in engaging male BMEs in education, raising aspirations and encouraging participation. Although beyond the scope of this book, the advantages of making use of sporting motivations to engage BME prisoners is certainly an area that warrants further attention, particularly in light of concerns around educational outcomes (Majors, 2001). It should also be noted that despite the fact that they are a recognised ethnic group for the purposes of the Race Relations Act 1976 and are over-represented in the prison system (Power, 2004), Gypsy-Travellers in prison are not routinely monitored and their experiences of incarceration and rehabilitation remain under-researched (see Meek, 2007). Evidently Gypsy-Traveller masculinities and violence (Levinson & Sparkes, 2003) and the importance of and role of sport in this context is an area warranting further research attention.

Detainees held in immigration removal centres

There are currently 10 Immigration Removal Centres (IRCs) in England and Wales with a total operational capacity of 3,500. Establishments are run by the U.K. Borders Agency and managed by either Her Majesty's Prison Service (three establishment detaining 747 detainees, Ministry of Justice, 2013b) or private providers. Immigration Removal Centres detain people who have no legal right to be in the United Kingdom but have refused to leave voluntarily. Detainees can leave at any time to return to their country of origin; over half of detainees are held for less than two months and fewer than 10% stay for over a year (Silverman & Hajela, 2012). Some illegal immigrants are also held within prisons: the vast majority of nonoffender inmates within prisons are illegal immigrants (Ministry of Justice, 2012b) and some of those detained within IRCs are foreign nationals who have completed custodial sentenced for criminal convictions but have failed to comply with immigration law by leaving the United Kingdom.

PE and sport provision has been identified as generally a positive aspect of life within IRCs (HM Inspectorate of Prisons, 2012), with ball games in particular being popular and well supported (Independent Monitoring Board, 2012a, 2012b). Although data are not available for privately run facilities, within Prison Service-managed IRCs participation levels in sport are comparatively high, with average prisoner participation levels of 72% (range 71%–74%) (Lewis & Meek, 2012). Despite language barriers presenting a unique challenge for delivering PE within such establishments, it is anticipated that the less constrained regimes allow detainees to utilise facilities without restriction, thus enabling higher levels of participation.

Interviews with Prison Service staff in IRCs showed that sport and physical activity was perceived to be an important element of the regime, in particular in promoting well-being:

> Helps to maintain a controlled environment and helps to relieve stress and tension in the detainees. (Staff, IRC)

However, the diverse nationalities of detainees held in IRCs was identified as presenting a challenge in terms of catering for different groups and their sporting preferences:

> A challenge is ensuring activities are attractive to all nationalities. (Staff, IRC)
> Due to the high number of different nationalities, there is always the risk of conflict between them. We also have to be flexible on the activities on offer, changing the weekly programme to suit the nationalities of the establishment. (Staff, IRC)

Language barriers were also noted as a challenge in delivering courses and providing inductions:

> Translating written information is not always helpful as many cannot read and write in their own language. (Staff, IRC)

However, this was largely overcome by using pictorial forms of information and making use of other detainees with translation skills. Innovative methods were also identified as being required in the delivery of courses due to cultural differences and sensitivities.

Innovative practice case study: Promoting participation of foreign nationals

Haslar Immigration Removal Centre detains approximately 160 male foreign nationals who typically have short lengths of stay (under a month). The diverse nationalities and numerous languages spoken present a challenge in terms of PE delivery, requiring flexibility of approach to inducting, delivering and promoting activities within the centre.

In order to cater for the diverse languages spoken all written information is translated into a range of languages. However, members of staff report that written translations are not necessarily sufficient for those with literacy issues and therefore induction materials, the PE timetable and other PE materials rely heavily on images to supplement written information. Detainees employed within the gym also act as translators at inductions (although Language Line – a telephone interpreting service – is used for the translation of sensitive medical information) and have an active role in promoting activities throughout the centre.

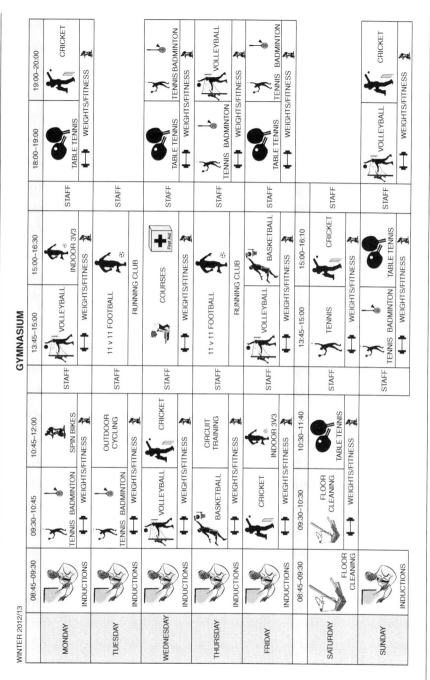

Figure 4.1 An example of an illustrated gym timetable for those with literacy difficulties, provided by a participating prison.

The transient nature of the population and influx of differing populations requires activities to be reviewed frequently. The PE programme is reviewed fortnightly in order to ensure it is meeting the needs of the population and specific activities; for example, badminton and cricket are run on an ad hoc basis as requested.

Principles of best practice

Illustrating induction material and timetables.
Utilising employees within the gym as translators.
Promoting activities through peer networking.
Frequently reviewing activities on offer based on the population's preferences.

Given that prisoner participation levels are used as an indicator of the efficiency of a prison gym and that inclusive participation is recognised as being a priority, ongoing attention needs to be paid to specific subpopulations of prisoners, for example older, vulnerable, and foreign national prisoners and detainees and those with learning difficulties. Although beyond the scope of this chapter, further consideration also needs to be paid to the way in which sport has the potential to minimise exclusions (for example, by integrating those who are excluded from sport or by bringing together conflicting groups in sport) just as it also has the power to create and maintain inequalities and conflicts, for example in segregating sex offenders and other vulnerable prisoners from the rest of the population and by targeting and delivering sporting sessions to these groups separately. Efforts to promote widening participation in sport need to be supported and resourced (by prisons as well as sporting organisations) and will be strengthened by a growing recognition of the need to identify and respond to the diverse needs of those held in prison custody, some of which have been explored here.

Innovative practice case study: Engaging with the diverse population at HMP The Verne

Category C prison HMP The Verne in Dorset has a substantial number of foreign national prisoners: they make up over 60% of the population held there and the prison is home to men representing over 50 nationalities. Recognising and building upon this diversity within the prison, gym staff use the international football tournaments they organise to celebrate the different nationalities held in the prison and to promote cultural awareness and educational opportunities. The prison also holds a considerable number of men over the age of 50. Recognising the need to cater specifically for this age group, gym staff have consulted with and tailored activities for older men, many of whom also make use of the prison's successful GP referral programme which is coordinated by the gym in partnership with healthcare and draws on the expertise of trained prisoners who manage their own caseload. Men who are held in the Care & Containment Unit (previously referred to as segregation) are able to participate in one-to-one classes with a member of gym staff through outreach sessions, and outdoor equipment is located throughout the recreation areas for prisoners to use in their own time. The gym also provides a smoking-cessation clinic and specialist sessions for those engaged in drug-treatment programmes, and the department boasts among its staff one of the few female PE officers in the country.

Note

1   Twenty-seven per cent of the current 31,981 'officer and operational support' and 'operational manager' staff are women (Ministry of Justice, 2012b).

5 The benefits of and barriers to participating in sport and physical activity for women and girls in prison

The preceding chapters have confirmed that, despite the strong potential of sport in contributing to beneficial outcomes in custody, official data verifies that female prisoners are significantly less likely to participate in sport and physical activity than their male counterparts. Indeed participation among female prisoners is not only lower than that of male prisoners but also typically lower than that of nonincarcerated females (Herbert, Plugge, Foster & Doll, 2012; Plugge et al., 2009). In community settings, in spite of the proliferation of national (Sport England, 2012) and international (International Working Group on Women and Sport, 1994) campaigns and initiatives that have aimed to increase women's participation in sport over the last 20 years, a long-standing gender disparity in sports participation has remained. Lower levels of participation among women have been explained in terms of women's multiple social roles and responsibilities (Verhoef, Love & Rose, 1992) and restricted access to sports facilities, particularly in areas of social deprivation (Rutten, Abu-Omar, Frahsa & Morgan, 2009). It may be that self-presentational concerns and low levels of motivation can be partially attributed to the social construction of sport as a predominantly masculine activity (Eitzen, 2000, 2006; Robbins, Puder & Kazonis, 2003; Sabo, 2001; Wellard, 2002) but also to the historic policy impetus to promote women's participation in sport for primary health benefits, which has consequently implied restriction and sacrifice rather than the benefit of sport for intrinsic enjoyment (Deem & Gilroy, 1998). Despite this, research with community samples indicates women do perceive the benefits of exercise to outweigh barriers to participation (Lovell, El Ansari & Parker, 2010) and strategies targeting the socio-psychological (Segar, Jayaratne, Hanlon & Richardson, 2002) and situational barriers (Rutten et al., 2009) to participation, and those promoting empowerment and offering women tailored activities and facilities (Kay, 2003) have had some success in increasing levels of participation in community settings in the short term at least. It may not be surprising that in prison settings the barriers to participation for women that have been identified in the community are likely to be exacerbated.

An accumulated body of evidence has identified the gender-specific gains associated with female participation in sport, including increased confidence, assertiveness, self-worth, empowerment and improved body image (Deem & Gilroy

1998; Humberstone, 1990; Richman & Shaffer, 2000). Reflecting this awareness, a number of community sports-based interventions have been developed to address a range of social problems among disadvantaged women and girls (Burdsal & Buel, 1980; Eitle & Eitle, 2002; Resnicow et al., 2000; Wichmann, 1990; Women's Sport Foundation, 1998), and the limited research assessing sport and physical activity among female prisoners confirms multiple beneficial outcomes in terms of addressing women's needs in prison. Ozano's (2008) small quantitative analysis of nine British female prisoners participating in at least three sessions of physical activity a week identified positive gains in terms of coping with prison life, physical and psychological well-being and the promotion of rehabilitation. The women in Ozano's study reported that sport served as a coping mechanism in prison, facilitating the release of aggression, stress and anxiety, while improving confidence, self-esteem and self-efficacy as well as physical fitness, body image, knowledge and motivation towards achieving a healthier lifestyle. Women described how they had developed transferable skills and knowledge through sports-based qualifications, work experience and participation that would support their rehabilitation in terms of gaining employment, leading healthy lifestyles and encouraging alternative and constructive uses of leisure time after release, so discouraging substance misuse and offending behaviour. Similarly, Leberman (2007) evaluated the effects of a 20-day experiential adventure-based course completed by 27 female offenders in New Zealand. Qualitative findings revealed positive gains in terms of enhanced self-confidence and self-awareness as well the development of transferable skills in team work, conflict resolution and goal setting. Those nearing the end of their sentences reported the greatest benefits, although the challenge of maintaining positive gains once back in the prison environment were also highlighted. Such research suggests that physical activity and sport within prison has the potential to ameliorate some of the negative psychological and physical effects of incarceration on women, as well as to facilitate resettlement processes and promote desistance from future offending.

Although women represent a relatively small proportion of the overall prison population (4,112 women were detained in prisons in England and Wales on 19 October 2012, Ministry of Justice, 2012d), recent years have seen a dramatic increase in the number of women sentenced to custody (Fawcett Society, 2007; Home Office, 2007) and the most recently available reoffending figures indicate that 57% of women who serve sentences of less than a year and 24% of women who serve sentences longer than a year reoffend within a year of release (Ministry of Justice, 2012e). The distinct sentence profile of women – coupled with high levels of vulnerability in terms of physical and mental health problems, substance dependency and adverse domestic and socioeconomic circumstances – continues to present a real challenge to policy makers and practitioners in a prison system largely designed by men for men. Consequently, there continues to be pressure exerted on prisons detaining females to adopt a holistic and uniquely women-centred approach (Fawcett Society, 2007; Hardwick, 2012; Prison Reform Trust, 2012) and a concerted effort has been made to address women's distinct needs, for example through the formation of additional resettlement pathways that recognise the need to support women in the criminal justice system who have direct experience of sex work and domestic violence (Home Office, 2007).

Sport and physical activity for women in prison

The Prison Service has acknowledged that female prisoners may be particularly difficult to engage in physical activity: gender specific guidance is outlined in the *Women Prisoners* Prison Service Order (HM Prison Service, 2008) which contains mandatory and discretionary directions to guide the operation of establishments detaining females. The order suggests that staff should promote physical exercise for women and have an awareness of the barriers to women's participation, including issues of age, body consciousness, and self-confidence. The directive also advocates physical activities for women that are integrated into the wider prison regime and meet the needs of women prisoners by fostering self-esteem, health and fitness and by providing opportunities for social interaction with other women. Activities such as yoga, aerobics, step activities and weight-management programmes, as well as specific provision for vulnerable and pregnant/post-natal women, are recommended.

International research has established that, historically, female prisoners are less likely to participate in sport and physical activity than their male counterparts (Goetting & Howsen, 1983) and analysis of the prisoner participation data generated from 107 public sector prisons in England and Wales (see Chapter 3) confirmed that at an overall average of 48%, women's participation remains the lowest of all incarcerated populations. However, there is also significant variability between different female prisons, with participation figures ranging from 29% to 89% and therefore representing the greatest variation across different types of prison establishments. Plugge et al.'s (2009) survey of 505 women entering English prison revealed that only 13% of those surveyed reported participating in the level of physical activity defined as sufficient by government recommendations (Department of Health, 2004) prior to incarceration, in comparison to 25% of females in the general population. There is a clear trend for women to remain sedentary once in custody, and even among the smaller number of female prisoners who have reported participating in physical activity frequently during their time in prison, most have had little involvement in sport prior to their incarceration (Ozano, 2008).

Women's participation in sport: Survey findings

As part of a larger prison-wide survey in one women's prison in the south of England, 190 female prisoners[1] between the ages of 18 and 70 (mean average age of 37 years) responded to questions relating to participation in exercise in custody. Participants predominantly self-identified as being White British (79%), were serving sentences of between two months and life and the duration that they had been detained within the prison at the time of data collection ranged from less than a week to over two years (an average of 19 weeks). Almost a third were on remand and just under a half had served one or more other prison sentences in the past. The questionnaire, completed anonymously, elicited information concerning frequency of participation in physical activities and sport in custody, actual and ideal engagement in differing types of activities and perceived barriers to participation. In order to increase participation, prisoners acting as peer supporters, mentors, classroom assistants and listeners ($n = 21$) were available to support those with literacy difficulties in completing the survey.

Over half (55%) of the women reported that they attended the prison gym at least once a week, but a substantial 43% reported never using the prison gym. Frequency of attendance at the gym differed significantly according to age, χ^2 (9) = 17.91, $p < .05$, with reported participation decreasing with age: two thirds of women aged under 25 years reported going to the gym at least weekly, compared to one quarter of those aged 50 years or over. Although this is consistent with women's participation trends in community settings, it appears to be exacerbated by a lack of provision for older women in prison. However participation in some activities (badminton and exercise classes for example) was not affected by age, suggesting that offering non-gym activities may increase participation among older women.

Participation also varied dramatically, depending on whether or not women had been to prison before, χ^2 (3) = 8.52, $p < .05$, with significantly lower levels of participation among those serving their first sentence, suggesting a lack of awareness of active opportunities and a need to promote opportunities to women who are less familiar with prison regimes. Those who didn't have jobs within the prison were statistically less likely to report engaging in sport and physical activity, χ^2 (3) = 21.11, $p < .001$, with 70% reporting never going to the gym. Almost a third (30%) of those who had a job within the prison reported going to the gym five times or more a week, in comparison to only 9% of those who did not have a job. Although this contradicts somewhat the interview findings that revealed that women's multiple roles (including work) could be a barrier to participation, it may be explained by those in employment within the prison being more able or motivated to participate in other aspects of the regime. Lastly, those who reported having a disability were less likely to engage in gym-based activities, χ^2 (3) = 14.67, $p < .01$, with 69% of women with a physical disability 'never' going to the gym, suggesting a lack of provision for this group and inequality of access. Ethnicity, duration in custody, sentence length, mental health problems, self-harming behaviour and drug use did not have a significant impact on self-reported participation in sport and physical activity.

In terms of types of activity, attending the gym and participating in exercise classes were the most prevalent, with three quarters of women reporting taking part in these whilst in custody, with smaller numbers involved in netball, badminton and football. Age was a significant predictor of whether or not women had used the prison gym, χ^2 (3) = 12.17, $p < .01$, and whether or not women participated in football in custody, χ^2 (3) = 10.84, $p < .05$, with participation in both decreasing with age.

Barriers to participation

When asked to identify reasons for not participating in physical activities in prison, over a half of the women reported a lack of interest, there being no activities available that they wanted to take part in (including specifically a lack of designated activities for older women), or physical health reasons, including pregnancy, despite the *Women Prisoners* Prison Service Order (HM Prison Service, 2008) stating that specific provision should be made for pregnant women. Other prominent reasons for not participating were represented in negative attitudes towards participation, manifested through a lack of confidence (in what was often perceived by non-gym users to be an intimidating or over-competitive environment), seeing physical activity as a form of punishment, or a concern that decency rules were not adhered to in the gym. A prominence of such negative attitudes highlights the importance of promoting a safe and non-threatening environment in the gym (particularly considering the number of women in custody with mental health issues and self-image anxieties) and ensuring that activities offered include those that are designed to be noncompetitive. In terms of practical barriers, women reported not having sufficient time to participate, not being unlocked from cells in time, being restricted from attending (for example due to being temporarily segregated), and clashes with other regime activities. The most frequently requested activities that were unavailable were aerobics, dance classes (in particular, Zumba) and yoga.

To supplement the survey findings, in-depth interviews were carried out with 45 women between the ages of 17 and 64 (mean age 34 years), either while they were in custody or soon after release. The women included those on remand, and those serving sentences of between two months and life, and the interviews they participated in aimed to explore the perceived benefits of and barriers to participation in sport and physical activity in prison. These discussions generated a rich qualitative data set of the women's sporting experiences, concerns and aspirations.

The importance of sport in promoting the physical and mental health of female prisoners

Prisons aim to provide health care equitable to that available in the community, and this is especially pertinent in the female estate where the physical and mental health needs of women prisoners are greater than those in the general population. Mental health problems are far more prevalent among female than male prisoners, and female prisoners are much more likely to have experienced physical, emotional or sexual abuse and trauma. Substance misuse contributes disproportionately to female offending with two thirds of female prisoners reporting substance or alcohol addiction in the year prior to imprisonment (Social Exclusion Unit, 2002). Although 83% of women in prison report having a long term illness (Plugge, Douglas & Fizpatrick, 2006), women have typically had less contact with health care professionals such as general practitioners, dentists and opticians prior to custody than women in the community, and they are also more likely to engage in negative health behaviours: 85% smoke, few exercise regularly (Plugge et al., 2009) and many have distinct perinatal health needs (Edge, 2006; Knight & Plugge, 2005).

In interviews, a significant number of women reported that imprisonment had resulted in substantial weight gain, which further served to impact adversely upon self-esteem. Many perceived attending the gym to be the only way to ameliorate the effect of the carbohydrate rich prison diet and reflecting this the women's reported motivations were typically focused on weight loss and socialisation (Plugge, Neale, Dawes, Foster & Wright, 2011). The *Women Prisoners* Prison Service Order (HM Prison Service, 2008) recommends providing weight management programmes to women, and where such provision was available and required, women clearly valued being supported to lose weight and develop healthier lifestyles ('I put on two stone when I first came in but I have almost lost it all now just by coming here [gym]'). Reflecting concerns in the male estate that, despite health initiatives being available, uptake can be low (Lester, Hamilton-Kirkwood & Jones, 2003), even in establishments where there were weight-loss programmes it was acknowledged that women were sometimes put off, or did not want to engage in these. However, an interview with a woman who had been released several months earlier (following a six month sentence) highlighted how the development of a more healthy lifestyle while in prison could be sustained after release:

> I used to run 5K everyday on the treadmill, and the gym staff would encourage me, run next to me. Now I do 5K everyday on the road instead – I never did that before.

Such experiences suggest that health behaviours adopted in custody can be translated into healthier lifestyles after release. However, although previous research has indicated that prisoners often intend to maintain healthy behaviours after release (Nelson et al., 2006; Ozano, 2008), intentions alone are often insufficient for behavioural actualisation (Ajzen, 1985) and further support may be required in ensuring that healthy living habits initiated in prison can be maintained in the community.

In terms of psychological needs, women in prison are more than five times more likely to have a mental health concern than women in the community (Plugge et al., 2006) and almost a half of all women in prison suffer from anxiety and depression (Ministry of Justice, 2010b). Whereas mental health in-reach teams are perceived to be effective in supporting women with severe mental health problems in prison, those with less severe mental illness often receive little intervention (Durcan, 2008) and if not appropriately treated the prison environment can exacerbate poor mental health (Harner & Riley, 2012; Nurse, Woodcock & Ormsby, 2003). Levels of self-harming among female prisoner are disproportionally high: whereas women represent only 5% of the prison population they account for nearly a half of all self-harm incidents in prison, and female prisoners are at a higher risk of suicide than male prisoners (Hardwick, 2012).

Interviews with women in prison highlighted the straightforward importance of physical activity as a way of coping with incarceration ('It gets rid of tension, like therapy as well as exercise'), particularly as a way of dealing with frustration ('I'd go off my trolley if I didn't have the gym, from a psychological point of view it gives you something to focus on'). Reflecting previous findings of improvements to self-esteem among female prisoners involved in intensive interventions based around physical activity (Leberman, 2007; Ozano, 2008) sporting achievements were also described by the women as being important contributors to self-esteem ('I thought I couldn't achieve anything, but then I did achieve').

Employment is not often perceived as a high priority for female prisoners and is frequently overshadowed by more pressing resettlement concerns such as accommodation, custody of children, and substance misuse problems (Gelsthorpe & Sharpe, 2007; Sheffield Hallam University, 2012). Previous research has identified that 20% of women in prison have not worked in the five years prior to custody (Hamlyn & Lewis, 2000), that women prisoners are less likely to have been in employment immediately before custody than their male counterparts (Stewart, 2008b), and that if employed, work was often low skilled and short term or temporary (Hamlyn & Lewis, 2000). Women entering prison are far less likely to have educational or vocational qualifications than women in the general population, and yet prison-based employment and training tend to be poorly integrated into the regimes of female establishments and opportunities to gain vocational qualifications whilst in custody are rare. Few women leave prison with employment to go to and over 50% of women anticipate returning to unemployment or domestic duties on release (Hamlyn & Lewis, 2000). However, many participants directly attributed their sports-based qualifications to an enhanced likelihood of successfully desisting from crime, for instance in overcoming financial motivations for offending by increasing their chances of gaining employment.

Innovative practice case study: Using physical education to promote the reintegration of female prisoners into the work force

HMP Downview is a women's working prison detaining adults and juvenile girls in southeast England. The physical education programme incorporates both a recreational and an educational element with a clear focus on developing self-esteem, confidence, employability skills and qualifications.

Up to 20 women at a time have the opportunity to enrol on HMP Downview's Physical Education course where they are supported to obtain qualifications in Leisure and Fitness, progressing from Level 1 and 2 to Level 3 courses, provided by a local college for women eligible for Release on Temporary Licence (RoTL). Theoretical learning is coupled with a strong emphasis on practical application: women are supported to develop skills to enable them to lead exercise classes within the prison and are then given the opportunity to design, organise and deliver classes on a regular basis, thus providing them with valuable experience which they can draw upon when applying for jobs in future. Women completing the course also mentor fellow prisoners through individual exercise programmes.

Recognising the importance of gaining relevant experience as well as qualifications, the department has developed links with local leisure centres in order to facilitate work placements for women eligible for RoTL whilst in custody and to foster employment opportunities for women upon release. Five women who completed work placements in the community whilst at Downview in the last year and have since been released have gone on to secure employment or progressed onto higher education.

> I started volunteering in the evenings, which I still do now, and I got a job as a Chiropractic Assistant. I learnt a lot of knowledge on the sports course that applies to my job now. I would never have been able to do this now if I hadn't had the support, I thought I couldn't achieve anything. Sometimes I have to pinch myself, because I just think, wow look what I have achieved. (Ex-offender released from Downview)

Principles of best practice

> Access to qualifications of a level high enough to meet employer's requirements.
> Providing opportunities for practical application and mentoring.
> Establishing links with colleges and national organisations to facilitate work/ educational placements and post-release educational and employment opportunities.

Although educational opportunities are available to women in prison, those with no presentence qualifications are significantly less likely to be working towards a qualification, and opportunities to gain qualifications are limited for those serving shorter sentences (Anderson with Carins, 2011; Hamlyn & Lewis, 2000). Nevertheless, female prisoners typically value and express positive attitudes towards educational opportunities (Hopkins, 2012), and sports-based opportunities evidently have an important role to play in engaging those who feel intimidated by formal learning environments. Female prisons where such motivations were nurtured in the gym were able to work alongside teaching staff and make use of gym-related teaching materials, and strong supportive relationships with staff were clearly important in encouraging women to achieve and progress from sports related qualifications and goals. At HMP Low Newton, for example, gym and education staff described how they had recognised that although a significant proportion of women were anxious or lacked the motivation to engage in education or pursuing qualifications, the gym was consistently well attended. As a result of tutors being brought into the gym, prisoner interviewees reported feeling less anxious about embarking on education and were able to establish trusting relationships with tutors and as a result were more confident to return to classes.

In terms of the delivery of activities, the women's comments echoed guidance in the *Female Prisoner* Prison Service Order (HM Prison Service, 2008) which recommends provision of a range of activities offering the opportunity for social interaction in order to increase participation. Although the women who participated in interviews clearly valued and recognised the benefits of engaging in sport and physical activity, these women also reported experiencing significant barriers to participation. Extrinsic issues relating to the regime and structure of delivering activities ('You have to make choices because you're locked up. You have to choose between going to the gym, using the phone, going outside'), as well as intrinsic reasons for nonparticipation, such as lack of motivation or anxieties about feeling intimidated when participating in exercise ('Women are conscious about people watching them when they are exercising, they are paranoid about what people think').

The prison environment not only emphasises existing marginalised and stigmatised groups within society but also introduces new divisions – for example between those serving differing sentences or with distinct needs such as substance abuse problems (Plugge et al., 2011) – and competitive environments can exacerbate social comparison concerns among those already susceptible to such anxieties (Andrews & Andrews, 2003; Slater & Tiggemann, 2011). Finally, for women who have had especially negative relational histories with men, or those with particular cultural beliefs such as Muslim and Gypsy/Traveller women, a lack of female staff was also thought to prevent some women from participating in sport and physical activities. Given that only 7.5% of prison gym staff are female (and there is no more likelihood of female staff being located in female establishments) this raised concerns for some women, although interviewees were generally very positive about gym staff and reported being able to establish far more constructive relationships with them than other members of prison staff:

> They [PE officers] are looked at just as prison officers but they are so much more than that, they take your circumstances into consideration. The way they are with you, the rapport it's different, they were my rocks, if I had a problem I would go to them rather than my personal officer.

While the evidence clearly points to multiple benefits for women participating in sport and physical activity in custody, barriers to participation can limit the opportunities for these to be realised, and within the female estate, sport and physical activity may not necessarily have the same allure or offer the same instant rewards as it does for male prisoners, thus raising additional challenges in promoting participation. Many of the interviewees had not been involved in sport and physical activity prior to prison and unless actively encouraged by staff or other women were unlikely to do so, but those who had participated during their time in prison – often for the first time since their school years – reported finding it rewarding. Previous research with incarcerated women in North America has established that the most popular recreational activities in prison are exercise programmes such as aerobics, weightlifting and gym activities (Belknap, 1996). Consistent with findings within the community (Kay, 2003), activities which the women felt would promote participation were typically those which conformed to traditional notions of femininity. Access to a broad range of individual and team-based activities were welcomed by the women, but in particular yoga, dance and aerobic activities.

Despite women's participation in sport and physical activity in prison remaining, on average, lower than that of men, women clearly recognise and value the significant physical, mental, social and resettlement benefits of participation in physical activity in prison, particularly in ameliorating the negative psychological effects of imprisonment, providing a coping mechanism and boosting self-esteem, whilst offering the opportunity to address physical health issues. Gym-based learning, qualifications and work experience in particular were perceived to be highly valuable in facilitating resettlement processes, but – as with the wider prison estate – the availability of such opportunities was locally contingent and highly variable from establishment to establishment, often reflecting the priorities of different senior management teams and the facilities/resources available.

Despite evident benefits, and a policy impetus towards tailored women-centred physical education provision (HM Prison Service, 2008), participants identified institutional as well as intrinsic gendered barriers to participation. Extrinsic institutional barriers included poor promotion of sporting activities to women, a lack of choice, conflicts with other aspects of the prison regime such as work and a dearth of female physical education staff. Self-presentational concerns and a lack of motivation were also identified as barriers to participation. Although women articulated such barriers, the findings also suggested that many of these could potentially be overcome by innovative practice and enthusiastic and supportive staff. Principles of best practice in engaging women prisoners in sport and physical activity includes providing a diverse programme of activities, promoting physical and mental health through sport and physical activity as a result of well-developed links between healthcare and gym departments, blending literacy and numeracy into physical education, offering sports-based qualifications alongside opportunities to gain work experience in the community and providing through-the-gate support to establish links with potential employers and community groups. Where such integrated practices were evident, sport and physical education contributed to meeting the complex well-being and resettlement needs of women in prison, thus demonstrating the considerable potential of such activities in contributing to the promotion of women's desistance from crime.

Note

1   Representing a response rate of 39% which signifies a high response for prisoner populations (Fazel & Danesh, 2002).

6   Sport and youth crime

How far has our understanding developed?

Contemporary youth justice policy and practice is a particularly complex and convoluted feature of the wider justice system, especially in the context of incarceration. Indeed, the question 'What is prison for?' is further complicated in the context of children, where the contradiction between the competing goals of welfare and 'justice' are reflected in what may be seen as public and political ambivalence towards young offenders. For example, whilst forms of *moral panics* (Cohen, 1972) have contributed to the popularity of particularly punitive measures, or what Muncie (2004) refers to as a 'neoconservative authoritarian approach' to youth crime, others are more likely to see young offenders as children in trouble, as reflected in the competing discourse of a *welfare paternalist* approach, where the care and guidance of young offenders is recognised as of most importance.

Within the youth justice system, despite a strong awareness of the importance of intervention and a growing policy impetus towards the use of sport for targeting youth crime and antisocial behaviour (Bloyce & Smith, 2010), attempts to engage and work with children in criminal justice settings can be especially challenging, and sporting initiatives are considerably less prevalent in incarcerated populations than in a community context. Although sport has become well-established as a useful social cohesion/inclusion strategy in community settings and despite the fact that many community-based sports projects are aimed at children and young people, particularly those who are on the verge of or at risk of entering the criminal justice system, few of these approaches have been translated into custodial settings, despite the fact that child-specific outcomes and rights that relate to sport and physical activity are equally applicable in prisons as they are in communities.[1]

The United Kingdom is not the only country to have a history of promoting sport as a way of tackling youth delinquency, but the issues of, and importance placed on, sport as a 'moral good' has become particularly ingrained in British politics (Conservative Party, 2009, 2010; Labour Party, 1997; TNS, 2011), despite there being little definitive evidence to support the assumption that sport is effective in reducing youth crime (Coakley, 1998; Coalter, 2009; Robins, 1990). Indeed, academic research in community settings which focuses on the re-engagement of marginalised young people through sport has yielded inconclusive results in terms

The challenge of using sport in youth justice practice in community settings

As a professional working with children who have been in custody or are serving community sentences, a stakeholder interviewee located within a Youth Offending Team emphasised the level of structured support necessary to enable children and young people to benefit from participation in sport, exacerbated for those with complex needs and chaotic lifestyles:

> The majority of the young people I work with are quite chaotic and have difficult personal circumstances. I have tried to use my sports and gym background to engage some of my young people in either using a gym or getting them into a sport. The majority have attended the gym induction, completed a few sessions with my support but then they have stopped going. A minority attended the session with me, but wouldn't go on their own. I've only had one young person who attended regular sessions with me and also went on his own: as a result his friendship group and his self-esteem improved and he started to question and change his drug use, for example thinking about reducing so as not to spoil the improvements he is making to his fitness. I've also had a few young people who have expressed an interest in sports. I have generally provided them with contact details and found out the sessions when they can attend. In a couple of cases I attended the initial session. Again, due to their difficult personal circumstances none of them were able to continue going – for some they had little external motivation due to having friends into drugs, no one to go with, and no parental support.

Despite not having the professional capacity and resource to provide the level of support necessary to encourage sustained participation in sport and physical activity, the interviewee was optimistic that by introducing those he worked with to sporting opportunities they might be encouraged to return to such activities subsequently:

> Overall, I've not had great success, but you never know even in the future some of these young people may go back to the activities I introduced them to. I think the potential benefits are massive, in terms of positively affecting lots of areas of their lives. (Probation Officer seconded to Youth Offending Team)

of efforts to reduce offending, partly as a result of the inevitable methodological limitations of small scale evaluation studies. Established during the 1990s, the U.S. sporting initiative Midnight Basketball claimed to reduce crime by up to 30% (Farrell, Johnson, Sapp, Pumphrey & Freeman, 1996; Hartmann, 2001; Hawkins, 1998) while in the United Kingdom, various community-based sporting initiatives have reported reductions in reoffending (Robins, 1990; Tsuchiya, 1996), including comparisons to matched controls (Nichols & Taylor, 1996). But as with many custodial interventions, such evaluations tend to be based on data generated from small sample sizes, lack the statistical techniques required to identify the contribution of sport as the cause of reductions to reoffending in a multimodal intervention, and rarely include comparisons to matched controls (but see Nichols & Taylor, 1996, for an example of this being successfully integrated into an evaluation). Furthermore, conflicting results arising from different indices of measurement within interventions – as well as differences across distinct programmes – also undermine the quality of the identified impact. For example, Berry, Little, Axford and Cusick (2009) found no difference between intervention and control groups on self-reported offending behaviour or substance use and yet established a modest significant improvement in official arrest and conviction rates among the intervention group compared to a control group.

Accumulated methodological shortcomings may have resulted in some commentators questioning the likely impact of youth sport schemes on recidivism (Smith & Waddington, 2004) but they remain one of the most prominent types of sport-based interventions. This may be because, as a developmental period, adolescence and early adulthood is seen as a time when the search for self-knowledge has particular importance (Harter, 1990; Heaven, 2001). Not only can sport and sporting aspirations have a powerful impact on identity development, but they also undoubtedly have the potential to address proximal risk factors for youth crime (Hodge, 2009), for example in improving poor social, interpersonal, and life skills (Coalter, 2005; Gould & Larson, 2008; Ravizza & Motonak, 2011; Theokas, Danish, Hodge, Heke & Forneris, 2007), negative peer groups and inappropriate use of leisure time (Nichols, 1997; Schafer, 1969), and in promoting psychological well-being (Coalter, 2005; Collins, 2009; Ekeland et al., 2005; West & Crompton, 2001). Collectively, such findings highlight the extent to which both the personal and social aspects of sport can impact positively upon young people and, of particular relevance here, how physical activity and sport can be an especially effective way of engaging young people in activities that they would typically be reluctant to participate in through conventional means, such as conventional classroom-based education (Sharpe, Schagen & Scott, 2004) or rehabilitative programmes (Nichols, 2007).

In contrast to community schemes, the use of sport with young people within the custodial context has received relatively little attention, although there is a common assumption that such initiatives might translate especially well into interventions aimed at juvenile (under 18 years old) and young adult (18–21 years old) offenders. This assumption may be a reflection of the fact that sports-based community programmes have typically had children and young people as their targets but also that young offenders have the highest rates of participation in physical activity of any incarcerated population in England and Wales (see Chapter 3 for a full discussion of comparative participation rates across different prison populations and Chapter 8 for an in-depth analysis of a programme specifically designed for young adults between the ages of 18 and 21). In the case of juvenile prisoners, high levels of involvement in sport can be in part attributable to physical education being a compulsory element of the curriculum outlined in the *National Specification for Learning and Skills* (Youth Justice Board, 2002) which ensures equitable educational provision for those of school age in custody as in the community. Furthermore, policy guiding physical education in custody for juveniles stipulates that provision must offer accredited qualifications, promote constructive use of leisure time and address offending behaviour (HM Prison Service, 2004; Ministry of Justice, 2012c), whereas such elements are now discretionary when it comes to provision for adults (Ministry of Justice, 2011b). In terms of recreational physical activity, surveys of juveniles coordinated by the Inspectorate of Prisons have revealed that the number of young people attending gym sessions at least five times per week and exercising outside everyday has increased consistently in recent years (Cripps, 2010; Tye, 2009). However, rates of participation are highly variable and remain inconsistent across prisons holding young people. For example, in 6 out of the 18 institutions (and of the 1,159 respondents) surveyed by Parke (2009), fewer than 1 in 10 young men said that they were allowed to take daily exercise, although 77% reported that they visited the gym at least once per week. Enthusiasm for sport, particularly among young men, appears to be high, and focusing on alternative nonoffending activities such as sports, along with getting a job, has been consistently cited by young prisoners as one of the key factors that would help them to stop offending (Cripps, 2010; Summerfield, 2011; Tye, 2009).

The importance of sport for children in prison

The number of children under the age of 18 who are imprisoned in England and Wales has decreased of late, with official figures indicating that the current population of just over 1,500 has halved over the past five years.[2] But levels of reoffending among children remain the highest, and almost three quarters of young people released from prison custody are reconvicted within a year (Ministry of Justice, 2012e). In England and Wales we have the youngest age of criminal responsibility in Europe, meaning that children as young as 10 are held accountable for criminal offences and can be incarcerated for serious enough crimes. In practice, the majority of those held in youth custody are aged 16 and 17 and will typically have incredibly complex social, psychological and educational needs.

Despite a plethora of evidence documenting the benefit of sport for young people (Busseri et al., 2011; Ekeland et al., 2005; Kremner, Trew & Ogle, 1997), growing evidence for the gains associated with sport and physical exercise for incarcerated populations (Buckaloo et al., 2009; Elger, 2009; Martos-Garcia, Devis-Devis, & Sparkes, 2009a; Verdot et al., 2010) and a recognised potential for sport as a vehicle for promoting rehabilitation among young offenders (Nichols, 1997), only a handful of evaluative studies have addressed the role of sport for young people in prison.

Aside from the methodological challenges of carrying out a meaningful and robust evaluation, successfully engaging young people in sporting activities in custody requires careful programme planning and delivery. Moreover, while practitioners, politicians, and academics have promoted sport with young offenders for educational and rehabilitative purposes, prisoners themselves rarely express such motivations for engaging in physical activity in custody (Frey & Delaney, 1996;

Martos-Garcia et al., 2009a; Martos-Garcia, Devis-Devis & Sparkes, 2009b) and it is therefore especially important to explore young people's own perceptions of participation in sporting interventions in custody in order to assess their potential to impact upon the decisions that young people make in terms of their attitudes and approaches to life within and beyond custody. Parker and Meek's (2013) exploration of the perceptions and experiences of children in prison in terms of their participation in a sports-based resettlement intervention demonstrated the importance of prison sports in motivating, not only young men who had an existing interest in (and passion for) sport, but also those who had experienced little, if any, previous involvement (given that many of the young people in prison custody have had disruptive educational experiences and a history of exclusion from school and may not have taken part in sport during mainstream schooling). Young participants evidently recognised the importance of sport, not only as an important form of emotional release, but as a way of creating a sense of achievment – an opportunity which can be highly valued among young offenders (Dubberley, 2010; Taylor et al., 1999). Echoing previous research (Andrews & Andrews, 2003; Morris, Sallybanks, Willis & Makkai, 2003), Parker and Meek's qualitative study also highlighted the importance of receiving encouragment and positive reinforcement, demonstrating the significance of an enthusiastic and engaging member of staff in establishing relationships with even the most diasaffected young people and in managing and improving behviour.

Innovative practice case study: Using a diverse sporting programme to promote well-being, qualifications and employment opportunities for juveniles

At the time of data collection, Ashfield YOI in the South West of England was a privately run Young Offender Institute detaining young males between the ages of 15 and 18 years. Although it was announced in early 2013 that the prison would no longer hold young prisoners and would be reinstated as an adult facility, the prison's sports programme, overseen by the physical education manager, remains a credible example of the innovative use of sport in engaging with children in custody.

Incorporating a broad range of activities delivered as part of the core curriculum alongside daily recreational activities, the model for Ashfield's sports-based programme is structured around a series of 'academies', each 12 weeks in duration and designed around a specific sporting activity: football, rugby, cricket, boxing, basketball, table tennis and rock climbing. Each academy consists of six classroom sessions per week (each session of 1.5 hours duration) where participants study the 'theoretical' aspects of sport, supplemented with six 'practical' sessions per week (also 1.5 hours in duration) where young people participate in their chosen sporting activity. Wrapped around the theoretical and practical sessions, a comprehensive multi-agency individual support package, delivered in partnership with voluntary sector and statutory organisations, aims to improve opportunities for the youngsters involved. To this end, academies included sports coaching, sport education qualifications (such as Sports Leaders awards), life-skills mentoring, community placements, community/industry-related guest events and prerelease resettlement support providing assistance to young people in their negotiations with case workers, Youth Offending Teams and parole boards, and in relation to issues surrounding family re-engagement. Depending on the length of their prison sentence, participants could complete as many different academy programmes (and associated qualifications) as was practically possible.

As well as the opportunity to obtain an accredited qualification relating to the central sporting activity, delivery partnerships with community-based organisations were also used to facilitate opportunities for Release on Temporary Licence (RoTL). Indeed, half of all RoTL activities across the prison were sports based, giving those eligible an opportunity to participate in sporting activities and volunteering in the community, with the aim of promoting the development of transferable skills such as communication, teamwork and organisation, and in order to provide opportunities for work experience – some of which were translated into employment opportunities upon release. Participation in academies was also linked to an individual's Incentives and Earned Privileges status, with increased participation in sport being used as an incentive for good behaviour.

Principles of best practice

Providing a diverse range of sporting activities.

Offering opportunities to gain accredited qualifications across all sporting activities.

Developing a wide range of community partnerships to facilitate RoTL and post-release employment opportunities.

Incentivising sport using the Incentives and Earned Privileges system to promote good behaviour with the establishment more widely.

Provision for juvenile and young adult males: A secondary analysis of inspectorate reports

Secondary analysis of published inspectorate reports for all 34 establishments holding male young offender populations[3] in England and Wales provided a valuable insight into the provision, practices, and identified problems in delivery of PE and sport, particularly in relation to the priority areas of health promotion, education, offending behaviour, resettlement and community partnerships. The prison establishments under consideration included those holding male juveniles aged 15 to 17 only ($n = 6$), young adults aged 18 to 25 only ($n = 9$), both juveniles and young adults ($n = 4$) and split sites holding young offenders and adults ($n = 15$).[4]

Across the 34 establishments accommodating male juvenile and young adult offenders, a wide range of team and individual sports were available, including (but not limited to) football, rugby, cricket, basketball, volleyball, rounders, boxing, table tennis, dance, weight lifting, swimming, racquet sports, mountain biking, climbing, athletics, exercise classes and other gym-based activities. Most establishments were observed by the Inspectorate to offer a sufficient range of sporting activities and, not surprisingly, the reports indicated that the variety of sports offered within individual establishments were largely determined by local resources and preferences, mirroring the National Audit Office's (2008) finding that the range of activities offered to prisoners will be determined by the type of facilities available and the design of each prison. All establishments appeared to offer both individual and team sports, with most having a combination of both indoor and outdoor provision, although no outdoor provision was available at one of the YOI/adult split sites, and access to outdoor provision was lacking at one of the juvenile establishments and one split site.

The amount of time that prisoners were able to participate in PE per week and the resulting participation levels varied substantially across different establishments holding young people, although the majority of establishments were found to achieve the minimum recommended provision of two hours per week for those aged under 21 years old. It should also be acknowledged, however, that establishing baselines for participation in physical activities and making meaningful comparisons across establishments is difficult since few YOIs hold identical populations or have comparable facilities. In the reports analysed, prisoner participation levels ranged from 93% in one juvenile establishment to 37% at a split site holding young offenders and adults. Participation levels in three establishments holding young adults, one prison holding both juveniles and young adults and one other split site for adults and young offenders, were also deemed to be low, and in a minority of instances, Inspectorate reports identified that access to PE was perceived to be insufficient or not equitable due to unclear selection criteria. In contrast, the provision at some establishments far exceeded minimum requirements. For example, one juvenile establishment scheduled six hours per week of core PE, plus additional access to recreational PE, thus offering young people up to 10 hours of sport and physical activity a week. Promisingly, survey findings from juveniles (Cripps, 2010) have revealed that the number of young people who said they attended the gym at least five times a week and could exercise outside everyday has increased steadily over the last four years. The type of prison establishment also appears to have a direct effect on participation levels, whereby higher proportions of young men attending the gym regularly were identified in dedicated sites for young offenders as opposed to split sites holding diverse age groups.

Consistent with findings from across the prison estate, Inspectorate reports have also indicated that increased access to PE in YOIs was often related to the prisoners' Incentives and Earned Privileges status, which should come as no surprise since access to the gym is widely acknowledged to be an important tool in encouraging good behaviour among those who value their time in the gym or involvement in sport. For example, an inspection of an establishment holding young adults in 2011 noted that those on 'basic' status and 'standard' unemployed prisoners were entitled to one session of PE a week, whereas a standard level employed prisoner would be entitled to two sessions of PE per week, and an 'enhanced' status prisoner would be entitled to three sessions per week. As such,

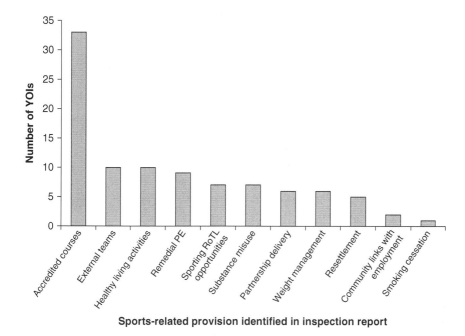

Figure 6.1 Frequency of wider sports-related policy provision within the YOI estate.

although policy advocates equitable access to physical education among prisoners, in practice involvement in sport and physical activity is often used as a reward for good behaviour, with activities withheld as a form of penalty. However, as research continues to explore how physical activity can be used most effectively in prisons, efforts may need to be made to ensure that prisoners who have reduced privileges or specific needs have the opportunity to participate in appropriate and effective forms of physical activity.

In practice, analysis of Inspectorate reports across the male juvenile and young adult secure estate indicates that there is a substantial variation in delivery of sports activities within young offender institutions. Figure 6.1 provides an overview of this variation, illustrating the number of establishments that, according to Inspectorate reports, successfully endorse the use of sport in promoting varied aspects of education, health promotion, resettlement and community partnerships.

Physical and mental health

Inspectorate reports for almost a third of the establishments holding children and young people explicitly referred to healthy living activities or exercise referral programmes incorporated into PE programmes, reflecting good working relationships between prison gyms and health care departments. Remedial PE was noted as available in nine of the establishments and clear links to substance misuse programmes were identified for seven prisons. Several PE departments also offered specific weight loss/gain programmes, and one PE department was responsible for facilitating a smoking cessation programme.

Education, training and employment

Offering accredited courses represents one way in which delivery of PE can be aligned with the reducing reoffending agenda by equipping young prisoners with the necessary skills to increase their employment options and education opportunities during the rest of their sentence and after release. Inspectorate reports for all but one of the youth establishments explicitly mention availability of accredited PE courses, although the range and level of such provision varied greatly across establishments. Whilst sports-based educational provision was considered limited or basic in some establishments, the overall range of accredited courses across the juvenile and young adult estate was broad, including awards in specific sporting activities and sports leadership, certificates in diet and nutrition, football coaching and junior manager awards, NVQs in sport, leisure, and recreation, GCSE (General Certificate in Secondary Education) PE and gym instructor qualifications. There was also widespread evidence of associated qualifications which could provide learners with a broader portfolio in sports, fitness and health, offered in areas such as communication in the workplace, developing customer service and understanding personal physical fitness, Active IQ, HeartStart, First Aid, manual handling training and Duke of Edinburgh Awards.

Supplementing qualifications, sports-based activities and placements for those young offenders eligible for Release on Temporary Licence (RoTL) provide an especially valuable work experience opportunity for involvement in community-based sports clubs. However, Inspectorate reports indicate that fewer than 20% of youth establishments took advantage of the RoTL scheme to offer further opportunities for sport, physical activity and sports-based work placements in the community.

Community partnerships

RoTL placements provide a valuable form of community involvement and can be an effective way of utilising and developing community partnerships and promoting prosocial networks, but such opportunities rely on local placements being available and are only offered to the small number of prisoners considered to be at a low enough risk to participate. Another more inclusive way of promoting community involvement with young people through sport is through partnerships with individuals, organisations and sporting teams who come into the prison to deliver coaching sessions, give motivational talks or establish supportive professional relationships that can be continued after sentences have been served. Although the relevant Prison Service Instruction, as well as policy documents such as *Every Child Matters in Secure Settings* advocate this form of community involvement, the actual practice is varied and irregular and established links with community sporting organisations and teams were noted in Inspectorate reports for fewer than half of the youth establishments considered. For those establishments that had developed external links, the resulting community partnerships had varying purposes but were predominantly used to facilitate matches with external teams or in order to receive specialist coaching or accredited courses. Given that partnership working and community links have been highlighted as a key element of best practice in the delivery of community-based sports initiatives for young offenders (Big Lottery Fund, 2009) and in light of the elevated risk of social isolation following release from prison, a prominent recommendation is that positive community partnerships should continue to be advocated and expanded in the delivery of youth sport in prisons.

Attitudes, thinking and behaviour

Existing policy clearly states that sport should also be promoted as a means to address offending attitudes and behaviours, but in practice few YOIs explicitly target offending behaviour through sporting activities and only five out of the 34 Inspectorate reports identified sporting initiatives explicitly targeting offending behaviour. Given that in community settings sport has been effective in attracting young people or in improving performance in activities which they are not normally motivated to engage in (Nichols & Taylor, 1996; Sharpe et al., 2004), and that active learning has been identified as a key element in the 'what works' literature on reducing reoffending, sport may be an especially valuable resource in motivating young prisoners who are reluctant to engage in classroom-based offender behaviour programmes. In practice, however, such incentives are not yet widespread in the juvenile and young adult estate, and their success is often contingent upon innovative delivery, drawing on community partnerships as well as internal expertise.

In summary, the practical delivery of sport to young offenders in custody in England and Wales is highly diverse and variable across establishments. While the majority of establishments meet minimum policy standards in terms of access to physical education, the degree to which the wider policy agendas of health promotion, education and training and reducing reoffending are ingrained into the delivery of sport varies substantially. The observation from the Chief Inspector of Prisons, that 'the high reoffending rate among young adult men is unlikely to reduce without significant changes in approach, funding and focus' (HM Chief Inspector of Prisons, 2010) serves to highlight the importance of exploring innovative and effective ways of working with young prisoners, particularly those who are not engaging with or responding to other prison-based interventions. Given its widespread popularity among young people as an interesting and appealing pursuit, sport should clearly not be underestimated as a valuable medium through which to achieve a broad range of positive outcomes. As with the wider prison estate, the distinct populations held and the availability of local resources may dictate the format of and extent to which sport is delivered across juvenile establishments and YOIs, but well-coordinated initiatives that promote education, health and desistance and make use of meaningful community partnerships have enormous potential in improving the immediate and longer term prospects of young prisoners.

Innovative practice case study: Supporting young offenders in the transition from custody to community through sports-based volunteering and employment opportunities

Street Team is one of several initiatives developed by Cricket for Change, a U.K.-based charity set up in the wake of the 1981 Brixton riots which has been using the game of cricket to change the lives of disadvantaged young people nationally and internationally. Taking referrals from prisons holding juveniles and young adults in London and the South West, the programme aims to support young ex-offenders in the transition from custody to community through a training for work programme, using an individual's enthusiasm for sport and personal experiences to improve their life opportunities and in turn to change the mindsets of other 'at risk' young people. The programme offers ex-prisoners between the ages of 16–25 the chance to gain skills, qualifications and experience to become trained coaches. Individuals are mentored by an ex-offender and other project staff and supported with a holistic resettlement package which adopts a model of training and support. The initiative uses a multi-agency approach and has the advantage of being able to involve those participating in the Street Team initiative in other projects run by the charity, encompassing cricket and rugby in a range of community, educational and secure settings. Expectations are managed through an agreed plan for each individual which builds on relationships established while participants are still in custody and with the support of probation staff can be written into licence conditions upon release. Specifically the programme prepares young people for release from custody by offering intensive support from the first days of release for up to a year, providing training and supervision and facilitating voluntary opportunities that can develop into paid coaching and sports development roles as part of the organisation's wider remit which includes preventative sports-based work in Pupil Referral Units to encourage young people to making positive choices. Over a three year pilot period the organisation has worked intensively with 12 young men who have achieved an accumulated total of 34 accredited qualifications, contributed 1,041 volunteering hours and engaged directly with 193 children in Pupil Referral Units.

Principles of best practice

> Partner with prison-based community organisations in order to make referrals and with probation staff to establish expectations and establish levels of involvement.
> Make use of the enthusiasm of ex-prisoners to participate in development work by using sport to engage with young people in Pupil Referral Units.
> Embed programmes for ex-prisoners in organisations that have responsibility for a broad range of sport-based initiatives that operate in different contexts.

Notes

1   Of particular relevance to sport and physical activity, Being Healthy and Enjoying and Achieving are two of the five specified outcomes that underpin the agenda for children's services in the 2003 Green Paper, Every Child Matters (Department for Education and Skills, 2003). Article 31 of the United Nations Convention on the Rights of the Child (United Nations, 1989), ratified by many countries including the United Kingdom, stipulates 'the right of the child to rest and leisure, to engage in play and recreational activities'.

2   Figures published by the Youth Justice Board state that there were 1,523 young people aged 18 and under in the secure estate at the end of the year 2012, compared to 3,037 in November of 2008 (Youth Justice Board, 2013).

3   All establishments holding young offender populations in September 2010 were considered, although for some of these establishments their reception criteria have since been reconfigured and they no longer hold young adults.

4   Analysis was conducted on the most recent inspectorate report published for each establishment by September 2010, and in cases where a more recent Inspectorate report had been published by April 2012 these were also analysed.

7 The role of sport in reducing reoffending and promoting desistance

It is coincidental that the annual cost of reoffending in England and Wales is roughly equivalent to the cost incurred in hosting the 2012 Olympics,[1] but it serves as a stark reminder of the problematic scale of reoffending: in the year 2012, over 86,000 offenders were discharged following a prison sentence (Ministry of Justice, 2013a),[2] and latest figures confirm that approximately half of all offenders released from custody will reoffend within a year[3] (Ministry of Justice, 2013b). It is not surprising, then, that reoffending by those released from prison is seen as a significant problem within the criminal justice system, recognised with government reforms packaged as a 'rehabilitation revolution' (Ministry of Justice, 2012a) which reflect an increased focus on rehabilitation processes in the management of offenders.

Aligning sport with resettlement pathways and criminogenic needs

In 2002, the *Reducing Reoffending by Ex-Prisoners* report produced by the now disbanded Social Exclusion Unit identified the primary factors which contribute to reoffending; these were then categorised in seven 'reducing reoffending pathways' formulated by the *Reducing Reoffending National Action Plan* (Home Office, 2004). These would come to guide resettlement service provision in the domains of accommodation, education, employment and training, health, drugs and alcohol, finance, debt and benefit, children and families, and attitudes, thinking and behaviour.

Although broadly welcomed as a more effective way of responding to the needs of offenders, there has been some concern that the pathways approach risks compartmentalising resettlement practice and commissioning processes, potentially suppressing more holistic services (Hucklesby & Hagley-Dickinson, 2007), and that the resulting resettlement policy has tended to concentrate predominantly on the provision of practical services to offenders, to the detriment of approaches which focus instead on the development of offenders' cognitive skills and self-motivation to desist from crime (Maguire & Raynor, 2006). Partially mapping onto these resettlement concerns are the more internationally recognised 'criminogenic needs' which have been identified following research into the major risk factors associated with criminal conduct. Whereas some of these risk factors,

Innovative practice case study: Partnerships between prisons and football clubs

Drawing on the recognised and valued brand of a high profile football club is a well-established way of promoting participation and encouraging good behaviour in prison. For example the Duke of Edinburgh scheme at HMPYOI Reading is delivered in partnership with Reading Football Club and the club's social inclusion officer. The promotion of education and employment opportunities through a partnership between Bournemouth Football Club, the PE department at HMP Guys Marsh and the Princes Trust has enabled the prison to offer an intensive six-week programme which leads to participating prisoners gaining a Football Association recognised coaching qualifications and volunteering opportunities at the football club for those returning to the area after release. Similarly, in partnership with Cardiff City Football Club, the PE department at HMP Parc also deliver a six-week programme which uses football-based learning materials to improve engagement in literacy classes offered by the prison. The course supports prisoners to gain accredited qualifications in communication skills at Levels 1 and 2 and engagement in the classroom-based literacy learning is rewarded with football coaching sessions delivered by professional Cardiff City FC coaches. The formal partnership with the football club also provides participants with links in the community which have been used to secure employment upon release.

Demonstrating the potential of extending community-based social inclusion programmes to involve offenders, Chelsea Football Club works in partnership with HMP and YOI Chelmsford, engaging with the young men held within the prison as well as youths at risk of crime. Chelsea staff visit the prison to coach football sessions and cofacilitate the delivery of accredited coaching qualifications, with the ultimate aim of creating a workforce of accredited coaches within the prisoner population. Under the supervision of Chelsea coaches, prisoners then have the opportunity to gain qualifications and apply their skills in coaching their peers, and prisoners meeting risk assessment criteria also have the opportunity to work alongside Chelsea FC after release in order to engage with young people at risk of crime who have been referred to the club's social inclusion projects.

Principles of best practice

Developing community partnerships with recognised football clubs to encourage uptake and deliver industry recognised qualifications.

Collaborative delivery of sporting activities to foster links for offenders with organisations in the community.

Blending literacy with sport to increase engagement.

Using sport as a reward for achievements in non-sporting domains.

Drawing on community partnerships in order to provide post-release employment and volunteering opportunities.

Integrating prison and community based initiatives.

such as a family history of criminality, are static (i.e. not possible to change through intervention), others are recognised as being dynamic (such as attitudes and values or employment status) and these have subsequently been termed the criminogenic needs which in turn can be targeted for change in seeking to reduce the likelihood of reoffending. These form the basis of the need component of the Risk-Need-Responsivity model for the assessment and treatment of offenders (see Andrews, Bonta & Hoge, 1990; Andrews et al., 1990), whereby the risk principle confirms the need to target those most at risk of offending, the need principle refers to the need to assess and subsequently target those previously identified criminogenic needs and the responsivity principle dictates that an intervention will be more effective if it is adapted to the circumstances, individual learning style, motivation and abilities of those being targeted.

The role of sport and physical activity in meeting resettlement needs: Staff perspectives

In identifying the direct benefits for prisoners who engage in sport and physical activity, prison staff referred most frequently in their survey responses to improvements in physical health, mental health and self-esteem, better management of emotions, the achievement of transferable skills and recognised qualifications, engagement in education and offending behaviour programmes, the development of positive values and a more constructive use of leisure time. Whether or not the identification of these factors by staff represents a direct result of attempts to align PE provision with the reducing reoffending agenda, the benefits reported by staff certainly map on to the recognised resettlement and criminogenic needs of offenders (see Chapter 3 for further discussion of staff perceptions of the value of delivering sports initiatives in prison).

However, as well as linking sport to specific aspects of resettlement, rather than working in isolation, there was also evidence of prison staff maximising the impact of their work by coproducing their activities with colleagues based elsewhere in the prison, outside the gym:

> I believe the benefits of engaging offenders in sport here are numerous. We make maximum use of our resources and work with education, healthcare, violence reduction and safer custody – contributing towards reducing reoffending pathways, whilst also improving offender health, fitness, education, social skills and well being, as well as empowering them with vocational qualifications and engaging them in purposeful activity. Sport has the opportunity to reduce reoffending in so many ways. (Staff, Category B)

Although sport and physical activity may be more obviously aligned with resettlement needs associated with health, education, employment and improvements to attitudes, thinking and behaviour, there was also evidence that use of the prison gym can play a role in maintaining positive family relationships, which are not only recognised as representing a significant factor in preventing reoffending, but can also contribute to the promotion of physical activity (Thompson et al., 2010). Where prisons offer family visit days, in many establishments the gym plays an important role during such occasions. Aside from the practicality of a sports hall offering the necessary space to accommodate a substantial number of visitors at one time, the more creative use of the available facilities and activities (typically organised by gym staff and orderlies in collaboration with family liaison staff or organisations supporting the families of prisoners) enable prisoners to interact with their children in a more natural way than they would otherwise:

> A prisoner came up to me afterwards and was so grateful, he said it was the first time he had ever been able to play with his daughter outside of a visit room. We had set up this soft play area and other activities in the sports hall – for many it was the first time they got to play sport with their children. PE can link into many of the resettlement pathways. (Staff, Category C)

However, while highlighting various ways in which the gym could contribute to meeting resettlement needs, stakeholder interviewees were also keen to distinguish between the standard model of recreational PE and more creative practices, placing responsibility for the latter on individual establishments and their staff rather than national standards:

> Establishments delivering the minimum service specification with a focus on recreational PE will not directly impact on offending behaviour. Prisons with a balanced, needs-driven programme can and will contribute to offending behaviour provision. (Senior Manager)

Using sport to promote desistance from crime

Key to the contemporary understanding of desistance is the recognition that, in order to abstain successfully from crime, ex-prisoners need to 'make sense' of their lives as nonoffenders. The desistance literature has identified a range of factors associated with no longer being actively involved in offending, many of which are concerned with the acquisition of something meaningful to the offender which promotes a re-evaluation of their sense of self. In interviews, prisoners consistently referred to the role that sport had played in transforming their outlook on life and in developing their social and cultural capital:

> I'm someone who had never achieved anything in life before I came to prison, it's let me set myself challenges and reach them and get that sense of achievement. Like I'd never played football before coming to prison and then when I tried it and got better and realised I could do it, it really boosted my self-esteem. You feel that you're part of a group and are actually capable of doing something. It gives you pride on a personal level, it gives you back that self-worth which prison takes away from you. (Prisoner, Local)

In particular, desistance from crime is recognised as relying on the successful negotiation of a reformed alternative identity, be that of student, sportsperson or employee. One important aspect of prison-based sport in this capacity is its role in promoting a shift of identity away from that of offender, offering alternative positive identifies – many of which may be represented through sport. Related to this, a critical feature of desistance is finding an activity or change of circumstance which has the potential to engage and motivate individuals and enable them to develop alternative prosocial identities, as well as contributing to the development of positive social networks. It may not be surprising that when McMurran, Theodosi, Sweeney and Sellen (2008) asked adult male prisoners to identity their goals, alongside employment and accommodation concerns, improving self-control and desisting from offending, 'finding new leisure pursuits' and 'getting fit and healthy' were prominent responses, demonstrating the salience of physical activity in efforts to develop an alternative positive identity to that of offender.

Individualised strength-based approaches rely on constructive relationships but can be especially effective if managed skilfully enough to instill a sense of possibility and opportunity and a meaningful way out of a cycle of incarceration and reoffending. Reflecting this, staff were well aware of the potential role of sport, not just as a constructive use of ex-prisoners' leisure time, but as a way of improving social capital:

> Constructive use of their time here may encourage them to participate in sport and leisure pastimes upon their release and represent a better use of their free time – and hopefully less time to commit crime. (Staff, Local)
>
> If an ex-prisoner joins a local club after release it can reduce criminogenic factors and they may well even get the opportunity of work etc. from fellow club members. (Staff, Category D)

In their commissioning criteria discussion paper, National Offender Management Service (2012c) assert the need for evidence-based practice which relates to desistance literature. Desistance theorists have identified the importance for offenders of a 'hook for change'; in the context of sport this has the potential to be an activity which can engage a broad range of people in prison, promote the development of prosocial identities and contribute to the building of positive social networks. For many of the prisoner interviewees who were asked to describe their involvement in sports-related projects, there was a consensus that the projects they took part in – as with other physical activity based projects (Dubberley, 2010; Ozano, 2008) – were less likely to represent a series of false hopes and empty promises (which unfortunately seemed to be a common perceived shortcoming of many prison-based initiatives), and instead offered a sense of possibility and opportunity and a meaningful way out of a cycle of incarceration and reoffending.

It should come as no surprise that creating and sustaining motivation is considered to be a key factor in bringing about positive change (Prochaska & DiClemente, 1986), including desistance from crime (Farrall, 2002; Maruna, 2001). Reflecting this, the accounts of prisoner interviewees suggest that using sport as a means of generating initial engagement and sustaining sufficient enthusiasm to overcome motivation-depleting experiences (such as financial or accommodation problems) can be an effective method of promoting significant processes of change, even if this is dependent on the provision of ongoing resettlement support. Many prisoners and ex-prisoners described how involvement in sport had not only motivated them and provided them with the support to identify positive and alternative futures, but had also enabled them to challenge their attitudes towards crime, encouraging them to adopt an alternative lifestyle upon release.

Although such dialogues suggest that sport may act as a diversion from offending behaviour after release (Hawkins, 1998; Nichols, 2007), it is also possible that engagement in these activities can provide a legitimate means of reintegration into the social world. If an individual has access to limited mainstream opportunities to gain a sense of inclusion and satisfy identity development needs, cultivating an interest in sport whilst ensuring access to ongoing participation after release may help fulfil identity needs and create the potential for positive new peer relationships.

Sport as a feature of identity transformation

Exploring the social psychological processes underlying role transition among offenders has emerged as a critical question for theory and empirical research on the desistance process (Shover, 1996; Maruna, 2001), and social identity theory (Tajfel & Turner, 1986) provides an especially useful mechanism for specifying the significant transitions which ex-prisoners negotiate upon release. Broadly, the theory proposes that individuals are motivated to act in accordance with group norms in order to achieve a positive identity and that behaviour is therefore guided by the norms attached to a particular identity (Jetten, Postmes & McAuliffe, 2002). A small body of research has paid attention to the 'criminal identities' of offenders (Byrne & Trew, 2008; Taylor, Gibbs & Merighi, 1994), the ways in which offending identities are created and confirmed in prison (Little, 1990; Waters, 2003) and processes of identity 'loss' as a result of incarceration (Harvey, 2005) or the presence of a dichotomous identity, where the dominant criminal identity contradicts with alternative identities present in the community (Corey, 1996). Alternatively, Jewkes (2002, 2005) explains that although becoming a prisoner can diminish or subsume other identities, attempts to avoid internalising the public image of 'prisoner' are reflected by an increased effort to maintain preprison identities or through the construction of new identities from within the prison. Meanwhile, a separate body of literature has explored the importance of sporting identities in community settings (see MacClancy, 1996) implying that sport can provide an important alternative identity to that of offender. An implication of this is that the adoption of sporting identities may serve a particular social psychological function, not just in coping with the existential crisis of imprisonment but also in re-establishing oneself as a nonoffender after release from prison.

Of course, however motivated an individual may be to assert him or herself as 'reformed', to take up alternative identities and to depart from a previous existance to that of offender or prisoner, research into the psychological effects of stigma (see Major & O'Brien, 2005) has established that its direct and indirect effects (for example manifested through mechanisms of discrimination, stereotype activations, and expectancy confirmation), coupled with explicit foms of stigma and hostility towards ex-offenders (Dale, 1976; Uggen, Manza & Behrens, 2004) can undermine even the most determined attempts to 'go straight'. But for those individuals who remain inspired by and comitted to sport, ongoing involvement in such activities can not only help to remove the stigma which often undermines rehabilitative efforts but also provide a meaningful and effective way of promoting the type of *civic reintegration* which Uggen et al. (2004) recognise as being as important as the better established factors of work and family in promoting transitions. According to this model, participation and volunteering can provide a valuable opportunity for ex-prisoners to 'try on' idealised roles as active, responsible and productive citizens, which can in turn help to reinforce a commitment to desistance. Illustrating this, ex-prisoner interviewees who were participating in voluntary youth coaching though a community organisation described the benefits of improved self-confidence and in establishing a positive identity:

> I go round Pupil Referral Units and the community sessions too, teaching young people rugby and about how to get over aggression and stuff. It is amazing giving back, having tomorrow's generation looking up to you. I say to them 'the future is whatever you want it to be.' It feels good, it's changed my life around totally. I'm appreciated more and my family and my friends look up to me now – I'm like a role model. (Ex-prisoner, YOI)
>
> I was glad to be in that environment, people looking up to me again and that is where I want to stay in life. Now I can stand up and coach 50 kids at a time and believe in myself. I never used to. I learned that I can actually achieve things. I wish I was like this ten years ago. (Ex-prisoner, YOI)

Furthermore, engaging in sports volunteering activities has been recognised as an appealing form of civic engagement for young males (Mawson & Parker, 2013), including those from marginalised and disadvantaged groups (Farooq, Moreland, Parker & Pitchford, 2013), suggesting that sport may play a particularly important role in promoting the citizenship strand of the Coalition government's Big Society agenda.[4]

The importance of community partnerships developed through sport

A common criticism of our criminal justice system is that despite the accessibility of structured programmes of support within custody and the provision of multi-agency assistance within the community, there remains insufficient integration of the two. Upon release from prison, individuals risk finding themselves without the necessary skills or resources to engage with the agencies designed to support them and as a consequence they may find the easiest way to survive is by a return to offending. Empowering and motivating ex-offenders to engage in constructive and supportive relationships after release has been found to contribute to desistance in a number of ways: in developing the skills required to think positively about life; to develop a more coherent sense of the self; in developing a sense of active citizenship and prosocial behaviours, and, where appropriate, in re-establishing familial connections and relationships. Establishing meaningful and trusting support networks which can be maintained after release will not necessarily guarantee desistance from crime but such supportive relationships can enable individuals to be better equipped to identify and articulate their needs which, in turn, increases their chances of receiving appropriate help and support to make the transition back into society.

Talleu (2011) highlights the importance of bringing sporting organisations into prisons as a feature of efforts to promote reintegration of prisoners and ongoing postintervention support has already been identified as a key element of successful sport-based interventions for young people in community settings (Morris et al., 2003; Nichols & Taylor, 1996; Taylor et al., 1999). In criminal justice settings, an important part of the role of such community organisation partnerships can be making the connections which prison staff may not have the resources to explore, referring individuals to other partnering organisation and support agencies and ensuring that the specific needs and interests of those concerned are appropriately and adequately met during the transition from custody to community. The importance of post-release support was specifically acknowledged by prison staff:

> We must, in my opinion, be able to deliver support throughout a prisoner's sentence and into the community, seamlessly. We often develop trust over many years with offenders, to expect them to leave prison and suddenly engage with a community worker or sport development officer is in my experience unlikely to succeed. (Staff, Local)

Innovative practice case study: Using community partnerships to mediate the transition from custody to community for young adults

Chapter 8 details a qualitative and quantitative evaluation of a sports-based resettlement project at HMP and YOI Portland, which provides an overview of the significant influence that a relatively small scale project can have on the individuals involved. Running over a period of 12–15 weeks, at the heart of the initiative was a structured process of individually tailored resettlement case work which was embedded in the sporting programme during the course of the initiative, with scope to continue after release on a voluntary basis for up to six months, depending on levels of individual need and engagement. The provision of structured post-release support was recognised as being an important way of meeting the initiative's aim of reducing reoffending and promote desistance from crime by enhancing the young men's skills and opportunities. A key element of the academy model was the one-to-one resettlement support delivered by a 'transitions caseworker' in order to support the young men to prepare for their release while in custody but also as an ongoing support system after release. The resettlement element of the programme was delivered alongside and integrated into the more traditional sports coaching and exercises, with group activities and individual case work aiming to identify and improve resettlement needs, challenge negative attitudes and establish positive and supportive working relationships between the participants and a network of professionals, with the ultimate goal of preparing individuals for a successful transition from custody to the community following completion of a prison sentence. Participants reported that the independent resettlement support offered surpassed any available from statutory organisations, since as a community-based organisation they were directly concerned with and knowledgeable about post-release support and able to establish supportive relationships well before the time of release. Although sport was not at the heart of the positive and constructive relationships observed between the caseworker and academy participants, it was critical in promoting initial engagement in the initiative and providing a lens through which to explore issues as they arose.

Principles of best practice

Use sport to establish supportive and trusting therapeutic relationships.
Draw on community partnerships to provide effective through-the-gate provision.
Use sport as a way of delivering and reflecting upon transferable learning opportunities.

Using sport to reduce stigma and enhance social capital

Community partnerships are not only good for the prisoner, they can also be a real eye opener for people involved in delivery, challenging the notion that offender are all just a waste of space. It makes them realise that they are people who may have made mistakes in the past but shouldn't all be written off. (Senior Manager)

There is an increasing awareness among practitioners and academics that rehabilitation may be as much concerned with the social and legal processes of delabeling and destigmatisation as it is about individual transformation. Successful transitions from custody to community are inevitably partially dependent on positive community relationships, with the stigma of ex-prisoners recognised as a major barrier to reintegration. Of relevance here is Putnam's (2000) work advocating participation in civil organisations (including sports clubs) as a way of promoting societal integration. In particular, Putnam highlights the importance of activities such as sport contributing to the bridging form of social capital which refers to the processes by which activities are shared with people who are different from each other.

Innovative practice case study: Using football to engage prolific and persistent offenders in the community

Sussex and Surrey Probation Trust's In2Sport project is a football-based initiative jointly funded by the Sussex Police and the NHS and delivered to Prolific and Persistent Offenders (PPOs) in the community who are supervised under the Integrated Offender Management (IOM) initiative. The project is jointly delivered by a probation officer and a police officer in partnership with Street Games, a U.K. charity working with young people in disadvantaged communities. The project aims to reduce the risk of reoffending, to promote self-confidence and pro-social behaviour, improve interpersonal skills and self-awareness and create opportunities to engage in training or employment. The initiative also aims to increase and improve the quality of engagement between ex-offenders and IOM teams and other relevant agencies following an individual's release from custody.

A motivation for establishing the scheme was a recognition of a lack of structured programmes for those who have left prison, in contrast to the provision available while still in custody:

> There are good programmes and provision in prison but then nothing when people come out and they often quickly disengage. (In2Sport Project Leader)

Delivered over a year, the programme consists of weekly practical football coaching sessions and theory-based learning sessions. Group sessions are supplemented with one-to-one work focusing on personal goals and signposting individuals on to organisations who can provide further support or opportunities for development. Each session targets a specific area of skills development linked to offending behaviour including communication, leadership and organisation skills, managing emotions and taking responsibility for behaviour. Where appropriate, participants also have the opportunity to attain accredited qualifications and throughout the programme the achievements of and skills developed by each participant are tracked in personal portfolios incorporating staff progress reports as well as participants' written/artistic work, self-assessment and peer assessment. Portfolios can consequently be drawn upon when applying for education, training or employment in the future.

Despite the clear benefits of delivering sports-based initiatives to offenders in a community context, there are significant challenges to promoting engagement outside custodial settings. However, the In2Sport project has proved to be effective in re-engaging individuals with the probation process:

> It's like 'stealth probation' . . . it gives an inroad to hook them in and work on other issues like attitudes and thinking. Attending football sessions instead of probation appointments can be offered if people are not attending – nine times out of ten people go for it and then re-engage with their probation officer. (In2Sport Project Leader)

However, in contrast to custody based initiatives, participant retention within the community can be a significant challenge in light of the complexity of needs facing individuals following release:

i didn't anticipate just quite how chaotic some of these people's lives are. They get out and there are continuous distractions – friends and in some cases families encouraging them back into crime, some don't have any accommodation and so on. Trying to retain people is a real problem and out of 19 people who have signed up for the course only six people have ever turned up all at the same time for a session. Many are recalled for minor offences . . . so we lose people all the time. (In2Sport Project Leader)

Despite such challenges, initial evaluative evidence for the scheme suggests that offenders who have completed the programme have increased engagement with probation and improved relations with statutory organisations including the police, as well as reductions in arrests and improved employment prospects. However, ongoing funding from statutory organisations to continue delivering the programme is uncertain, with project staff concerned that the policy impetus towards privatising probation services will further threaten funding for such projects in future.

Principles of best practice

Recognising the need for post-release structured support and the role that sport can play in enhancing such provision and in maintaining sustained engagement.

Integrated working in project delivery across criminal justice professionals.

Targeting those most at risk of disengagement.

Clearly stated session objectives with a rationale for change.

Integrating attitude and behaviour change objectives into sports based and theory sessions.

Developing personal portfolios of progression and skills development.

Signposting to other agencies for further support.

Sport evidently has a significant role to play in enhancing social integration processes, and not just in enhancing the significant social capital opportunities associated with belonging to sporting social networks. In responding to the recognised need to improve public attitudes towards prisons and prisoners, staff as well as prisoners spoke with enthusiasm in interviews about the positive impact of prisons hosting visiting community teams, typically in football and rugby. Such perceived benefits extended beyond the evident exhilaration of having the opportunity to engage in a friendly competitive experience with an opposing team and included the impact of being able to interact briefly with members of community teams informally after matches had taken place. The research identified occasions where prison staff had attempted to recreate some of the post-match sporting rituals that are typically undertaken in community club settings – for example by each team nominating their man of the match for the opposition and by sharing refreshments. Observations of such interactions also confirmed the positive impact on community members, many of whom had no previous experience of visiting prisons or of interacting with a serving prisoner.

Notes

1   Initial estimates of the annual cost of reoffending at £11 billion (Social Exclusion Unit, 2002) have been replaced with more recent estimates (adjusting for inflation and changes to crime levels) of between £9.5 billion and £13 billion (National Audit Office, 2010). The financial cost of the 2012 Olympic Games and Paralympic Games is reflected in a figure of £9.3 billion in Public Sector funding, reported by the National Audit Office (2012).

2   This figure excludes discharges following recall after release on licence, non-criminals, persons committed to custody for nonpayment of a fine, persons reclassified as adult prisoners and deported prisoners.

3   A proven reoffence is defined as any offence committed in a one year follow-up period and receiving a court conviction, caution, reprimand or warning in the one year follow-up or a further six month waiting period. The data source is the extract of the Police National Computer held by the Ministry of Justice.

4   Soon after the 2010 election, British Prime Minister David Cameron formally launched the Big Society initiative which had been a flagship policy of the Conservative election manifesto. Encouraging people to take an active role in their communities was one of a number of stated priorities, alongside promoting localism and supporting social enterprise. Exactly what is meant by the concept in practice remains unclear (Evans, 2011) and surprisingly little research has looked at the impact of Big Society initiatives on sport, but in criminal justice settings the Big Society agenda has seen a growing emphasis on extending the role of third sector organisations in work with offenders (Meek, Gojkovic & Mills, 2013).

8 Rugby and football initiatives for young men in prison

A quantitative and qualitative evaluation

Activity-based interventions for young men: Setting the scene

Well-designed and delivered sports initiatives can evidently have a positive effect on prisoners' well-being and the wider prison community, but evidence of its impact on rehabilitation (or re-entry) and successfully reducing reoffending is less clear, with only a handful of studies addressing these issues. Contradictory findings have emerged from activity-based interventions targeting behavioural and attitudinal changes alongside efforts to reduce reoffending. For example Farrington et al. (2002) presented evaluations of two controversial regimes for young offenders introduced in England by the then Conservative government – Thorn Cross High Intensity Training Centre in the North of England and the Colchester Military Corrective Training Centre in the South of England. Both regimes were based on military activities, such as drilling and physical training and Outward Bound courses. The Colchester Centre operated for only 13 months in the late 1990s and was run partially by military staff and overseen by an Army Commandant Governor. The Thorn Cross regime combined military activities with a rehabilitative element, which included educational, life skills and vocational training, programmes designed to address offending behaviour based on developing thinking skills and a prerelease work placement in the community. In addition to studying reconviction rates, Farrington et al.'s evaluation assessed changes in cognitive patterns relevant to criminal behaviour, the ability to control aggression and attitudes to staff and inmates. The psychological assessments showed mixed findings, with those participating in the Thorn Cross regime displaying improved attitudes, self-esteem and control of aggression, along with reduced reoffending rates. However, the same offenders displayed increased pro-offending attitudes, and responsibility and behaviour assessments did not improve following participation. Although the Colchester sample displayed improved attitudes, self-esteem and physical fitness, there was no improvement in attitudes towards offending, control of aggression or self-control. However, fewer reconvictions were observed in the Thorn Cross sample, which Farrington et al. attributed to the cognitive-behavioural skills element of the programme and the considerable efforts made to find work placements for participants in the final weeks of the programme and after release. Such findings highlight the challenge of locating the effective component in holistic sports-based interventions and demonstrate the difficulties faced when trying to draw conclusive evidence from a range of highly diverse sports initiatives.

Further independent evaluation of the Duke of Edinburgh Award (a programme encompassing volunteering, physical activity, the development of life skills and orienteering techniques) delivered in the Young Offender secure estate (14–21 year olds) in England and Wales offers some promise in terms of the role of physical activity interventions in rehabilitation (Dubberley, Parry & Baker, 2011). Quantitative measures of offenders' attitudes and beliefs using the CRIME PICS II measures administered at the beginning of award (n = 64) and approximately six months later (n = 46) revealed improvements in participants' attitudes toward offending, anticipation of reoffending, victim hurt denial, evaluation of crime being worthwhile and perception of current life problems. However, Dubberley et al. acknowledge that their findings must be considered with caution since the initial and follow-up samples did not comprise all of the same participants, and therefore the results may reflect differences between individuals rather than improvements resulting directly from participation in the intervention.

Further attention clearly needs to be paid to the psychological and social processes underpinning how sport can be used positively in custodial contexts and under what circumstances it can best be delivered, along with the wider role of sport in offender rehabilitation. To this end, the aim of the evaluation study reported here was to assess the effectiveness of a series of prison-based football and rugby academies which used sport as a way of engaging young male prisoners in identifying and meeting their needs in the transition from custody to community.

Summary of the intervention

In order to assess the effectiveness of a series of football and rugby initiatives, an in-depth qualitative and quantitative evaluation study was carried out. Observed changes in a spectrum of self-report psychometric measures from baseline (Time 1) to completion of the programme (Time 2) and at longitudinal follow-up (Time 3) were used to assess changes in attitudes and behaviours, with sustained improvements shown on measures of aggression, impulsive behaviours, attitudes towards offending and conflict resolution skills. The psychometric results were examined in tandem with one year reoffending rates which, at 21% for participants, compared favourably with national and institutional averages of 53% and 50%, respectively. These quantitative findings were supplemented with qualitative insights into the impact of the programme, generated by interviews with participants and delivery staff and reflecting on the process and impact of the initiative. Responses given were overwhelmingly positive towards the programme, confirming that the project served to provide not only practical support in terms of offering employment options and information, signposting, generating contacts and new interests, but also the benefits of psychologically focusing, motivating and reassuring individuals about their resettlement needs and concerns. In addition to receiving specialist resettlement support within custody, many participants also cited the reassurance of knowing that ongoing support was available after release, with someone in the community to turn to for help if required. Staff and prisoners also emphasised the ways in which the sports initiative had promoted more positive relationships and improvements throughout the prison.

Over a two year period, four consecutive sports academies (two based on football and two on rugby[1]) were delivered to 79 young men serving sentences at HMP and YOI Portland, a prison in the South West of England holding approximately five hundred sentenced young adult males. Each academy was three to four months in duration, incorporating intensive football or rugby coaching, training and matches (including fixtures against visiting community and student teams), supplemented with classroom-based exercises focusing on goal setting, thinking skills, team skills training, presentations from guest speakers and peer review exercises. Activities were delivered by prison gym staff in collaboration with community-based voluntary sector providers and representatives from sporting organisations, including Chelsea Football Club and the Rugby Football Union. Those participating in the football initiatives completed their Level 1 coaching qualification while rugby academy participants achieved a Level 2 in First Aid and the RFU Rugby Ready coaching award. Three of the rugby academy participants also completed their RFU Young Leaders Rugby Award.

Central to the academy model was the resourcing of and importance placed on individually tailored resettlement case work which was delivered intensively during the course of the academies and continued after release by a caseworker, employed by Second Chance, the community organisation with overall responsibility for academy management. The primary role of the caseworker was to identify and improve resettlement needs, challenge negative attitudes and establish positive working relationships between the academy participants and a network of professionals, with the ultimate aim of preparing and supporting each individual for a successful transition from custody to the community.

Recruiting participants within the prison

Forthcoming academies were advertised around the prison, and prisoners wishing to be considered submitted their applications to gym staff. Once these were collated, the prison's Head of Learning and Skills was then responsible for identifying any offenders who would not be eligible to participate (for example, those serving sentences for sexual offences or those shortly due for transfer/release). Participants were screened by security and the Offender Management Unit and any queries or concerns about suitability for working with children/community groups were raised and dealt with. However, a number of participants were released or transferred from the prison partway through their participation in the academy, representing one of the inevitable challenges of delivering prison-based interventions.

In total, 79 young men took part in the sport academies over the two-year delivery period. Fifty-four participants completed an academy in full, 11 completed the majority of their academy but were released or moved prior to completion, and

14 participants withdrew or were excluded.[2] Five individuals serving longer sentences completed two different academies, and their data for each academy has been treated independently. Ages ranged from 18–21 years with a mean of 19 years and 8 months. In terms of ethnicity, 46% of academy participants were White, 33% Black and 21% were mixed race, Asian or 'other'.

Participants' offence profiles indicated that academy participants were most likely to have been convicted for offences against the person (40%), robbery (20%), drug offences (18%) or burglary (13%), which closely resembles the offence profile of the national young adult make prison population. Table 8.1 summarises the distribution of participants across the four academies.

Table 8.1 Participant demographics, offence profiles and retention rates

(Number of participants)	*Academy*				*All Academies*
	1 (n = 12)	*2 (n = 22)*	*3 (n = 24)*	*4 (n = 21)*	*(n = 79)*
Age (*Mean Years*)	19 yrs 11 months	19 yrs 1 month	19 yrs 10 months	19 yrs 11 months	**19 yrs 8 months**
Ethnicity %					
White	16.7	45.5	47.8	60.0	**46**
Mixed	16.7	4.5	8.7	5.0	**8**
Asian	0.0	4.5	0	0.0	**1**
Black	58.3	40.9	5.0	20.0	**33**
Other	1.0	4.5	4.0	15.0	**12**
Offence(s)%					
Violence Against the Person	26.7	24.0	38.7	63.3	**40**
Robbery	33.3	27.6	12.9	13.3	**20**
Burglary	6.7	13.8	16.1	13.3	**13**
Theft/Handling Stolen Goods	0.0	3.5	6.4	0.0	**3**
Fraud/Forgery	0.0	0.0	0.0	3.3	**1**
Criminal Damage	0.0	6.9	3.2	0.0	**3**
Drug Offences	33.3	20.7	19.4	6.7	**18**
Other	0.0	3.5	3.3	0.0	**2**
Retention % (*n*)					
Completed	100 (12)	50.0 (11)	66.8 (16)	71.4 (15)	**68 (54)**
Completed majority before being released or transferred	0.0	18.2 (4)	16.6 (4)	14.3 (3)	**14 (11)**
Removed/Withdrew	0.0	31.8 (7)	16.6 (4)	14.3 (3)	**18 (14)**

Note: Offences were coded according to Home Office (2011) counting rules. Percentages for offence types were derived from the total number of offences recorded (105 offences) since 22 participants reported being sentenced for more than one offence (14 participants reported two offences, 4 participants reported 4 offences and 2 participants reported four offences). Offence type data were not disclosed by two participants.

Those taking part in the academies were serving prison terms which ranged in length from seven months to indeterminate sentences. In terms of criminal history, participants had received an average of four previous convictions before the age of 18 (range: 0–15) and a further two previous convictions from the age of 18 onwards (range: 0–15). The age at first conviction ranged from 12–18 years (mean age 15.9 years) and the age of first contact with the police ranged from 12–18 years (mean age of 14.9 years).

In order to evaluate the degree to which any intervention has been successful, it is important to identify the extent to which participants can be seen as representative of the general prison population or whether they represent a particular group of offenders. This is especially important when participation is voluntary, since there are associated self-selection factors to take into account. In an effort to explore whether academy participants could be seen as representative of the national sentenced prison population of young male adults (aged 18–21 years), the percentage spread of the academy participants' offence category was compared to national figures of the male young adult sentenced population at the time (Ministry of Justice, 2011d). As demonstrated in figure 8.1, academy participants were broadly representative of the national young adult population according to sentence category.

The Offender Assessment System (OASys) is the primary risk/need assessment and management tool used for adult offenders in England and Wales, and is used to assess – amongst other things – suitability for programme participation. It has been in operation for over 10 years, but is not mandatory and coverage is not yet universal. OASys assessments were available for 40 of the participants. The Offender Group Reconviction Scale (ORGS) is a risk assessment measure used to predict the likelihood of reconviction after one year for individual offenders based

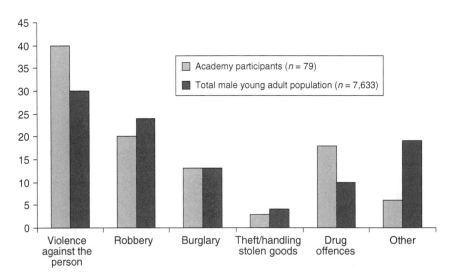

Figure 8.1 Offence category for academy participants and national young adult population.

on static risks (age, gender and criminal history). For the academy participants, OGRS scores ranged from 10%–85%, with a mean score of 46% (identified as medium risk).

Reconviction analysis

When seeking to explore recidivism rates within a sample, Shepherd and Whiting (2006) suggest that at least six months should pass between release from prison and attempts to follow up, since that is the average time that elapses before reoffending, even though this figure varies according to offence type. However, a longer period of one year is widely used in official reconviction data, with national and local figures published annually by the Ministry of Justice. In accordance with this, one year reconviction data were retrieved from central records for the 42 academy participants who had been released from prison for 12 months or more in November 2012. Of these, 33 (79%) had successfully desisted from reoffending and nine had been convicted of a new offence,[3] representing a one year reconviction rate of 21%. A full breakdown of these figures appears in table 8.2. The reconviction rate for these participants was compared to the reconviction rate within one year for prisoners released from the same institution during the closest equivalent time period (released January–December 2010). Inspection of raw data released by the Ministry of Justice (2012f) has confirmed that, of the 411 prisoners released from the prison where the programme was delivered in 2010, 50% were reconvicted within one year[4] and nationally, 53% of young adults released in this time period were reconvicted within one year. Assuming that the academy participants are representative of the wider prisoner

Table 8.2 Status of all academy participants (at 1 October 2012)

	Academy				All Academies
	1 (n = 12)	*2 (n = 22)*	*3 (n = 24)*	*4 (n = 21)*	**(n = 79)**
Status % (n)					
Released 12 months/ more and desisting	58% (7)	50% (11)	29% (7)	19% (4)	**37% (29)**
Released and recalled due to breach of licence within 12 months	8% (1)	14% (3)	0%	0%	**6% (4)**
Released and reconvicted of a new offence within 12 months	17% (2)	18% (4)	4% (1)	10% (2)	**11% (9)**
Released for fewer than 12 months	8% (1)	9% (2)	42% (10)	48% (10)	**29% (23)**
Remains in prison custody	8% (1)	9% (2)	25% (6)	24% (5)	**18% (14)**

population at the institution (and according to offence category and reoffending risk they broadly are), this suggests that academy participants are less likely to reoffend than those who haven't participated in the academy. However, this comparison must be considered in light of the fact that as an experimental group, 42 remains a relatively small sample size, thus placing further importance on the role of the intermediate measures that will be considered next and the qualitative data that will be explored later in this chapter.

Intermediate measures of the impact of the sports-based initiative

In order to complement the reconviction analysis, questionnaires assessing attitudes towards offending, behaviours and psychological constructs such as self-esteem and self-concept were administered to participants in small groups or individually at three points in time. The psychometric measures were completed prior to commencing the academies (Time 1) in order to gain a baseline measure and again immediately following completion of each initiative (Time 2) in order to assess changes in attitudes and behaviours from commencing to completing the academies. Follow-up quantitative measures (Time 3) were collected from 22 of the participants 3–16 months after completion of the academy (mean = 6.86 months; $SD = 3.71$) in order to establish any short term longitudinal development of attitudinal and behavioural change. Twelve of the participants who completed follow up measures were still in prison custody at the time of follow up and 10 had been released.

Each participant completed a questionnaire containing a total of 95 statements, which they were asked to read (or to have read to them if preferred). They were asked the extent to which they agreed or disagreed to the statements, responding predominantly on a five-point scale. The statements mapped onto a number of psychometric measures, as follows.

Beliefs about Aggression

The Beliefs about Aggression scale was adapted from Farrell, Meyer, and White (2001) for the evaluation of the Multisite Violence Prevention Project (2004), an intervention aimed at reducing violence among young adolescents. The scale has since been utilised in psychological research concerning aggression among young adolescents (Zhen, Xie, Zhang & Wang, 2011). The scale was compiled from responses to six statements and measured individuals' beliefs about the use of aggression in hypothetical situations. A high score on the Beliefs about Aggression scale indicates more favourable beliefs supporting the use of aggression. The scale was found to have satisfactory internal consistency ($\alpha = .69$) in line with previous research ($\alpha = .72$) (Farrell et al., 2001), suggesting that the scale is a reliable measure for use with older incarcerated samples in addition to the younger adolescent population it was originally designed for.

Use of Non Violent Strategies

The Use of Non Violent Strategies scale, adapted from Farrell et al. (2001), consisted of responses to five statements and measured individuals' endorsement of nonviolent responses to hypothetical situations. Higher scores indicate higher levels of support for using nonviolent strategies. Consistent with previous research (α = .72) the scale demonstrated adequate internal consistency (α = .69), demonstrating its potential to be utilised as an evaluative measure with older adolescents and young adults.

Self-esteem

The self-esteem measure was drawn from the Weinberger and Schwartz (1990) adjustment inventory which reflects an individual's perception of their self-value. The Weinberger and Schwartz adjustment inventory has previously been utilised in psychological research with young offender populations (Cauffman Piquero, Brodidy, Espelage & Mazerolle, 2008; Trejos-Castillo, Vazsonyi & Jenkins, 2008) and has also been established as a valid measure among young adults and adult populations (Weinberger, 1997). Answers to seven items are combined to create a self-esteem score ranging between seven and 35, with a high score indicating low self-esteem. Internal consistency (α = .77) exceeded that reported in previous research with young adolescents (α = .55–.72) (Feldman & Weinberger, 1994) suggesting that the scale is a reliable measure of self-esteem among young adult offenders.

Self-concept

The self-concept measure was drawn from Phillips and Springer's (1992) individualised protective factor index which was developed for use with 10–16 year olds but has subsequently been utilised with older populations (Basca, 2002). The measure was created to ascertain an individual's sense of self-concept and self-confidence. Responses to 12 items were combined to create a self-concept score, with the maximum score of 48 indicating a strong self-concept. In applying the scale in the context of the academy evaluation it had especially good internal consistency (α = .80), exceeding previous reliability findings with adolescent samples (α = .58–.59) (Gabriel, 1994).

Impulsivity

Bosworth and Espelage's (1995) impulsivity scale is a measure which has previously been used in the evaluation of violence prevention interventions among inner-city adolescents (McMahon & Washburn, 2003). Questions relating to impulsivity measured frequency of impulsive behaviours such as lack of self-control and difficulty finishing things. Answers to four statements were combined to create an impulsivity score ranging from four to 16, with high scores indicating higher self-reported impulsivity. The scale demonstrated satisfactory internal consistency ($\alpha = .60$), consistent with prior findings with young adolescents ($\alpha = .62$) (Bosworth & Espelage, 1995).

Conflict Resolution, Impulsivity and Aggression Questionnaire (CRIAQ)

The Conflict Resolution, Impulsivity and Aggression Questionnaire contains 26 items which focus on impulsivity and conflict resolution and were designed specifically to measure changes in levels of aggression among violent offenders. The CRIAQ measures developed by Honess, Maguire and Vanstone (2001) specifically focus on the features of aggression targeted in prison and probation interventions aimed at reducing offending behaviour and have been developed in partnership with prison and probation staff. The measures have been found to possess good validity across diverse groups of offenders in the United Kingdom (Honess et al., 2001). The CRIAQ measures have also been used in the evaluation of cognitive behavioural therapy interventions aimed at reducing alcohol-related violence in the community (McMurran & Cusens, 2003).

Participants responded to 26 statements on the CRIAQ questionnaire (e.g. 'I often find that I have got aggressive without meaning to'). Items corresponded to seven psychometric measures (created by totalling scores across items corresponding to the same scale): Overall Impulsivity; Impulsivity without Aggression; Impulsivity with Aggression; Problems in Conflict Resolution; Aggression in Conflict Resolution; Physical Violence in Conflict Resolution; and Lack of Compromise in Conflict Resolution. On all seven scales a higher score indicates a greater identification with that particular mode of operating. Good internal consistency ($\alpha = .79–.83$) was observed in the current sample for the three Impulsivity-based CRIAQ scales, although the coefficient alphas were slightly lower than those found in previous research[5] ($\alpha = .83–.89$). Similarly, internal validity for both the Problems in Conflict Resolution ($\alpha = .78$) and Aggression in Conflict Resolution ($\alpha = .72$) scales was good, though lower than previously found ($\alpha = .82$ and $.79$, respectively). Conversely, reliability on the Physical Violence in Conflict Resolution ($\alpha = .48$) and Lack of Compromise in Conflict Resolution ($\alpha = .56$) scales was substantially lower than previously identified ($\alpha = .78$ and $.72$, respectively), suggesting that these scales may be less reliable in young adult offender populations. That said, the current reliability estimates depend on a smaller sample which can negatively affect Cronbach's alpha calculations (Shevlin, Miles, Davies & Walker, 1998).

Attitudes towards offending

CRIME PICS II psychometric measures are widely used in the evaluation of offender interventions, and have previously been used in assessing prison-based Enhanced Thinking Skills programmes (McDougall, Clarbour, Perry & Bowels, 2009; Sadlier, 2010) and the Going Straight Contract pilot project (Hudson &

Meek, 2007). The 35-item structured CRIME PICS II questionnaire was designed to measures individuals' attitudes towards offending on five distinct scales (Frude, Honess & Maguire, 2009). In the first section of the questionnaire participants rated their level of agreement with statements on a five-point scale ranging from strongly agree to strongly disagree. Answers were numerically coded and combined to create four scales: 1. The General Attitude to Offending Scale, a measure of the offender's general attitude towards offending with a low score indicating that an individual believes an offending lifestyle is not desirable; 2. The Anticipation of Reoffending Scale, a measure of the offender's anticipation of reoffending with a low score indicating that the individual does not anticipate reoffending; 3. The Victim Hurt Denial Scale, a measure of the offender's attitude towards his/her victims, such as whether they believed they caused harm, with a low score indicating the individual recognises their actions impact on the victim and 4. The Evaluation of Crime as Worthwhile Scale, a measure of the offender's evaluation of crime being worthwhile, with a low score indicating that the individual perceives the cost of crime as being greater than its rewards.

The second section of the CRIME PICS II questionnaire, the Problem Inventory, required participants to report the extent of their problems on a four-point scale ranging from no problem at all to a big problem. Struggles associated with money, relationships, employment, controlling temper, sensation seeking, family, health, boredom, housing, substance use, gambling, depression, self-esteem, confidence and anxiety were assessed. Answers to the problem inventory were numerically coded and combined to create a composite scale measuring perceptions of current problems. The higher the score the greater the number and gravity of problems identified. Internal consistency information concerning the CRIME PICS II scales is not available for the current sample due to use of a computerised scoring system. However, previous research with 422 offenders (Frude et al., 2009) has confirmed that overall, the CRIME PICS II measures demonstrate good internal consistency.

Changes in attitudes and behaviours

In order to identify longitudinal improvements in participants, repeated measures ANOVA analyses (with time as the repeated measure) were conducted on each of the quantitative measures across three critical time points: prior to commencing the academy (Time 1); immediately after completing the academy (Time 2); and at longitudinal follow-up (Time 3, carried out on average six months after completion of the academy, range: 2–16 months; SD = 3.71). Table 8.3 illustrates the results of the ANOVA analysis along with mean scores at each time point.

Significant positive improvements were observed for mean scores on six out of the 17 measures and are illustrated in figure 8.2. Beliefs endorsing the use of aggression decreased significantly from commencing the academies (M = 15.0) to completing the academies (M = 13.89) and continued to improve longitudinally when measured at the latter follow up (M = 13.39), ($F(2, 34)$ = 3.00, $p < .05$), suggesting that the young men endorsed the use of aggression less over time following their participation in the academies. Significant improvements were identified

Table 8.3 Changes in attitudinal and behavioural mean scores pre-academy, postacademy and at longitudinal follow up

Psychometric measure	Immediately before	Immediately after	Follow up	F	df
Beliefs about aggression	15.0	13.89	13.39	2.98*	2,34
Use of nonviolent strategies	14.12	14.65	14.41	.62	2,32
Self-esteem	17.39	16.67	16.72	.45	2,34
Self-concept	37.67	37.44	37.11	.13	2,34
Impulsivity	10.00	10.39	9.00	4.09*	2,34
Overall impulsivity	31.29	30.36	25.07	4.85**	2,26
Impulsivity without aggression	16.64	15.71	12.79	4.95**	2,26
Impulsivity with aggression	14.64	14.64	12.29	3.06*	2,26
Overall problems in conflict resolution	34.36	34.43	30.00	2.54	2,26
Aggression in conflict resolution	15.71	15.79	13.5	2.13	2,26
Physical violence in conflict resolution	8.71	9.29	7.29	2.47	2,26
Lack of compromise in conflict resolution	9.93	9.36	9.07	.47	2,26
General attitude towards offending	40.39	39.50	35.67	2.62*	2,34
Anticipation of re-offending	11.89	11.22	10.50	1.00	2,34
Attitude towards victims	5.33	5.67	5.44	.16	2,34
Evaluation of crime being worthwhile	12.67	11.94	10.72	2.49	2,34
Problem inventory	23.5	22.4	20.6	1.58	2,34

Note: * $p < .05$, ** $p < .01$

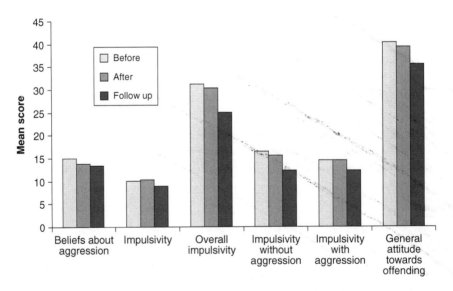

Figure 8.2 Statistically significant changes in attitude and behavioural measures.

longitudinally on both generic impulsivity measures, scores on the 'impulsivity' measure increased from 10.00 to 10.39 from pre- to postacademy, before decreasing significantly to 9.0 at Time 3 ($F(2, 26) = 4.09$, $p < .05$), while scores on the CRIAQ measure 'overall impulsivity' also significantly improved ($F(2, 26) = 4.85$, $p < .01$), reflected by mean scores reducing from 31.29 pre-academy to 30.36 postacademy and 25.07 at the subsequent follow up.

A significant progressive improvement was observed in impulsivity without aggression ($F(2, 26) = 4.95$, $p < .01$) which decreased from 16.64 pre-academy to 15.71 postacademy, reducing further to 12.79 at follow up, with participants reporting less identification with nonaggressive impulsive behaviour over time. Impulsivity with aggression remained the same from pre- to postacademy, with the mean score remaining at 14.64 before significantly decreasing at follow up to 12.29 ($F(2, 26) = 3.06$, $p < .05$), suggesting that participation reduced identification with aggressive impulsive behaviour in the long but not short term. Significant improvements in general attitudes towards offending were also observed ($F(2.34) = 2.623$, $p < .05$) with mean scores decreasing moderately from 40.39 at commencement of the academies to 39.50 upon completion, before significantly decreasing at follow up to 35.67.

Positive changes that were approaching significance were also observed for overall problems in conflict resolution, physical violence in conflict resolution and evaluations of crime being worthwhile. In particular, overall problems in conflict resolution remained static from Time 1 to Time 2, before decreasing at follow up to reveal a nonsignificant improvement ($F(2, 26) = 2.54$, $p = .10$) suggesting that participation may improve conflict resolution skills in the longer term, though not immediately following completion. Similarly, identification with physical violence in conflict resolution was initially observed to increase slightly from preparticipation (8.71) to initial follow up (9.29) but then reduced to a mean of 7.29 at the subsequent follow up, a positive change approaching significance ($F(2, 26) = 2.47$, $p = .05$) which suggests a decreased reliance on physical violence to resolve conflict. A near significant progressive improvement in evaluations of crime being worthwhile was also observed over the three time points ($F(2, 34) = 2.49$, $p = .06$), suggesting that participants increasingly perceived the costs of crime to outweigh the rewards following participation in the academies.

Lastly, trends towards positive improvements in attitudes and behaviours over the three time points were identified for lack of compromise in conflict resolution, participants' anticipation of reoffending, and perception of their current problems. However, no significant changes or clear trends were observed in the use of nonviolent strategies, self-esteem, self-concept, aggression in conflict resolution or attitudes towards victims.

How useful are reconviction data in small-scale evaluations?

Provisional one-year reconviction rates of 21% (compared to an average of 50% reconviction within one year for the institution as a whole) appear to support the effectiveness of the intervention in efforts to reduce reoffending. The range of sentence lengths served by academy participants and consequent dispersal of release dates over time prevent an analysis of one year reconviction rates for all participants, as this would not be possible until further time has elapsed. This is likely to be a common methodological challenge in other small prison-based interventions where, unless specifically targeting individuals in the final weeks and months of their sentence, participants will have a range of time left to serve on their sentence and provisional release dates may be brought forward or put back, depending on whether or not applications for parole are accepted. Whilst highlighting these challenges, the data presented here provides at least an initial comparative insight into one-year reconviction rates for those participants released for a sufficient period of time to warrant comparison analysis.

Given that the current analysis was based on the relatively small sample of 42 academy participants who had been released from prison for 12 months or more at the time of analysis, the dependence on a small numbers of participants to determine reductions in reoffending across interventions raises concerns over the statistical reliability of the findings. Similar concerns in the context of previous evaluations have led some commentators to question the likely impact of such schemes on recidivism rates (Smith & Waddington, 2004). Nevertheless, in the light of the average reconviction rate of 50% within one year (for 2010) in the prison studied, the 29 percentage point reduction in reoffending observed even in a small sample should be acknowledged as a positive indicator for the impact of such schemes.

The system of measuring reoffending is nevertheless a complex area and although reconviction rates are acknowledged as being an important indicator of intervention success, they should be used with some caution. Such rates are a proxy measure which may underestimate reoffending (for example they only capture data on whether or not an individual has been convicted of a new offence) and self-report data on offending behaviour may well paint quite a different picture. Although reconviction figures have descriptive value are not necessarily indicative of a programme's effectiveness (Friendship, Beech & Browne, 2002). Furthermore, one- or even two-year reconviction data may prove to cover too short a period for those who pose a serious risk to the public and an individual's offending history should also be taken into consideration when assessing their success in desisting from crime (Kershaw, 1997). For example, the achievement of desisting from crime for one year may represent significant change for one individual but not for another. Likewise, an individual who participates in a programme and is subsequently reconvicted but for a less serious offence could still be recognised as achieving a certain degree of success as reflected by their 'improved' offending behaviour (Lloyd, Mair & Hough, 1994). Consequently, the most appropriate form of measurement for small-scale prison-based interventions will depend on what the intervention is aimed at addressing. Despite all these shortcomings, reoffending rates certainly provide a valuable indicator of the impact of physical activity-based interventions on reducing reoffending, particularly in the light of the inconclusive evidence from the few previous evaluations of such initiatives (e.g. Farrington et al., 2002). However other quantitative indicators and qualitative data sources are evidently required to identify which aspects of the programme were successful and why they had the impact they did.

Usefulness of psychometric measures: Lessons from the current evaluation

Deciding on which measures need to be taken in a given intervention is a key issue for programme evaluators, and capturing irrelevant or inappropriate data is at best a waste of time and resources and at worst a disruptive or even potentially damaging process. In the case of the evaluation methodology for the football and rugby academies it was clear that the programme designers and delivery staff had a broad set of expectations and aspirations about the impact of the programme, but beyond efforts to reduce reoffending these were not necessarily clearly aligned to specific psychological constructs, which highlights the importance of an evaluator's involvement in the early stages of an intervention to ensure that the right kind of data are collected at the right time. The quantitative analyses revealed significant and sustained improvements in established measures of aggression, impulsivity and attitudes towards offending, and positive improvements approaching significance were also identified in conflict resolution skills, providing a valuable context to and detail behind the reconviction data. Consistent with theoretical contention (Czajkowska, Golemba & Popieluch, 1967) and empirical evidence (Wagner et al., 1999), significant improvements in aggression and impulsivity suggest that the initiative succeeded in its aim to reduce aggression and improve discipline. The current results extend previous suggestions of improvements confined to a custodial context over short periods and indicate that such gains can be sustained not only whilst still in custody but also following release.

Improvements approaching significance were identified in measures of conflict resolution, although scores initially deteriorated from commencement to completion of the academies before improving at longitudinal follow up. Hypothetically it is possible that engagement in competitive sport on an intensive basis may initially increase the frequency and intensity of conflict and an individual's perception of their capability to manage such situations before they have the ability to apply and reflect on the skills they have developed. This finding certainly warrants further attention but tends to provide support for the notion that sport can be an effective means by which to promote awareness of the importance of and practice in conflict resolution skills and socially acceptable behaviours among samples of disadvantaged youths (see also Ravizza, 2011; Ravizza & Motonak, 2011).

In the context of the current evaluation, no significant changes were identified in participants' self-esteem or self-concept, thus contradicting the theoretical premise (Coalter, 2005; Sabo, 2001), empirical evidence (Ekeland, Heian & Hagn, 2005) and previous evaluation findings of both community (Berry et al., 2009; Nichols & Taylor, 1996; Robins, 1990; Tsuchiya, 1996; West & Crompton, 2001) and custodial (Farrington et al., 2002; Johnsen, 2001) sports-based programmes which have associated participation in sport with bolstered self-esteem. One explanation for this finding is that young offenders do not homogeneously have low self-esteem: Lochman and Dodge (1994) found that although severely violent young offenders had low levels of perceived social competence and general self-worth, moderately violent offenders had unusually high levels of perceived social competence and general self-worth, and measures of self-concept indicate variance across offenders in strength of self-concept and negative self-perceptions (Frey & Epkins, 2002; Henderson, Dakof, Schwartz & Liddle, 2006). As a consequence of this, and since levels of self-esteem vary among young offenders, it may not be surprising that aggregated improvements were not identified, and future research should look at the specific effects of programmes on those identified as low or high in self-esteem. Importantly, the literature primarily proposes that sports such as football or rugby may provide alternative positive identities to delinquent young people (Carmichael, 2008; Gras, 2005; Kehily, 2007; Schafer, 1969) rather than specifically strengthening an individual's self-concept. The quantitative measure of self-concept strength and self-confidence utilised in the current research may therefore not adequately capture subtle changes in self-concept.

Sports-based programmes with integrated 'through the gate' resettlement support clearly have the scope to aid prisoner rehabilitation – even if the sport is used primarily as a hook to achieve engagement, thus supporting Mason and Wilson's (1988) view that, rather than promoting sport as a primary outcome, interventions need to adopt a holistic approach. There is clearly scope for such projects to promote the specific needs of offenders at least partially through sport, while recognising that, despite the potential for sport to offer a catalyst for rehabilitative efforts, it may not inevitably confer positive outcomes (Coalter, 2002; Hawkins, 1998) and should not be uncritically viewed as an entirely wholesome activity (Crabbe, 2000) given that differing sports in diverse contexts will inevitably have varying effects on delinquency which may not always be affirmative (Conroy, Silva, Newcomer, Walker & Johnson, 2001; Kavussanu & Ntoumanis, 2003; Rutten et al., 2007). For example, Begg, Langley, Moffitt and Marshall's (1996) longitudinal study showed that high involvement in individual sports – but not in team sports – was associated with increased delinquency. Of even more concern, Hughes and Coakley (1991) warned of the potentially negative effects of an overcommitment to the 'sport ethic' characterised by dedication, goal setting and perusal, defying adversity and making sacrifices, which they suggest although emphasising essentially positive norms, can result in deviant behaviours (referred to as 'positive deviance') such as excessive drinking or substance use. They hypothesise that men who have low self-esteem are more likely to overcommit to a sports ethic, with resulting positive deviance. This is certainly worth considering when looking to sport to engage marginalised young men since it suggests that there is a risk that the competitive environment can foster social comparison concerns in individuals already predisposed to high levels of such anxieties (Andrews & Andrews, 2003; Slater & Tiggemann, 2011). The overall evidence base maintains, however, that well-structured carefully delivered sports programs that address resettlement needs have the potential to achieve benefits in terms of individual psychosocial functioning, prison dynamics and reducing reoffending.

The findings of the current study provide much needed evidence of the efficacy of using sport as a mechanism to engage young prisoners in holistic resettlement programmes which can produce tangible reductions in reoffending as well as improvements in attitudes and behaviour. Although the research drew longitudinally on multiple measures in an attempt to address on-going widespread concern regard the lack of rigorous evaluation of sports based programmes for young offenders (Coalter, 1989; Nichols, 1997; Nichols & Crow, 2004; Robins, 1990; Sandford, Armour & Warmington, 2006; Smith & Waddington, 2004; Tacon, 2007; Utting, 1996) the results are confounded by a number of largely unavoidable limitations. Firstly, further research should seek to establish whether or not the programme has a lasting impact or if the observed one-year effects have dissipated after two years, as was previously found by Cann, Falshaw, Nugent and Friendship (2003) in the context of cognitive behavioural programmes. Secondly, the lack of an experimental design means that the results of the present study may be a consequence of confounding variables as opposed to a direct effect of the intervention. Although a randomised controlled trial (RCT) is widely recognised as 'the gold standard' of evaluation methodologies (Friendship et al., 2002; Meek, 2010), these are not necessarily practical or achievable in the context of prison regimes and small-scale programme delivery, and they also raise concerns regarding the ethical implication of denying treatment to those not selected. Consequently, RCT's remain rare in criminal justice studies (Farrington, 1983; Friendship et al., 2002). The lack of a control group introduces confounding variables such as participant expectation and selection bias which could have influenced the results. The young men voluntarily applied to participate and were then screened by prison personnel for suitability. It is therefore possible that those who volunteered to participate (and were selected) may have been more motivated to change at commencement of the intervention, thus potentially undermining the quality of the reconviction data. Selection screening was essential to meet security requirements and voluntary participation is an essential element in the effectiveness of sports-based programmes (Coalter, 1996; Morris et al., 2003; Nichols & Taylor, 1996). Although limited resources and access prevented a quasi-experimental research design from being implemented in the present study, future research should prioritise this in order to compare the reconviction outcomes of participants with a matched comparison group who have not participated in the programme, using criteria such as risk of reconviction, age, ethnicity, drug use, accommodation, educational and employment status before custody, index offence type and criminal career histories of family as well as the individual prisoner concerned (as was done by Sadlier, 2010). Thirdly, the use of self-report measures presents problems when used in forensic settings (Crighton & Towl, 1995) or with individuals subject to community supervision such as probation who may perceive there to be an incentive for appearing successful following intervention. It has previously been established, however, that young offenders are less likely than adults to use impression management response styles to present themselves favourably when responding to measures (Weeks, 1993), and the study design emphasised the anonymity of responses, thus potentially reducing such concerns.

Further research is evidently needed to establish, in the context of prison-based sports initiatives, what works and for whom and how. Comparisons of outcomes across offence types are also required in order to target specific at risk groups in future research since different offence categories are associated with a higher probability of reoffending (Ministry of Justice, 2011e), and prior research has suggested that the relationship between sports participation and deviance varies depending on the type of offending behaviour examined (Hartmann & Depro, 2006; Hartmann & Massaglia, 2007). Methodologically, future evaluative studies should incorporate a sample of matched controls, extend the duration of reconviction analysis, distinguish between reconvictions for breach of licence or new offences, and draw on self-reports as well as official databases (Falshaw, Friendship, Travers & Nugent, 2003).

Over the course of two years, semistructured individual interviews, focus groups discussions and written feedback exercises were carried out with the prisoners who participated in the initiative. Initial qualitative data gathering focused on their expectations of what the academies might offer, with subsequent discussions following programme completion concentrating on individuals' subjective experiences of participation and how they perceived their involvement in the initiative to have impacted upon them. Where possible, further face-to-face and/or telephone interviews were carried out with academy participants following their return to the community; these discussions focused on individuals' experiences of the transition from custody to community, their perceptions of their resettlement needs, the extent and quality of support they had received to meet these needs and personal reflections on the academies as a whole. In seeking to explore the staff perspective, the 11 key members of prison and delivery staff involved in the programme were interviewed and/or submitted written feedback on their experiences and observations of the academies following delivery.

The perceived impact of participation on the prison environment

Although not a primary aim of the programme, participation in the academies was perceived by the young men, as well as by prison and delivery staff, to offer benefits within the prison environment at both individual and cultural levels. Participants reported that taking part in the academies improved their quality of life within prison by providing something to focus on, alleviating boredom and frustration and providing an incentive for good behaviour. At the level of prison culture, those involved described how the academies had served to dissipate previously existing barriers between groups of prisoners, as well as improving relations between prisoners and prison staff. Away from the gym and sports pitch, improved behaviour on the wings was attributed to the programme, as was a heightened sense of and culture of positivity throughout the establishment.

Many of the participants discussed how, prior to the academies, they experienced difficulties in managing their frustration and anger, which often culminated in conflict and adjudications whilst in custody, and in some cases had contributed to the offences for which they were incarcerated. As well as learning to manage emotion, impulsivity and aggression better, the opportunity to engage in sport was seen to be a positive way in which to manage daily stresses, partially reflecting what Johnsen (2001) has described as an opportunity for self-expression and escape from the disciplinary power of prison regimes, as this prisoner testified:

> Within the prison, rugby helped me release anger and stress, cos you're stuck on the wings and it builds up and you can just get rid of all that anger and stress and frustration.

As well as equipping prisoners to manage their emotions and behaviour better, participants consistently cited their involvement in academies as a motivating factor in promoting discipline. Participating in the academies required individuals to demonstrate continued good behaviour and thus introduced a new incentive for behavioural regulation, as reported by an individual who prior to taking part in the initiative had struggled with behavioural problems:

> Behaviour wise, when I was first sent down [to prison] I was always on basic [regime] for messing around. With the academies you have to be on enhanced [regime] so you have to be well behaved and work your way up, so they give you an incentive to behave.

In particular, the young men also described how their participation, although initially challenging, had enabled them to develop adaptive skills to respond to situations with staff and other prisoners which might previously have evoked negative responses:

> The football academy teaches you discipline, because it puts you in a predicament that you're not used to and you have to learn to adapt to the situation . . . And one day [prison staff member] said 'your attitude has changed, you don't answer back, you allow people to do their own thing and get on with what you have got to do.'

Staff also reported significant improvements to the behaviour of participants (including those notorious for disruption and hostility), in addition to the wider implications that this had on behaviour within the prison generally. Staff testified that the academies had not only prompted individuals to behave better but that there was also a knock-on effect of improved behaviour within the prison more generally:

> It creates good behaviour and leaders around the jail, through the perceived standing of the lads involved, leading to them openly challenging others' inappropriate behaviour either on the pitch or on the wings. Lads involved with this academy have openly stopped violent incidents and been strong enough to say why and lead others. (Prison Gym Staff)

Behavioural improvements identified by staff as a benefit of the academies corresponded with participants' own descriptions of improved relations between prisoners. In particular, the young men explained how their collaborative experiences on and off the pitch provided opportunities to break down social barriers between different groups of prisoners, thus supporting the notion of sport as a medium to dissipate social divisions (Joseph Rowntree Foundation, 2007; Kenyon & Rockwood, 2010; Townsend, Moore & Mahoney, 2002).

As well as improved relationships between different groups of prisoners, and consistent with previous findings that refer to sport as a facilitating factor in breaking down barriers between staff and prisoners (Johnsen, 2001; Sabo, 2001), academy participants and prison staff also reported that the initiative had led to improved prisoner-staff relations. Members of staff identified wider cultural shifts in their relations with prisoners, while participants confirmed that the academies brought prisoners and staff together, facilitating positive relationships which many of them did not anticipate or seek, but relationships which previous research (see Harvey, 2007) has identified as being crucial in the adaptation of young men to imprisonment. Consistent with the participants' perspective, staff also cited improved prisoner-staff relations as representing a professional benefit to them, with shared achievements allowing for more personalised relationships to be fostered:

> You can see the person within the prisoner, and hopefully the lads can see me as an ally. (Prison Gym Staff)

> Lads see us differently – rather than screws we are screws with individual personalities and interests. (Prison Gym Staff)

Such improved relations were reported by staff members to challenge the traditional barriers between prisoners and officers; barriers which might previously have impeded rehabilitative efforts gave way to more trusting and courteous interactions. Indeed, the significance of improved staff-prisoner relationships shouldn't be underestimated, particularly in young offender institutions which are typically characterised as the most violent and disrupted prisons, with staff-prisoner relationships more likely to be strained. Improving the quality of interactions between prison staff and the young people in their care will inevitably have significant implications, not least in facilitating more constructive relationships. Importantly, and in line with previous research (Sidney, 1987), staff members also indicated that the more individualised and supportive approach used in the academies cultivated a genuine shift in the attitudes and practices of prison staff, thus promoting a more humanistic and person-centred dynamic in their work:

> It has changed staff perceptions, creating a real interest in how the lads are getting on. Staff now use [prisoners'] first names openly rather than having to be told to. (Gym Staff)

Preparing for the transition from custody to community

The role of sport as a 'hook' to engage young offenders to engage in wider rehabilitative work was at the core of this initiative. Although sport was the initial reason for getting involved, participants soon reported that the individualised resettlement work enabled them to reflect upon their circumstances and focus on planning for their release in a goal-directed manner which many of them claimed not previously to have thought about in detail:

> It was good to actually look at what I'm doing wrong and how I can improve myself and what I want, because most of my life I've just been basically what everyone else wants me to do. Looking at what I want to do myself and how I can take smaller steps to reach the bigger goals in my life.

Encouraging the formulation of clear goals and action plans is particularly important when engaging in resettlement work, and research has shown that those who successfully desist from crime are more likely to have a plan of action and optimistic outlook, compared to reoffenders who possess little or uncertain future visions (Farrall & Calverley, 2006; Giordano, Cernkovich & Rudolph, 2002; Maruna, 2001), and that individualised and intensive post-release support has been associated with lower recidivism rates (James, Stams, Asscher, De Roo & van der Laan, 2013). In addition to directing individuals cognitively to look toward and plan for a more positive future, participants highlighted the benefit of receiving independent and personalised information and support in order to formalise their resettlement goals:

> Basically helping me look into my future. I came to [caseworker] with a couple of views of where I wanted to go when I left and he would research it for me.

This caseworker aspect of the initiative was entirely non-sporting, but it is clear that the constructive relationship developed within the project would not have been possible without the vehicle of sport in motivating those involved and providing a supportive community in which to develop as individuals and a group. Indeed, the independent resettlement support which was offered as part of the scheme was especially valued by participants:

> The prison guards look at it as though, at the end of the day, when we're in prison, we're there for them, and when they leave prison, we're not – so it's as simple as that. Whereas [caseworker's] problem is more keeping us out of jail than putting us in it.

It may not necessarily be accurate or fair to assume that prison staff are not concerned with supporting prisoners to lead law-abiding lives after their release from custody, but this is certainly a common assumption among prisoners and one that raises further questions about the need to improve the quality of interactions between prisoners and staff. These findings partially reflect earlier considerations of community-based sports interventions, wherein partnership working and the involvement of non-statutory organisations in delivery techniques is thought to be a key element of best practice (Big Lottery Fund, 2009; Morris et al., 2003; Nichols & Taylor, 1996; Taylor, Crow, Irvine & Nichols, 1999).

In post-release interviews, the young men attributed their desistance from crime either directly or partly to their involvement in the academies, the opportunities offered to them during the academy and the post-release support they had received. It could be argued of course that the positive and constructive relationships between the caseworker and academy participants were developed as a result of the caseworker's expertise and skills, with no relevance to the sports activities promoted within the project. However, the research process revealed that the sporting element remained critical, not only in promoting initial engagement and ongoing enthusiasm in the initiative, but also in instilling or rekindling a passion for sport which in turn had important implications for desistance. The evident capacity of the sports academies to endow *social capital* in the form of community contacts – in addition to building *human capital* in personal skill development – is of particular significance since building capability is futile if ultimately processes of change and desistance depend on being afforded an opportunity to make use of newly developed capabilities (Farrall, 2002; McNeill, 2006).

Strengthening a claim for sport's contribution to processes of desistance, participants frequently indicated that their commitment to sport would provide an alternative positive interest to pursue upon release. In turn this was recognised as a way of preventing a return to offending behaviour, thus lending support to the rationale that sport may act as a diversion from antisocial behaviour (Hawkins, 1998; Nichols, 2007):

> It's got me back into football so, obviously, that's a good thing and it's going to help me to take up more time, isn't it? So when I get out, I'm not just hanging around. I'm doing something and then not messing about.

Psychological 'work' in sport

Just as, or perhaps even more importantly than, the finding that involvement in sport while in custody could contribute to opportunities to 'go straight' after release, another prominent theme emerging from the research highlighted the way that participation in the academy had encouraged the young men to develop and practice their thinking skills ('It makes me think about situations more') which for many could have important implications in preventing impulsive behaviours ('I've learnt to think more before I act'). This is an especially promising finding considering the theoretical contention that offending behaviour is often linked to deficits in the cognitive skills required for social adaptation (Ross & Fabiano, 1985) and evidence of the efficacy of interventions which target such deficits in order to reduce reoffending (Friendship, Blud, Erikson & Travers, 2002).

Participants described how they had learnt to react to frustrations in an adaptive and responsive way by communicating and helping others, rather than by resorting to aggression, thus lending support to the notion that sport can be an effective way to promote conflict resolution skills (Ravizza, 2011; Ravizza & Motonak, 2011). The development of such techniques is of course reliant on a facilitator skilled in the principles of emotional regulation and in this case was cultivated both on and off the pitch by dealing with incidents as they arose. Perceptions of improved skills in domains such as communication, conflict resolution and team work are certainly of theoretical importance since habitual offending is thought to be partly predicted by an individual's acquired negative or pessimistic responses to common practical problems (Zamble & Quinsey, 1997). Consequently, equipping young people with alternative positive response styles can have important implications in supporting rehabilitative efforts.

Aside from skills development, the young men described affective benefits in terms of being, for example, 'more positive about myself, more confident', thus identifying the kind of improvements to self-concept and self-esteem which are consistent with the broader sports literature (Coalter, 2005; Ekeland et al., 2005; West & Crompton, 2001). An increased sense of self-efficacy was also observed as a result of taking part in and 'graduating' from the academies ('It has made me realise that if I try hard enough I can succeed'), which has important implications for promoting the psychological processes of adaptation (Dulmen & Ong, 2006) and resilience (Luthar, 2003) both of which feature in 'strength-based' models of desistance (Burnett & Maruna, 2006).

An examination of the ideographic experiences of the delivery staff, and of the young men who participated in this innovative scheme, highlights the practical and emotional importance of ensuring that resettlement interventions offer sustained post-release support. The need to facilitate opportunities to develop human capital as well as social capital to ensure that gains made can be maintained after release (Farrall, 2002; McNeill, 2006) is also apparent. As such, integrated partnership working and the development of community links should be key elements of effective prison-based sports resettlement programmes. Some of these themes – peer relationships, partnership working and the development of positive relations between staff and prisoners as well as different groups of prisoners – will be explored further in the subsequent chapter devoted to the prison regime itself.

Notes

1   An initial survey of 67 young adult male prisoners sought to identify which sports would be most effective in attracting participation. Although at the time it was not authorised in public prisons, boxing was the most popular response (45%), followed by football (35%) and rugby (17%). Cricket was cited by 5% of prisoners surveyed, and the remaining 9% referred to other sports, including basketball, athletics and weightlifting.

2   For analytical purposes these have all been included. Completers of intervention programmes are often found to have a stronger effect than noncompleters which may be due to a self-selection effect whereby completers may be more motivated, or have fewer needs, or have a lower risk of reoffending. Therefore, it has been suggested that

effectiveness of the programme should not be evaluated against completers alone, whose outcomes may have been better even without the intervention. Rather, the true effect of the intervention as it is used in practice should be evaluated by considering all participants, both completers and noncompleters (Colledge, Collier & Brand, 1999; National Offender Management Service, 2005), and more weight should be placed on the findings for all participants (Sadlier, 2010).

3   Four participants were recalled to prison as a result of breaching licence conditions. Official reconviction data does not include those recalled to prison due to a breach of licence conditions so they are not included here, but if they were the reconviction rate would increase to 31% which is still significantly lower than the institution and national comparative figures.

4   Reconviction data are not yet available for prisoners released throughout 2011 so it is assumed that there was no significant change in the 2010 and 2011 cohorts.

5   The reported α statistics for previous research are based on Honess et al.'s (2001) British research with a sample of 145 male adult offenders (70 with a violent offending history) and 45 male young offenders (17 with violent offending history).

9 The contribution of sport towards education and employment opportunities in prison

> There is no point having gym if you can't do any courses. You need courses so when you get out you can use the qualifications to get back into work. (Prisoner, Category C)

> I've learnt how I could work in an outside gym. It gives you responsibility, confidence, you learn how to be professional and project yourself. (Prisoner, Category B)

There is undoubtedly a link between improving educational opportunities, raising levels of numeracy and literacy, equipping prisoners with meaningful qualifications and skills and the likelihood that they can successfully desist from crime after release. It is not surprising, therefore, that education, employment and training are well established in representing one of the seven 'resettlement pathways' formulated by the *Reducing Reoffending National Action Plan* in identifying the factors that influence reoffending. In this chapter I explore the role of sport firstly as a way of engaging offenders in education and secondly as a meaningful and realistic route into vocational training and employment.

The role of sport in promoting education

As well as being a significant risk/protective factor in itself, education (or the lack of it) evidently has an especially powerful impact on many of these other recognised resettlement needs, for example health outcomes and family relationships, and interventions such as offending behaviour programmes risk having less impact on prisoners with poor levels of literacy (Davies, Lewis, Byatt, Purvis & Cole, 2004). An enduring paradox, however, is that those who have the most to gain from education are often those who are least likely to have benefitted from it, or to do so in the future, raising particular challenges for educators in the prison estate.

Despite evidence of pockets of good practice, prison education has experienced something of a crisis in recent decades, resulting in provision being stripped to a core curriculum. Historically education has not been prioritised by the government, the prison regime or by prison staff, but more recently it has become something of a competitive commodity, with prison education contracts being prioritised and resourced. The setting of educational targets has forced providers and prisons to be held more accountable for learning provision and outcomes, thus emphasising the importance of education within prisons. The development of the government's now defunct Prisoner Learning and Skills Unit marked a new focus on prioritising offender learning, and the subsequent procurement by the Skills Funding Agency of Offender Learning and Skills Services (OLASS), together with the appointment of Heads of Learning and Skills in prisons, has generated an increased focus, not just on prisoner education, but on the importance of encouraging imaginative teachers to bring innovation into their teaching practices. Teaching can be demanding whatever the context, and especially so in a prison environment with its higher prevalence of negative previous learning experiences, behavioural problems, mental health problems and other needs and anxieties, coupled with a greater frequency of unrecognised learning difficulties, such as dyslexia.

Prisons by their very nature are closed and harsh environments and it can be especially difficult for teachers to cater for the varied needs and abilities of each learner, especially in local establishments where prisoners rarely stay long enough to complete standard length learning modules. However, teaching can be enhanced by the development of a more innovative and adaptive approach, creating positive learning spaces throughout the prison and taking education to nonlearners outside the classroom – to the wings, the kitchens, the workshops and of course the gym.

Engaging reluctant learners through sport

> They resent a desk because it represents authority. Gyms are less intimidating than education departments and once we get them through the door we can encourage literacy and numeracy, encourage them to write letters or to work out BMIs or weight-lifting calculations. (Prison Staff)

Sport has long been recognised as an incentive or way of increasing motivation among those who might otherwise be unlikely to participate in other activities, and in the context of offender education, sport can obviously be effective in engaging with prisoners who are initially reluctant learners, by exposing them to learning in a non-threatening environment. Apprehensions about attending education and training often stem from previous negative and disrupted educational experiences, which offenders are significantly more likely to have experienced than nonoffenders (Stewart, 2008b). Indeed, many prisoners will entirely avoid going to the education department of a prison – which will typically contain traditional-style classrooms and predominantly use conventional teaching methods – due to the negative connotations of these rooms and teaching styles. So in order to engage reluctant or anxious learners, embedding learning into other more appealing activities can evidently be an effective way of making it more relevant and less intimidating.

Exploring prisoners' motivations for undertaking sports-related qualifications

The grant making charity Prisoners Education Trust funds over 2,000 prisoners a year for distance learning courses in a range of academic and vocational subjects and at levels not otherwise available in prison, thus enabling them to progress from basic skills qualifications gained either in custody or in the community. Sports-related courses are especially popular: in 2011 alone the Trust funded 162 prisoners to engage in exercise and fitness courses leading to qualifications such as gym instructor, personal trainer and sports nutritionist, and ranging from basic qualifications through to degree-level courses offered through the Open University.

When prisoners apply to Prisoners Education Trust for funding, they are required to do so with the approval of the prison and to write a personal statement explaining their motivations for embarking on the course. Recognising the potential value of these letters as a research tool, a close analysis of the content of 314 personal statements written by prisoners to support their applications for the funding of a sports-related qualification between 2010–2012 provided insights into the applicants' key motivations. These strongly mapped on to the resettlement priority area of education, training and employment – which is one of the key pathways which guides resettlement service provision. But aside from these primary motivations, several other resettlement pathways were strongly represented in the content of the applications; for example, some learners indicated that the qualifications would encourage them to lead healthier and more active lifestyles after release, thus improving their physical health. Others reported being motivated to improve their mental health and psychological well-being, to deal with substance addiction or to increase self-confidence – whether through the desire to seek employment and/or education or to lead a life free of crime.

In terms of how the completion of sports qualifications related to their time in custody, the majority of prisoner learners saw undertaking such courses as a way of complementing or supplementing the existing qualifications they had gained since being sentenced, enabling them to progress onto further study at a higher level or simply as a way of using their time in custody more constructively. The data demonstrates the role of such courses in prisons, not only in terms of the improved confidence, skills and motivation of prison learners but also in contributing to the current *Prisons with a Purpose* agenda to promote purposeful activity within prisons (Conservative Party, 2011). A smaller but still substantial group of learners (particularly those serving longer sentences) reported intending to use the requested qualification in order to improve their physical or psychological health or to help fellow prisoners, highlighting the potential impact on prosocial behaviours and peer mentoring roles.

Interviews with prison staff confirmed that initial sports-based learning opportunities were seen as a valuable way of promoting a culture of learning among those who might not have been likely to embark on learning without being inspired by sport:

> It gets them started on other educational courses by doing entry level sports qualifications – makes them have a go at something else. (Staff, YOI)

> Gaining credits through a PE qualification can be a building block for going onto education, giving people confidence that they can achieve. (Staff, High Security)

> Taking what might be seen as a low level qualification in PE can give prisoners confidence and motivation to go on to education, it enables them to build skills like the ability to create a portfolio which they may not have thought they were capable of. (Staff, High Security)

> A significant proportion are not interested in education. What we've done is tried to concentrate learning in the gym. It doesn't work for all the women but it opens the door. Once they're engaged in this informal environment they often want to go on more formally. (Staff, Female)

Numerous prisoner interviewees confirmed that gym-based qualifications were seen as a worthy achievable to work towards ('the chance to do more qualifications gives us something to aim for,' Category B), with educational outcomes being valued as much as the psychological and physical benefits ('Gym is very important as it keeps minds stimulated, challenges frustrations, helps me get fit and gives a chance to get qualifications,' Local).

Sport and higher education

> I'm even considering going to university to do a foundation course, then possibly doing physiotherapy. Before I never had anything like that in my mind. (Prisoner, YOI)

Aside from career-oriented motivations, a substantial 20% of all prison learners reported the opportunity to progress onto further study after release as a primary incentive for undertaking a sports qualification in prison, identifying it as a valuable catalyst in the promotion of lifelong learning. In a population where ambitions for higher level learning are not typically prominent or promoted, the power of sport to create aspirations of this kind should not be underestimated. Despite concerns regarding basic numeracy and literacy skills tending to overshadow the promotion of higher level education in prison, many interviewees reported being sufficiently enthused by their involvement in sport to embark on degree level studies or to go into higher education after release:

I'm going to study Sports Science on an access course and hopefully off to university the year after. (Prisoner, YOI)

The *Review of Offender Learning* published by the Department for Business, Innovation & Skills and the Ministry of Justice (2011) acknowledges the importance of higher education as an important learning progression route for some prisoners. In the academic year 2011/2012 there were 38 prisoners studying for modules as part of the Open University (OU) Foundation Degree in Sports and Fitness and funded by the Prisoners Education Trust. These studies were undertaken despite not having access to the Internet or the online tutor support that OU students outside of prison benefit from, demonstrating the high level of motivation among these learners given these restrictions. However, a potential barrier to completing the OU foundation degree is the requirement to achieve the prerequisite Level 2 qualification in practical coaching or fitness instruction, which not all prisons offer.

Although the impact of embarking on distance learning courses during a period of incarceration is significant and has been explored elsewhere in the context of positive transformations (Hughes, 2009), of particular interest when considering the sustained impact of sports education in prison are prisoner learners' post-release motivations and perceived benefits of undertaking sports qualifications in prison. The majority of the learner applications referred explicitly to the post-release employment-related benefits of undertaking sports qualifications in prison, with aspirations of careers in the sports and leisure industry, for example as gym instructors, personal trainers or nutritionists. Reflecting a general awareness that self-employment may be a more successful career path in light of restrictions imposed by criminal convictions and that the sport and leisure industries remain relatively robust even during a period of economic recession, many prisoners specifically stated that increasing the chances of being able to pursue self-employment after release was a primary motivation of embarking on sports education in prison, as was the realisation of finding genuine enthusiasm for a career in the sports industry: one prison learner embodied this optimistic attitude towards working within the sport and leisure industry with the statement 'I have finally found a career that I would enjoy.'

Using sport to develop a more holistic approach to learning and employment

An unrestricted diet of literacy or numeracy will not provide the motivational hook to start an offender on their journey to becoming a more responsible citizen. (Department for Business, Innovation & Skills and Ministry of Justice, 2011)

As well as recognising the importance of generating 'hard skills' in the form of qualifications and employment, there is a need to acknowledge the importance of education in developing those 'soft skills' (such as communication techniques and emotional literacy). Sports-based learning can provide a valuable opportunity to develop these soft skills, most notably through team games, and the need to develop effective communication strategies and the ability to manage emotion (for further discussion of this in the context of the evaluation of a sports-based initiative see Chapter 8).

Acknowledging a growing recognition of the need to provide more holistic learning processes and a more widespread culture of learning throughout prisons, the government initiated the procurement process for Offender Learning and Skills Services in 2012 which specified not only a greater focus on employability in custody than previously, but also actively promoted embedded basic and

---

Innovative practice case study: Embedded learning and industry-led programme development

The gym at HMP Wandsworth is a typical gym but with a notable difference. While other prisoners pump weights or run on the treadmill, sitting on one of the benches away from the main activity is a teacher. Rather than teaching sports and fitness though, she is a literacy and numeracy skills tutor helping a prisoner, who explains how he previously avoided the prison education department 'like the plague' as he struggled at school due to dyslexia and had negative earlier experiences of schooling. He was, however, a keen boxer and so when he was sentenced to custody he spent a lot of time in the prison gym. It was here that he saw other prisoners sitting with the tutor doing work, and soon she had encouraged him to start working through some learning tasks whenever he was in the gym, which led to his first achievement in basic skills qualifications, followed by further qualifications in gym instruction, football coaching and public health. He hopes the sports-based qualifications he has accumulated while at Wandsworth will enable him to make a career in the sports and fitness industry after his release from prison.

Gym staff at HMP Wandsworth have also arranged for potential employers to come to the gym to meet the prisoners and give advice about careers in the fitness industry. During these visits they emphasised that soft skills, such as approachability, good eye contact, politeness and confidence were as important as industry-recognised qualifications. Staff reported modifying their programme in response to the employer advice, with the inclusion of role-play scenarios and an increased focus on the development of soft skills in order to prepare prisoners for interviews after release. Establishing relationships with sports and fitness employers can therefore directly inform the design and delivery of sports-based programmes, as well as providing a resource for potential placement opportunities.

Principles of best practice

    Embed literacy and numeracy tuition in the gym.
    Engage industry employers in careers and employability advice.
    Prepare prisoners for interviews after release through the inclusion of role play in gym activities.

functional skills in literacy, numeracy, language and ICT (Information and Communication Technology) in vocational programmes, including sport. However, Prison Inspectorate reports have drawn attention to the fact that although high pass rates indicate a good level of engagement with and motivation for undertaking sports-related qualifications in prison, many of the courses offered are only of a basic level and therefore do not necessarily satisfy the requirements of potential employers:

> Although the range and number of accredited PE courses tended to be limited, pass rates were generally high. Where the range of courses was better, the qualifications and the work experience prisoners gained gave them the opportunity of finding employment in the leisure industry on release. However, in some prisons accredited courses were unavailable due to staff shortages. (HM Inspectorate of Prisons, 2012)

Offering higher level qualifications, as well as equipping prisoners with soft transferable skills, is evidently an important way in which prison gyms can support the resettlement pathways of education and employment. This is especially critical since the publication of new Prison Service guidance (Ministry of Justice, 2011b), which states that education is no longer a mandatory requirement in physical education provision within the secure estate.

Developing employment opportunities through sport

For a substantial number of prisoners, as well as inspiring participation in formal education, from basic skills right up to degree-level studies, sports-based learning and training also offer a meaningful and rewarding route into employment. But given the popularity of sports-related courses among prisoners and the high numbers of prisoners and ex-prisoners who have ambitions to work in the sports, fitness and leisure industries, it is important to explore how well prison education and training currently prepare prisoners for employment or self-employment in these industries. Are such aspirations realistic or are we at risk of encouraging undue optimism, particularly in the current economic climate where competition for vacant posts is fierce? Analysis of advertised posts for personal trainers, fitness/gym instructors, and coaches, coupled with consultation with existing employers in the sports industry, revealed the importance of relevant previous experience and qualifications (specifically at Level 2 and 3) in potential candidates, together with demonstrable leadership, interpersonal, and other soft skills.

An ex-offender interviewee who gained a Level 1 coaching qualification while in custody was released on electronic tag after serving one year in a Young Offender Institution, whereupon he participated in voluntary football coaching which enabled him to complete his Level 2 and led to paid employment. As he testified, 'If young offenders have jobs when they're out then they won't re-offend. They need qualifications that can get them jobs, ones that are of a high enough level for employment' (Ex-Prisoner).

Other ex-offender interviewees who had gone into non-sports employment had still attributed their success in gaining employment after release to participation in sport whilst in custody, as the following young male confirms:

> Since I've got out I've got a job. I think because I was able to explain in the interview that I didn't just sit around in jail and I was involved in sport, that made the employer realise there was more to me than just an ex-criminal. (Ex-Prisoner)

Although organisations and individuals who had employed ex-prisoners reported some challenges and risks associated with doing so, and despite recognising that some offence categories would exclude a considerable number of ex-offenders from a career in sports and leisure, employers clearly recognised the benefits of employing former prisoners. Such benefits were especially important for organisations running social inclusion programmes and activities for young people at risk of crime, thus demonstrating the value that offering appropriate sports qualifications – particularly those that equip individuals with relevant skills and experience – can have, not only in terms of improving prisoners' employment prospects upon release, but also in creating skilful and valued employees:

> These guys speak with knowledge and understanding about how it really is and the consequences associated with this type of behavior. (Sports Employer)

> Employing ex-offenders helps us prevent offending, but also helps us as an organisation to engage with hard to reach young people as the ex-offenders have been there and done that. (Sports Employer)

Staff responses from across the prison estate referred to the generation of particular skills through participation in sports, most notably team work, organisation skills, better communication and a sense of achievement, all of which were seen as important in increasing employability. Staff were also aware of the need to prove the impact of their work through demonstrable outcomes which would contribute to the prison's performance targets, while utilising resources with care:

> People with less than 18 months left on their sentence – we try to link them up with employment on the outside. You have to build it up, and get the right people to do it as it is expensive and you need to be realistic about whether they are going to get a job on the outside. (Staff, Category C)

> Physical activity and sport are an integral part of our provision and it is the participation in these that can, if nurtured, lead to quality achievements within the learning process. We have regular correspondence from learners who have left us and been released, who have been successful in gaining employment in the Active Leisure Sector, both in full and self-employment. (Staff, Category C)

Innovative practice case study: YMCA placements for offenders

In legislative developments, the *Breaking the Cycle* Green Paper sets out to deliver 'reformed and revitalised' training that involves employers and education providers collaborating with senior prison managers to adapt their training to the needs of the labour market. It also commits to improving offenders' work skills and connections with employers through an increased number of employer-led training workshops. Consultation with prisons throughout England and Wales revealed evidence of the type of innovative practice with industry partners that the Ministry of Justice may have been seeking. For example, a number of YMCA gyms run a volunteer programme which enables people with a qualification in fitness to gain valuable work experience as gym instructors and have extended this to involve those still in custody. For several years they have offered prisoners on temporary licence (RoTL) volunteer placements and additional qualifications to make them ready for a career in the fitness industry after release. As a YMCA manager reports:

> What I'm looking for is someone who really wants to do it. There are often too many applicants for the volunteer spaces we have available. Sometimes I refer them to another YMCA centre or if they have a low level of knowledge I give them feedback and ask them to improve their knowledge and re-apply in the future . . . Normally they start with a couple of shifts a week, but most of them enjoy it and quickly want to take on more shifts, up to four or five a week. All volunteers are provided with an experienced gym instructor to supervise and coach them throughout the placement. We try to give them as much training as possible so they will be able to find a job in the future. I can't guarantee that vacancies will be available with the YMCA after the end of the volunteer period, but the aim is to get them ready for interviews and to get a job in fitness anywhere . . . I would encourage other gyms to work with local prisons to run similar schemes for prisoners.

Principles of best practice

> Establishing partnerships in the fitness industry.
> Providing work experience to build on existing qualifications whilst on RoTL.

Although prisoners acting as gym orderlies and volunteer coaches can gain valuable work experience while in prison, interviewees who had previously tried to secure employment in community gyms after being released from prison were frustrated at the difficulties they faced, for example:

> Last time I got out I tried to get a job in a gym but it didn't happen because I didn't have the qualification or any experience. (Prisoner, Category B)

Interviews with representatives from professional organisations confirmed the need to align the professional experiences offered in prison gyms with the priorities of community gyms:

> It's hard to come out of prison and work in a professional gym if you have only ever worked in a prison gym. In real gyms people pay membership and they expect good service . . . When people come from the prison the main problem they have is lack of confidence and social skills . . . I would say prisons should do more activities encouraging teamwork to help them build social skills. (Community Gym Manager)

One way in which prison staff have responded to this challenge is demonstrated at HMP Dorchester, where the gym is run as much like a commercial gym as possible, as summarised in the following case study.

Innovative practice case study: Gaining valuable work experience in gym orderly roles

An effective way in which prison gym staff have responded to the challenge of enabling prisoners to gain the most relevant types of work experience is demonstrated at HMP Dorchester where the prison gym is organised and operated to represent a community gym as much as possible. Orderlies are an integral part of the staffing team and follow a schedule of activities, overseen by the most experienced orderly who acts in an assistant manager role. Duties include responding to the varied demands of gym users (prisoners and staff), conducting assessments, setting up equipment for staff and prisoner sessions, working with and supporting vulnerable prisoners and visiting community groups and generally representing the gym, including at meetings with other departments within the prison. Orderlies are provided with opportunities to gain industry-recognised qualifications, with responsibilities increasing as qualifications are acquired. PE staff members compile reports reflecting each orderly's responsibilities, achievements and attributes, and are regularly used as referees by ex-prisoners seeking employment in the industry after release.

Principles of best practice

> Organisation and structure replicate community gyms.
> Increasing meaningful opportunities and responsibilities for prisoner gym orderlies.
> PE staff are able to provide references post-release.

Sports education provision: Operational challenges

Analysis of reports published by HM Inspectorate of Prisons confirms widespread good practice in integrating education through accredited sports courses across the secure estate, in spite of accredited qualifications no longer being a mandatory requirement of the Prison Services PE specification. Inspectorate reports for the majority of prisons identified the availability of accredited courses, but also revealed less availability of accredited courses within high security (75%) and local (88%) prisons. This may be partially explained by the elevated security and risk concerns within these establishments and the difficulty of delivering accredited courses, which take time to complete, to transient remand populations.

Despite being aware of the powerful impact of sport in motivating prison learners, staff were also acutely aware of the limitations imposed on them according to the type of establishment they were working in. For example, PE staff in local prisons have to adapt to the fact that many of their population will not remain in the establishment for long before being moved to a different prison, with obvious repercussions on developing relationships or completing courses:

> Retention of prisoners allocated on to courses is a challenge. Being a local establishment can sometimes limit the variation of courses given: trying to do a seven week gym instructor is near impossible. (Staff, Local)

Despite this, there was still awareness of the ability for local prisons to establish a training plan that could be picked up in subsequent prisons, subject to effective information sharing:

> We do not keep prisoners here long enough to achieve much in the way of qualifications, however we do put in place the foundations for them to build on through their sentence. (Staff, Local)

Staff interviewees in high-security establishments reported that, although they may not experience the frustrations that their peers in local prisons experience in working with a transient population, the priorities may be quite different:

> We have a fairly static population. The priority is treatment so there may be less time for qualifications. (Staff, High Security)

Despite the wide availability of accredited sports courses, opportunities to translate skills into tangible employment opportunities after release – which can play a significant role in reducing reoffending (Social Exclusion Unit, 2002) – remain scarce. Analysis of Inspectorate reports identified clear links from PE departments to employment in the community among 40% of juvenile and 30% of YOI establishments, but such links for other types of establishments were either nonexistent or rare. Furthermore, only 4% of Inspectorate reports considered across all establishments referred to sports-related Release on Temporary Licence opportunities, and those that did were predominantly prisons holding younger offenders or females.

However, just as different types of prisons were restricted in the form of provision they could offer, prisoner interviewees also confirmed that support for pursuing gym-based qualifications varied across the estate, depending on the perceived priority of qualifications in specific PE departments:

> I've been to quite a few different prisons on this sentence, and the PE department here really encourages and helps you to get qualifications. At other places they just didn't care what you did. (Prisoner, Category B/YOI)

Members of staff were obviously well aware of the need for sports-based qualifications to be targeted only at appropriate prisoners, with calculations of risk being continuously applied when providing courses and training:

> The main risk is delivering qualifications to offenders who may use them on release for inappropriate purposes. (Staff, Category B)

However, whereas offence category will inevitably restrict access to some types of courses, staff were also clear that, given the broad scope of sport-based qualifications, numerous alternative opportunities were also available so as not to exclude specific types of offender (see Chapter 4 for further discussion of the needs of diverse populations):

> We have a very large sex offender population, who by the nature of their offences are not allowed to hold sport coaching qualifications. (Staff, Local)

> Risk needs to be carefully managed depending on the offence of each individual. We encourage PE via the educational route and encourage prisoners to engage with and promote direct links with the Library / Education department. (Staff, High Security)

When discussing the challenges of promoting education gym staff referred to the need to set realistic and useful training goals:

> A challenge is ensuring that those undertaking the courses are realistically going to use the skills on release. (Staff, Category D)

Despite acknowledging the difficulty of securing funding and sufficient resources to be able to do so, there was a strong recognition amongst gym staff of the potential to motivate prisoners to make significant achievements:

> We continually risk assess for suitability. It is always challenging working with prisoners but with experience and dedication to motivate and be enthusiastic you can achieve some very positive outcomes. (Staff, Category C)

Innovative practice case study: Promoting employment opportunities for those nearing release

HMP Leeds is a local adult male prison with a highly transient population. The prison has a dedicated resettlement wing from where prisoners nearing the end of their sentence are released during the day in order to receive individual support with employment issues and to attend employment placements.

A partnership between the resettlement wing and the physical education department has enabled the prison to develop links with local sporting clubs in order to facilitate placements for prisoners which aim to develop prisoners' soft skills, familiarise them with the working routine in preparation for release, and create post-release employment opportunities.

Consistent with the aim of preparing individuals for release and mirroring physical activity patterns among employed populations in the community, recreational sports activities are available to individuals on the resettlement wing at 7 in the morning prior to work and again at 7 in the evening.

Principles of best practice

Embedding sport and physical activity within one-to-one resettlement support.
Developing sports-based community contacts to facilitate work placements.
Offering recreational activities consistent with typical patterns in the community, a principle with particular relevance within working prisons.

The role of sport in education, training and employment: Implications of the findings

Prison education in England and Wales is certainly going through a time of significant change: the implementation of new education contracts, alongside an increased policy focus on prisons as places of education, employment, rehabilitation and restoration; the rolling out of Payment by Results initiatives, and the development of the Virtual Campus scheme (a customised search engine allowing prisoners secure access to sites relevant to education and employment). In the context of these changes there is potential for sport and physical activity to play a greater role. Those who are not inspired by learning are quite likely to be enthusiastic about other activities (an obvious example being sport) and there is evidently plenty of scope to integrate the gym with broader educational objectives. Drawing on examples of good practice from across the estate tutors can, where safe to do so, spend time in the prison gym in order to engage with and motivate reluctant learners through embedded learning. In promoting a culture of learning throughout the prison the gym has a role to play in initiating reading, for example by establishing stronger links with prison libraries and/or developing a small library of books and learning materials relating to sports and fitness. In making better use of technology, prison gyms should contain a computer, if possible linked to the virtual campus, for prisoners to develop their ICT skills, for example in creating session plans and tracking fitness progress using spreadsheets. Sporting activities – in particular team sports – when used effectively can help develop a whole range of soft skills concerning communication, leadership, problem solving and group work. More specifically, prisons can develop the transferable soft skills that employers want by running specialist programmes such as the leadership awards and qualifications that are offered by the charity Sports Leaders UK. These soft skills can be developed both on and off the pitch but in order to have a sustained impact they need to be recognised and recorded, ideally through learning records so that prisoners can reflect on these skills and refer to them in interviews and on application forms.

As well as stimulating education opportunities by establishing links with prison libraries and education departments, in promoting employment opportunities the research has highlighted the importance of partnership working with sporting organisations and clubs in the community. Prisons can benefit from direct links with employers, but in turn employers may need support and guidance on employing ex-prisoners, effectively managing risk and the benefits that employing an ex-prisoner might bring to their business. For example, the Employers' Reducing Reoffending Forum is a group of local and national employers who provide job opportunities for offenders, supported by the Ministry of Justice and the European Union, is an example of resource meeting need in this domain. Drawing on better established links, prison gyms can also provide advice and information to prisoners nearing release about ways to continue sport and fitness activities in the community, whether through volunteering or participation at a gym or sports club, apprenticeships or college courses in the community after release.

In sum then, despite many having histories of disrupted and negative educational experiences and prolonged periods of worklessness, interviews with prisoners of all ages and backgrounds from across the prison estate revealed strong motivations to engage in sports and fitness studies and to explore employment opportunities in the sports and leisure industry. The findings have highlighted the powerful impact that sport can have, particularly in inspiring those who have been unwilling or unable to engage in other aspects of prison life. But, as has been confirmed elsewhere in this text, however enthusiastic individual prisoners are, initiatives need to be driven by enthusiastic and capable staff and supported by broader prison structures in order for them to have the best impact. However, although the pursuit of sport in itself may not automatically improve educational and employment outcomes, it is important to recognise its capacity as a vehicle to increase motivation, improve attitudes towards learning and establish more constructive and meaningful relationships with staff, which can then be translated into more effective learning and employment opportunities. This theme will be revisited in subsequent chapters, when considering the impact of sport and physical activity on the broader prison environment.

10   The role of sport and physical activity in prison-based health promotion

It is widely acknowledged in both national and international literature that offenders represent a group with complex and multiple health needs (McSweeney & Hough, 2006), many of which are not addressed prior to custody (Department of Health, 2009a; Mair & May, 1997) and yet which place considerable cost and resource burden on health services (Rodriguez, Keene & Li, 2006). Prisoners have poorer physical health (Harris, Hek & Condon, 2006; World Health Organisation (WHO), 2007) and elevated levels of substance misuse, mental health problems and vulnerability to self-harm and suicide (Department of Health, 2009a; WHO, 2007), and approximately half of all male prisoners (Fazel, Bains & Doll, 2006), and two thirds of female prisoners report substance dependency prior to imprisonment (Social Exclusion Unit, 2002). Over 70% of the prison population in England and Wales have two or more mental health problems, and it is widely recognised that access to mental health and substance misuse services can contribute to a reduction in offending (Home Office, 2004; Social Exclusion Unit, 2002). However, despite growth in these services within prisons, many prisoners still do not engage with treatment (Stewart, 2008a).

The concept of empowerment and the ability to make healthy choices is a central pillar of health promotion which is heavily curtailed by prison regimes (Sim, 2002; WHO, 2007). It has been suggested that voluntary participation in sports can offer a means by which to promote healthy living, as well as offering an active form of learning, which typically is preferred by offenders (Audit Commission, 1996; Evans & Fraser, 2009; Meek, Champion & Klier, 2012). Although prisoners can be unlikely to subscribe to ideas of 'healthy living' (National Audit Office, 2008), participation in sport in prisons is often high (Buckaloo et al., 2009) so physical activity has the potential to play a key role in promoting health objectives. In spite of this, and the wide acknowledgement that sport can confer both physical and psychological health benefits within the community (see Frank & Dahn, 2005, for a review), scant academic attention has been paid to the role of sport and physical activity in promoting health among prisoners, or the degree to which this is achieved in policy and practice.

Prisoner health: The policy context in England and Wales

Following the publication of the Social Exclusion Unit's (2002) *Reducing Reoff-ending by Ex-Prisoners* and the subsequent *Reducing Reoffending National Action Plan* (Home Office, 2004) physical and mental health needs and substance use have been established as key areas to be addressed in order to facilitate reductions in reoffending. National and international policies that specifically address prisoner health have promoted the notion of a 'whole prison approach' to improving the physical and mental health of prisoners in order to meet such objectives (Department of Health, 2002; WHO, 2007) and in an attempt to respond to prisoners' multiple health needs, recent years have seen an increasing emphasis on more holistic approaches within prisons, including the promotion of partnership working. In 2006 the responsibility for health care in public prisons was transferred from the Prison Service to the National Health Service, accompanied by the introduction of Public Service Agreements aimed to promote shared delivery (House of Commons Treasury Committee, 2007). Despite such strategic political attempts to address prisoner health, subsequent reports have continued to highlight the unmet physical (Bradshaw, 2008) and, in particular, mental health needs of offenders in custody (Department of Health, 2009b; Home Office, 2007), and there has been a resulting call for more integrated and innovative approaches (Patel, 2010). Nationally, the Department of Health's (2002) strategy for improving the health of prisoners and internationally the World Health Organisation's *Health in Prisons* both outlined a whole-prison approach to promoting health, thus explicitly placing responsibility for improving the health of prisoners on all relevant departments and staff within prisons, rather than solely with health care professionals. Furthermore, policy directives have indicated that local plans for health promotion must address active living as a minimum requirement (HM Prison Service, 2003) and that physical activity should be considered as an accompaniment to healthcare interventions and detoxification programmes (HM Prison Service, 2000), thus emphasising that physical education departments have an intrinsic role to play in the promotion of offender health.

Health promotion consideration has been outlined in local planning mechanisms, and national directives (e.g. Department of Health, 2002) have subsequently been implemented locally through the Prison Service Orders and Instructions, which contain compulsory and discretionary directions regarding the operation of prison establishments. Such guidance has been developed and implemented to address the primary areas of mental health promotion and well-being, smoking, healthy eating and nutrition and healthy lifestyles, including sex and relationships, active living and substance misuse (HM Prison Service, 2003). Prison PE departments are increasingly seen as having a role to play in delivering such provision and this is made evident in the Physical Education Instruction of 2011 which stipulates that PE programmes must incorporate access to remedial PE and should promote healthy living and diet opportunities as well as activities that boost self-esteem to improve psychological well-being. Likewise, clinical guidance on services for substance misuse advocates physical activity as an accompaniment to detoxification programmes (HM Prison Service, 2000), and the *Tackling Drugs through Physical Education* report (Ministry of Justice, 2009) provides a framework for such provision.

To give prisoners the opportunity to participate in physical activity for at least one hour per week (or two hours for those under 21 years old), physical education is routinely delivered throughout the secure estate and the majority of establishments fulfil the mandatory obligation (Ministry of Justice, 2011b). However the extent to which health promotion policies are effectively integrated in physical education provision in practice is less clear.

Physical health

As well as being increasingly likely to enter prison with unmet physical health needs, prisoners are at higher risk of noncommunicable diseases (Herbert et al., 2012) and periods of incarceration are also associated with deteriorating physical fitness (Fischer et al., 2012; Plugge et al., 2009; Plugge et al., 2011; Olaitan, Shnaila, Sikiru & Lawal, 2009). Prison sport and physical activity can be a relatively low-cost way of promoting offenders' physical health and targeting those who may typically be difficult to engage with in community settings (Woodall, 2010). As well as contributing to overall physical well-being and reducing obesity, regular physical exercise among prisoners has been found to reduce sleep problems such as insomnia (Elger, 2009) and the development or progression of disease (Ross, 2013).

Mental health

> It has given me a passion for something in life which I never had before prison. I have mental health problems and the gym helps me keep on the straight and narrow. (Prisoner, Local)

The Department of Health (2006) recommends the inclusion of a physical fitness element in the treatment of service users with mental illness, with physical activity widely recognised to improve psychological well-being (Frank & Dahn, 2005). Research with community samples has demonstrated that exercise can have a positive impact on psychiatric symptoms, including psychosis (Beebe et al., 2005; Ellis, Crone, Davey & Grogan, 2007), and a growing number of studies have documented such positive gains among prison populations (Johnsen, 2001; Martos-Garcia et al., 2009a; Martos-Garcia et al., 2009b). Buckaloo et al. (2009) found that male prisoners in a North American low-security prison who exercised regularly had significantly lower scores for depression, anxiety and stress compared to those who did not exercise, regardless of the type of exercise and number of sessions participated in (although a direction of causality was not identified so these findings should be used with caution). Such findings have been corroborated in diverse offender populations (Libbus et al., 1994; Verdot et al., 2010) and exercise in both male and female prisoners has been inversely correlated with

Innovative practice case study: Peer-led support through the Health Trainers initiative

HMP Bullingdon is a Category B local prison with a Category C training function detaining over 1,000 adult males. The prison's PE department has introduced an innovative Health Trainers programme, equipping prisoners with skills and qualifications in health promotion to improve health and well-being within the wider population.

The Health Trainers programme is a Primary Care Trust funded initiative, whereby prisoners gain a Level 3 qualification equipping them with the skills and knowledge to become Health Trainers, thus increasing employability and enabling them to support other prisoners to improve their health.

Individual health trainers work with a case load of between 15 and 25 prisoners, receiving referrals from other departments within the prison and from individual prisoners themselves. Health Trainers wear sweatshirts identifying their role to increase awareness and promote their services within the prison.

Health Trainers are trained to carry out basic health checks, develop individualised plans, and support their peers with health concerns such as weight loss, substance dependency and diabetes, delivered through group work as well as one-to-one provision. The Health Trainers work in partnership with other health care professionals, such as nutritionists, to develop holistic support plans for clients and attend quarterly Governor's steering meetings concerning health care within the prison.

> Lots of guys in here aren't in good shape, they come to me and want to get ripped up, drop weight or stop taking drugs or smoking. I do exercise programmes and diet plans with them, I can refer people to other agencies too like RAPT or smoking cessation . . . I give education classes and show people how to do cell exercises. (Health Trainer and Prisoner at HMP Bullingdon)

Principles of best practice

> Promoting health through peer-led initiatives.
> Partnership funding with local health authorities.
> Integrated working between health care professionals and prisoner Health Trainers.
> Equipping prisoners with qualifications of a standard to meet employers' needs.
> Promoting the services of Health Trainers through increased visibility and effective networking between departments across the prison.

feelings of hopelessness (Cashin, Potter & Butler, 2008). A qualitative evaluation of a British sports-based intervention with female prisoners (Ozano, 2008) established positive outcomes in terms of increased confidence and self-esteem, as well as in the provision of a coping mechanism for dealing with anxiety and aggression, which is especially important considering the elevated level of mental health problems among females in custody. Although it has been suggested that an excessive focus on sport among some prisoners has the potential to undermine the therapeutic impact of other psychiatric interventions (Tesu-Rollier, 2008), sport and physical activity in prison can clearly lead to psychological benefits and has the potential to be used as a medium through which to engage prisoners who may be reluctant or unable to participate in more traditional psychological work.

Innovative practice case study: The Mersey Care NHS Trust Positive Intervention Programme at Ashworth hospital

Ashworth hospital is run by Mersey Care NHS Trust, covering the North West of England, the Midlands, and Wales. It is a high-security psychiatric establishment detaining individuals who require treatment for their dangerous, violent or criminal tendencies. The Gym Seclusion programme is aimed specifically at patients in segregation who have extensive histories of violent and aggressive behaviour within community and psychiatric settings, and who often experience (or have experienced) psychotic spectrum disorder.

The programme aims to increase the quantity and range of physical activity, engage patients in low-demand social interaction, develop opportunities for modelling of prosocial behaviour and ultimately to reintegrate people into the mainstream regime in order for them to engage in insight-focused therapy.

Programme structure and outcomes

The Gym Seclusion project forms part of the patient's overall treatment programme which includes pharmacological, psychological and psycho-social components. Individual plans are developed outlining specific and achievable goals as well as assessing risks for sessions which are continually reviewed. Low-intensity physical activities are initially introduced on the ward, tailored to require only low-level social skills. Participants can then progress onto gym-based activities, such as cardiovascular resistance work, with staff participating in parallel activities, allowing for prosocial modelling. High-intensity sessions are provided for participants exhibiting high levels of distractibility or who drift into antisocial behaviour or fantasy. Participants who successfully progress through the programme are encouraged to engage in team-based activities, including games such as table tennis and pool. Activities are collaboratively delivered with input from nursing and ward staff, psychologists and psychiatrists.

Since 2005, over 30 patients who had been in long term seclusion have successfully been reintegrated into the mainstream regime. The programme has contributed to improved therapeutic relationships between patients and staff and played a part in reducing aggressive behaviour beyond sessions.

Principles of best practice

Integrating physical activity into a wider therapeutic model.
Carefully planned highly structured goal focused sessions.
Using a range of activities varying in intensity to promote engagement.
Multidisciplinary delivery of activities.
Prosocial modelling through staff participation in activities.

Substance misuse

Although the role of physical education in prison to address substance misuse and dependency has received little academic attention, evaluations of community sports-based interventions targeting substance use tentatively conclude that physical exercise may be correlated with decreased drug use and increased abstinence (Collingwood, Sunderlin & Kohl, 1994; Collingwood, Sunderlin, Reynolds & Kohl, 2000). For example, integrating substance misuse consultations into sports programmes for adolescents in the community has been found to reduce alcohol, drug and cigarette consumption 12 weeks postintervention and at one year follow up in a randomised controlled trial (Werch, Moore, DiClemente, Bledsoe & Jobli, 2005).

A small but significant body of evidence suggests that sport can make a positive contribution to addressing substance use in prisons, and there are several rationales which explain how physical activity may be a valuable addition to substance misuse interventions. Firstly, the psychological impact of exercise may have a positive impact on substance misuse risk factors and associated behavioural problems; secondly, alterations in neurotransmitters and endorphin levels as a result of exercise can lead to improved mood and provide an alternative 'high' to that achieved through drug use; and thirdly, the development of a health-enhancing lifestyle in which drug use is incongruent may promote abstinence. Furthermore, sport can be used as a valuable tool to encourage participation in wider drug interventions and the *Tackling Drugs through Physical Education* framework (Ministry of Justice, 2009) advocates physical activity to support those on compact-based drug testing and drug-free wings. Substantiating this, Stöver and Thane (2011) describe how Hungarian prisons have used privileges such as sport as a means to promote drug-free units and uptake in prison-based detoxification programmes.

Innovative practice case study: Using sport to tackle substance misuse. The drug recovery wing at HMP Bristol

HMP Bristol is a local prison detaining remanded and sentenced young adults and adult males in the South West. The drug-recovery wing within the establishment houses 150 prisoners at a time and adopts a multidisciplinary approach to tackling addiction: providing medical and physical support, group and individual psychosocial programmes, life skills and sports-based interventions to offenders with drug problems. Delivery is achieved through partnerships between the prison's substance misuse team, the prison gym and a number of community organisations, in order to achieve continuity in care between custody and community.

The Health through Sport element incorporates a range of low-intensity activities including walking, bowls, and team games such as cricket and rounders which are delivered in the unit's own sports facilities. In efforts to reduce self-presentational concerns and increase confidence and participation, these facilities are independent of the main prison gym. Prisoners learn about healthy eating and are supported to develop skills in planning and cooking healthy meals. Activities are designed to take prisoners' focus away from drugs, improve physical health, promote communication and team working skills, enhance self-esteem and promote ongoing active and healthy lifestyle choices in the community.

Those who participate in the Health through Sport scheme have been found to produce consistently negative drug urine tests, and more drug-using prisoners are taking up health and fitness activities as a result. There has also been an increase in people with a history of substance misuse gaining qualifications: some individuals have completed national vocational qualifications within the prison gym and have subsequently gone on to work in local gyms after release.

Principles of best practice

Integrating sport as part of a multimodal substance misuse intervention.
Partnership working between departments within the prison as well as with external organisations.
Providing stepped up opportunities for ongoing sporting involvement.

The National Audit Office's (2008) *Good Practice Guide to Promoting Healthier Lifestyles for Prisoners* recommends encouraging prisoners with drug dependency issues to participate in physical activity and linking physical education with healthcare drug strategies. Initial evidence suggests that implementing such guidelines has had positive outcomes, for example PE departments delivering healthy living and healthy balanced diets sessions within the Integrated Drug Treatment Systems (IDTS) in British prisons have experienced increased referrals and engagement in PE, as well as benefiting from physical education instructors' specialist knowledge in promoting interest in IDTS sessions.

Gym-based health provision across the estate: Analysis of inspectorate reports

In order to assess the extent to which health promotion policy agendas across the three domains of physical health, mental health, and substance misuse are delivered in practice through physical education departments across the secure state in England and Wales, data from the most recent reports (published between 2006 and 2012) made public by Her Majesty's Inspectorate of Prisons (HMIP) for 142 establishments (130 of which were publicly run, the other 12 being privately run) were analysed for content and comparisons made according to prison category. Establishments were grouped according to whether they were a juvenile ($n = 7$), young adult ($n = 18$), Category B/C ($n = 47$), local ($n = 32$), high security ($n = 8$), open ($n = 10$), female ($n = 16$) or immigration removal ($n = 4$) facility, based on their reception criteria (in instances where establishments held more than one population type they were categorised according to their principal population). In cases where the most recent inspection was a short follow up, the previous Inspectorate report was also considered, resulting in a total of 185 reports being subject to scrutiny. The content of each Inspectorate report was checked to ascertain if it stipulated whether or not there was provision for six elements of health promotion identified in policy (healthy living initiatives, remedial PE, weight management, mental health, smoking and addressing substance misuse) and the extent to which this was successfully integrated into PE practice in each establishment.

The analysis indicated that health promotion through physical education is widespread across the secure estate, but provision of differing elements of health promotion through physical activity vary greatly, with remedial physical education being widely available whereas targeted physical education programmes to address specific health concerns – for example smoking cessation and mental health – were available in only a small minority of establishments. Figure 10.1 illustrates the percentage of establishments across the entire estate with physical education provision across the six domains of health promotion.

Analysis of HMIP reports indicated that just over half (57%) of establishments integrated healthy living initiatives into PE programmes. Sports-related healthy living initiatives were most commonly found within the high-security estate, with seven out of the eight high-security establishments recognised as having such provision. Establishments detaining young people were least likely to have physical education programmes promoting healthy living: only 14% of juvenile and 22% of young offender institutions were identified as having such provision, whilst sports-related healthy-living programmes were identified in over 50% of establishments holding adult prisoners.

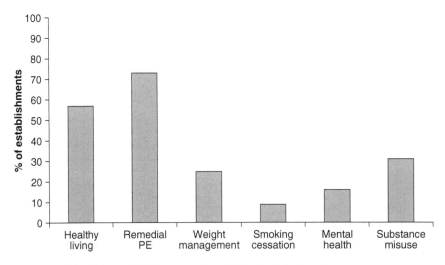

Figure 10.1 Provision of health promotion within physical education programmes across the secure estate in England and Wales.

HMIP reports for almost three quarters (73%) of establishments across the secure estate identified remedial PE provision of some form. Such provision was greatest within local establishments (88%) and least common within juvenile establishments (43%), but identified in over half of all other types of establishments. Programmes designed to address specific physical health issues – such as weight management and smoking cessation – through physical education were substantially more disparate: a quarter of physical education departments were identified as offering weight-management programmes, and these were most frequently identified in the women's estate (44% of female establishments), with comparatively low levels of prevalence in open prisons (10%) and high-security prisons (38%). Likewise, smoking cessation programmes integrated with physical education were infrequent, with HMIP reports for fewer than 10% (13 of the 142 establishments) identifying such provision; such programmes were identified most frequently within open prisons although this was still only reported in HMIP reports for 2 out of the 10. No smoking cessation programmes linked to physical education were identified in establishments for juvenile or high-security prisoners, or within immigration removal centres.

Innovative practice case study: Promoting physical health and healthy living among vulnerable and older prisoners

At HMP Parc (a privately run Category B prison run by G4S) the Fit for Living programme incorporates theoretical learning around healthy lifestyles (for example in terms of diet, nutrition and fitness) alongside low-impact physical activity. The programme aims to improve the fitness of and promote healthy living among prisoners who may have particular health needs or may not be ready to engage in mainstream physical activities.

The programme is delivered twice weekly over 12 weeks and is designed in particular for older and vulnerable prisoners who have the greatest need, with dedicated sessions being set aside for these populations. Engagement in a diverse range of activities is promoted, including walking, chair-based aerobics and Boccia, a form of bowls tailored for those with disabilities. These activities are particularly popular with older prisoners and suitable for those with a physical impairment or poor motor skills.

Individually tailored remedial plans are created for prisoners with specific physical health problems in collaboration with the health care department and a qualified visiting physiotherapist who attends weekly. The PE department also works closely with other departments within the prison, providing regular individual feedback regarding vulnerable prisoners' engagement and progress on the programme. Following completion of the Fit for Living programme prisoners are encouraged to continue participation and try different physical activities, with many progressing on to the mainstream physical education programme.

> ### *Principles of best practice*
>
> Tailored provision for older and vulnerable prisoners.
> A range of low-level noncompetitive activities to attract individuals who are not able or confident in engaging in mainstream gym activities.
> Cross-departmental working and partnership working with external professionals.

The analysis suggests that provision of gym-based programmes explicitly aiming to improve mental health are substantially less common than initiatives aimed at promoting physical health. HMIP reports for only 23 of the 142 establishments (16%) directly referred to instances of such programmes targeting or being tailored for those with mental health problems. In practice, these programmes were most commonly found within the juvenile estate, with reports indicating that three of the seven juvenile facilities had physical education programmes aimed at promoting psychological well-being. No such provision was identified within open establishments, only one such programme was identified across the 16 female establishments and under a quarter of all other types of establishments offered sports activities specifically aimed at improving mental health.

HMIP reports indicate that tackling substance misuse through sport and physical activity in English and Welsh prisons was not widespread: overall just under a third (31%) of establishments offered sports-related substance misuse interventions. The integration of sport into substance misuse programmes was most common within local and high-security establishments (half of these establishments had such provision) followed by prisons holding young people (43% of juvenile establishments and 28% of young offender institutions). Provision of such programmes in all other types of prisons ranged from a quarter of female establishments offering sports related substance misuse programmes to none of the immigration removal centres.

Conclusions

> It lets you relieve stress, use up energy and helps you get a good night's sleep. There should be more gym! (Prisoner, Local)

The highly variable but overall relatively infrequent extent to which health promotion is integrated into physical education across the secure estate highlights some examples of particularly innovative, inclusive, and positive practice but also raises the question of how effective the last decade's drive towards a 'whole prison approach' to improving the physical and mental health of prisoners has been. In terms of integrating health promotion into physical education within prison, generic efforts to improve physical health – such as promoting healthy living through sport – are common, but sporting provision targeting discrete physical and psychological health concerns is limited and delivered inconsistently, despite a strong potential for prison gyms to play a significant role in such endeavours. These observations were also confirmed in interviews, for example a senior manager reported that:

> Currently the link doesn't seem to be made between physical education and sport and the health promoting prisons agenda.

Given the joint responsibilities for prisoner healthcare, it is not surprising that variation in the provision of sport-based health promotion was commonly attributed by stakeholder interviewees not just to the senior management of individual prisons but also to the differing priorities of Primary Care Trusts. Although the Prison Service PE Instruction (Ministry of Justice, 2011b) stipulates that all PE programmes within English and Welsh prisons must promote healthy living, not all establishments achieve this. Of particular concern may be a finding which highlights an absence of PE related health programmes within Juvenile and YOI establishments: such initiatives were identified in fewer than half of all establishments detaining young people. This dearth of provision may reflect the stronger emphasis within establishments holding young people on providing sports-related educational and vocational opportunities which dominate delivery and leave little time for health promotion. However, considering that young prisoners have been identified as being particularly resistant to healthy living (HM Prison Service, 2004), the results suggest a discrepancy between need, policy, and consequent provision. Indeed, these results echo those of Condon et al. (2008) who identified that although facilities for physical education were generally good across the estate, there where large disparities in the availability of healthy living opportunities across prison departments. In contrast to healthy living, remedial physical education – also a mandatory requirement of the Physical Education Instruction – was available within the majority of establishments. This is particularly promising since exercise on referral has been found to promote ongoing engagement in mainstream physical activity (National Audit Office, 2008). Nevertheless, remedial PE was referred to less frequently in HMIP reports for establishments holding juveniles, although this may be explicable in terms of a reduced demand among a younger prisoner population.

In line with previous qualitative research which identified large disparities in the availability of specific health promotion programmes across prison regimes (Condon et al., 2008), the analysis suggested that the provision of specific health promotion programmes integrated with physical education such as those addressing weight management and smoking cessation were disparate. Greater provision of sports programmes targeting weight management in the female estate may reflect a response to recommendations made in the *Women Prisoners'* Prison Service Order (HM Prison Service, 2008) for PE activities to address issues of body image and self-consciousness. The overall paucity of physical education programmes addressing weight management in British prisons may also reflect a decreased perceived need for such provision given that a recent systematic review has revealed that male and female prisoners in the United Kingdom are less likely to be obese compared to the general population (Herbert et al., 2012). However, the scarcity of smoking cessation programmes integrated into physical education provision cannot be attributed to a lack of need, given that according to a 2003 report from the Health Development Agency and ASH, over three quarters of prisoners smoke. Comparative figures for England's general population gathered soon after indicated that less than a quarter of adults in the community smoked (Health and Social Care Information Centre, 2006) thus highlighting a significant health inequality in smoking status. Whereas some countries (such as New Zealand) have introduced total smoking bans in prisons, so far most English and Welsh prisons have implemented less stringent smoking restrictions whereby adult prisoners can still smoke within their own cells (Hartwig, Stöver & Weilandt, 2008).

Gym-based and PE programmes tend to focus on physical health significantly more than mental health, and initiatives aimed specifically at promoting psychological well-being were infrequent. However, the greater provision of such programmes identified within the juvenile estate may reflect a move towards more individualised, multimodal interventions to address children's needs on the part of the Youth Justice Board (which has responsibility for the juvenile estate in England and Wales). Indeed, tailored sports programmes targeting psychological well-being in young prisoners appear to offer particular benefits for mental health. For example the *Every Child Matters in Secure Settings* toolkit (National Children's Bureau, 2008) describes the ACCESS course initiative within the juvenile facility at YOI Wetherby which targets young people at risk of bullying and self-harm who are reluctant to participate in PE. The scheme combines sessions designed to promote coping, social, problem solving and emotional-management skills with physical activities such as trampolining, gymnastics, rollerblading and team games and is thought to have positive outcomes in terms of reducing the risk of self-harm and suicide as well as increasing self-esteem and motivation to engage in sport.

Despite evidence of good practice within the juvenile estate, only one sports programme specifically targeting mental health was identified in the female estate, where mental health problems are known to be most prevalent. Although it is widely agreed that sport and physical activity can be effective in promoting psychological benefits such as improved self-esteem and confidence, mental health problems are a key challenge for delivering physical education in prisons (Johnsen, 2001; Martos-Garcia et al., 2009a; Martos-Garcia et al., 2009b) and women's participation in physical activity in prison is lower than that of males. Consequently, challenges associated with engaging female prisoners in sport, coupled with a high prevalence of mental health problems, makes delivering such programmes particularly challenging and may help to explain the rarity of such provision within the women's estate. Nonetheless, isolated examples of good practice serve to demonstrate the extent to which carefully designed and delivered multimodal programmes can produce positive outcomes for those with severe mental health problems and self-harming behaviours, who are typically less likely to participate in sport.

Despite sport being advocated within official policy as an accompaniment to substance misuse programmes (HM Prison Service, 2000), and although a clear framework for implementing such provision exists (Ministry of Justice, 2011b), in practice this is not widespread. The greater prevalence of physical education programmes targeting substance misuse within local and high-security prisons is likely to be a reflection of the high level of substance misuse problems presenting within these populations. However, considering the elevated level of substance misuse problems among female prisoners and the ongoing call for tailored approaches to address women prisoners' needs, it is surprising that only a quarter of the female establishments considered appeared to offer PE-based substance misuse programmes. It may be the case that even if provision was made available, maintaining prisoner engagement and motivation to complete such programmes would be difficult, with high levels of attrition. Furthermore, the use of sport and physical activity to address substance misuse in prison is further confounded by the removal of the mandatory requirement to provide the minimum level intervention outlined in the *Tackling Drugs through Sport* from the latest Physical Education Instruction (Ministry of Justice, 2011b).

Despite the findings presenting a pessimistic picture of the way in which physical activity has been utilised in health promotion, innovative examples of how sport can be used to tackle substance misuse do exist. For example, the drug-free wing at HMP Bristol draws on partnerships between the substance misuse team, the gym, and community partners in order to incorporate within their wider multimodal Health through Sports programme as a means of diverting prisoners' focus away from substance use and towards the promotion of health and self-esteem. The programme has reported positive outcomes including better overall health, higher participation in physical activity and consistent negative drug urine tests among prisoners engaging in the sports-based element. Additionally, an increase in people with a history of substance misuse gaining qualifications was identified following participation in the programme, and with the support of prison gym staff participants had completed national vocational qualifications and secured work placements in local gyms (NHS National Treatment Agency for Substance Misuse, 2011). Previous research has identified that many prisoners, particularly young men, are more likely to participate in sport in prison as it is one of the few times when they are drug free (Condon et al., 2008) and such examples demonstrate the added value that physical activity can confer when integrated into holistic multimodal substance misuse interventions in prison.

Accumulated Inspectorate material and policy literature indicates that the degree to which health promotion is incorporated into PE programmes varies significantly across establishments, with some PE departments making a greater impact in health promotion than others. Initiatives promoting healthy living clearly have the potential to be integrated into PE delivery plans to ensure that the healthy prisons agenda is translated into practice within PE departments. For example, young prisoners have already been identified as being particularly resistant to healthy eating (HM Prison Service, 2004), and physical education departments are evidently ideally situated to encourage and educate for better eating habits and work in partnership with those involved in wider health promotion remits. Moreover, introduction to physical activities through health promotion incentives and exercise on referral may also encourage prisoners to attend mainstream sporting activities with greater regularity.

In accordance with British and international research (Condon et al., 2008; Hagan, 1989; Herbert et al., 2012) it seems that, although prisons in England and Wales are favourably placed to address health inequalities, such opportunities are not necessarily being fully exploited in the context of physical education and sport. Despite empirical evidence linking participation in sport to improved physical and psychological well-being in prison and community samples, and in spite of the promotion within policy of sport as a means of achieving health objectives in prisons, there is limited evidence of such responses being implemented, and practice across the secure estate remains variable. Such variation may be partially attributed to the discretion that governors can exercise in allocating resources and prioritising different aspects of the regime within their establishment, and likewise the effectiveness of integrating health promotion in physical activities and the gym will be dependent on the development and maintenance of good internal relationships between departments.

Despite uncovering disparity in provision, innovative examples of how physical education can effectively be integrated as part of multimodal initiatives addressing the physical, mental health and substance misuse needs of specific prison populations do exist. Successful sports-based health promotion interventions in prison typically embed tailored sports provision within a wider multimodal programme of learning and specialist psycho-social and medical intervention and draw upon internal and external partnerships in promoting opportunities for ongoing sporting participation. Physical activity is by no means a panacea which can resolve the disproportionate health inequalities evident within the prison population, and care must be taken to avoid the potential negative impact of sport. However it does offer an effective mechanism by which to involve and empower those who may prove to be particularly hard to engage with or motivate in health promotion.

Although this discussion has focussed specifically on the benefits of sport and physical activity in health promotion, that doesn't mean there aren't necessarily potential drawbacks – for example, since 2004 the Prison and Probation Ombudsman (2011) has investigated at least 20 deaths occurring during or shortly following exercise sessions in custody. But aside from the associated risks of injury and even death, and the potentially detrimental effects for those with low self-esteem or predisposed to anxiety (see Chapter 12 for further discussion of the potential drawbacks of promoting sport and physical activity in prison settings), there are clearly more positive potential outcomes as a result of promoting sport and physical activity, particularly if thorough health screening, monitoring and effective procedures are in place as a matter of routine.

In conclusion though, there certainly appears to be a strong case for sport and physical activity to be recognised as an effective way of promoting mental as well as physical health in prisons, even for those with the most complex physical and psychological problems. In extending the focus of physical activity to health promotion more globally in the context of attempts to reduce the cost of delivering prison healthcare (for example, see Schaenman, Davies, Jordan, & Chakraborty, 2013 for a discussion in a North American context where up to 30% of 'corrections costs' go to prisoner health care) sport and physical activity may increasingly be seen as worthy of further utilisation as a way of reducing costs without jeopardising service quality.

11 Promoting order and control, adaptation and citizenship in prison through sport

There are three things you need to get right in a prison: the food, the visits and the gym. Mess up any of those and you're asking for trouble. (Senior Manager)

The gym is the hub of prison life. (Staff, YOI)

Without gym in jail I would not survive. (Prisoner, Local)

There is no denying that physical activity, the gym, and members of gym staff remain central, even critical, to every prison, and more influential than might be assumed when first considering the organisation and formation of a prison environment. The physical, social and psychological effects of sport and physical activity which have been outlined in preceding chapters inevitably have a wider impact on the broader prison environment in subtle as well as obvious ways that reach beyond the specific focus of the gym. Although prison staff interviewees have recognised the potential role of sport in contributing to a reducing reoffending agenda, the positive impact of sport throughout the prison and most specifically its use as a tool in promoting compliance appears to be especially valued by staff, thus echoing early rationales for the use of physical exercise in prison as a way of *managing* prisoners:

Not only does sport occupy prisoner time, it helps promote good order and discipline within the establishment. (Staff, Local)

Sport certainly helps to maintain a controlled environment. (Staff, IRC)

When it is a balanced PE programme based on regular analysis of the prisoner population it can be a key lever of our order and control arrangements. Prisoners, on the whole, want to engage in PE activities which are often a useful diversionary activity. (Senior Manager)

Drawing heavily on a 'pressure cooker' rhetoric of prison, staff and prisoners alike would regularly refer in their interviews to the role of sport and physical activity as a way of channelling aggression or frustration and thus maintaining order and control within the prison:

> PE keeps a lid on the prison, it gives people somewhere to channel their aggression. The gym can handle large numbers of testosterone-charged guys who would otherwise be causing problems on the wings. (Staff, Local)

> Sport gives us a purpose, a goal and some determination to channel aggression and frustration rather than going out attacking people. (Prisoner, Category B)

> It helps you release frustration. We are locked up a lot and it hits you the hardest when there are extra lock ups, it gets you down. I'd go off my trolley if I didn't have the gym. (Prisoner, YOI)

> PE in essence stops people jumping off roofs and helps promote security and control in the prison. (Staff, High Security)

These observations also serve as a reminder of lessons drawn from previous investigations into prison disturbances, where instances of mass violence have been partially attributed to a lack of purposeful activity within the daily regime (Home Office, 1991). But as well as being recognised as fulfilling an important function in terms of proving a meaningful way to pass time, another recognised way in which sport contributes to the social control of a prison is by providing an incentive for positive behaviour, as reported widely in staff and prisoner interviews, and illustrated by this frank testimony:

> The gym is good for control. If I get in a fight I'm banned from here and the last thing I'm going to do is jeopardise my gym time. (Prisoner, Local)

Sport, adaptation and coping with prison

> Sport is a massive part of prison, if it wasn't here I don't know what I would do with myself. The gym was a real coping mechanism for me when I came to prison. (Prisoner, Category C)

As Harvey (2007) has previously stated, the transition to prison from the outside world is one characterised by a preoccupation with safety, uncertainty, deprivation of freedom and control and feelings of separation and loss. The concepts of adaptation and coping are relatively well explored in a sociological context (Sykes' 1958 explanation of how prisoners adapt to life in prison as a process of reducing 'the pains of imprisonment' has paved the way for subsequent analyses of 'prisonisation' – see Sim, 2008; Thomas, 1977) but until now the emerging literature on sport, physical activity and leisure as an adaptive strategy has not been applied specifically to prison settings. However, in prisoner interviews, physical activity was frequently cited as being critical to coping:

> Everyone suffers from stress here, it helps you get rid of that and cope with it. Whatever problem I've got I go to the gym and work out. It really works for me. (Prisoner, Female)

Coping was also regularly referred to in discussions about the frequency of visits to the gym and widespread concerns that staffing and regime changes might lead to less access to physical activity:

> The more you take away gym the more people will start self-harming and there will be more suicides. (Prisoner, Local)

A body of non-criminological research has developed which explores the role of sport and leisure in the prevention of – or 'inoculation' against – stress, and in coping with existing stress (see Caldwell, 2005; Patterson and Coleman, 1996). For example, participation in social and time-out leisure activities is recognised as contributing significantly to improving mental health, with leisure coping strategies also found to contribute significantly (Kelly, 2011). According to Iwasaki and Mannell (2000), leisure coping beliefs are maintained through socialisation processes and actual participation in leisure activities, constituting largely stable psychological dispositions which are theorised to act as a buffer or moderator between the negative effects of stress on health and well-being, and are thought to be of benefit predominantly when stress levels are high. In turn, leisure coping strategies refer to situation-grounded behaviours or cognitions generated through actual participation in leisure activities in order to help cope with stress. Although such research has not been applied to prison settings to date, there is clearly scope for it to do so. For example, Iwasaki and Mannell's (2000) concepts of leisure coping beliefs and strategies (and their associated measurement tools) may be especially pertinent in considering the role of sport as an adaptive strategy in prison and in identifying and developing the different activities which may be used as strategies to cope with stress and to promote well-being.

Related to the recognition by staff that sport serves a useful purpose in maintaining order throughout a prison, physical activity was also reported by prisoners to play an important role in breaking up the monotony of prison regimes and in alleviating boredom, with its perceived function ranging from one of simple distraction ('It means you're not thinking about being in prison all the time,' Prisoner, Category B) to occupation ('It keeps you out of trouble,' Prisoner, Local) and time allocation ('It breaks up your day and it's something to look forward to,' Prisoner, Category B). Considering the reported links between boredom, loneliness, depression, distractability and offending (see for example, Coalter, Allison & Taylor, 2000; Newberry & Duncan, 2001) activities that can provide a healthy and prosocial form of interaction or activity are especially important in prison settings. Indeed in interviews, prisoners and staff referred to instances where individuals who had initially chosen to participate in sport simply as an alternative to the boredom of incarceration were then able to benefit from a range of unexpected positive consequences.

As has already been established, sport and physical activities are recognised as playing an important role in improving physical and psychological well-being, but they can also contribute to fewer instances of violence and conflict (Martos-Garcia et al., 2009a; Murtaza & Uddin, 2011; Wagner et al., 1999). Indeed, Johnsen (2001) and Sabo (2001) suggest that for prisoners, the practice of sport represents a particular way to express masculinity while also offering a form of temporary virtual escape from the prison regime itself.

The contribution of sport in efforts to reduce prison violence

Violence is typically seen as a normal part of the prison routine, sustained and legitimated by wider cultures, not just of masculinity, but of retribution and fear. Age is one of the strongest correlates of prison misconduct and the highest incidences of violence are reported in Young Offender Institutions,[1] but levels of prisoner on prisoner violence can also be partially explained by factors such as staff to inmate ratios and the wider prison regime. As Gaes and McGuire (1985) state, crowding is the most influential variable on assault rates which may in part explain the higher levels of misconduct amongst younger inmates (Franklin, Franklin & Pratt, 2006). However, it is an interactionist approach to prison violence (Bottoms, 1999) – the need to consider the dynamic interaction between prisoners, prison staff, and the social and physical context in which they are placed – which best recognises the various processes at play in escalations of prison violence. Indeed, O'Donnell and Edgar's (1998) exploration of the functions and meanings of violence in prison concludes that there are complex and varied causes and functions of assaults, including conflict management, a desire to enhance one's status, retaliation, material gain and boredom. But it is the ever-present threat of violence that Edgar, O'Donnell and Martin (2012) suggest leads to a social order where the perception of a need to use force in order to protect oneself can rapidly develop, in the tense and highly stressful environment of a prison, into further violence.

Prisoners who have a history of conflict with staff and/or other prisoners are disproportionately disruptive within the prison community, both in terms of cost and resourcing and also in terms of the significant disruption to the wider regime that each incident causes. For instance, a serious disturbance will lead to a 'lockdown' where all meaningful and recreational activity is cancelled to free up staff. National Offender Management Service (2012a) acknowledges that reducing violence and self-harm can create safer environments in which prisoners can engage more effectively but despite the widespread implementation of violence reduction initiatives, effective and long-lasting ways of preventing violence are yet to be identified and violent episodes remain a significant concern within all establishments.

Theories concerning the link between aggression and sport remain contentious: despite strong evidence of sport as a way of reducing violence, encouraging individuals to manage their emotions and resolve conflict (see Chapter 8 on evaluation) and improving relations not just among prisoners but also between prisoners and staff (Murtaza & Uddin, 2011; Wagner et al., 1999), there has also been much discussion about the perpetuation and perceived legitimacy of violence within organised sport (see Conroy, Silva, Newcomer, Walker & Johnson, 2001; Russell, 2008). Overall though, the most robust discourse is that which sees sport as a way in which to control or manage violence, or as a form of catharsis whereby sport provides a legitimate release for aggressive instincts (Bushman, Baumeister & Stack, 1999). Indeed, this theme was especially prominent in interviews with staff who saw sport as a way of managing emotions in prison – not just in the short term, but also longer term in learning to regulate emotions more effectively:

> Using the gym in prison channels their aggression and frustrations into something positive. (Gym Staff, Local)

> It gives them something to focus their mind on and release their day to day stress that prison can build on them. (Gym Staff, Category C)

> I feel it is excellent and motivates, whatever the sport, and helps challenge aggression and self-discipline, with very little risk or problems. (Gym Staff, Open)

> A high percentage of individuals are introduced to sport and find it helps to control temper, as well as reliance on drugs and alcohol. (Gym Staff, YOI)

Promoting social cohesion through sport

Politicians, social commentators and academics have long proclaimed the social benefits of sport: leadership, teamwork and self-sacrifice are words and concepts which are commonly used in association with sporting endeavour (Collins, 2009) and sport is recognised as an important way of promoting social cohesion and interaction. Given the isolating aspect of incarceration it is not therefore surprising that sport can be seen as having an especially important role to play in promoting relational interaction and the development of social skills in prison settings. Reflecting this, and in line with Woodward's (2012) claim that it is the source of some of the most powerful personal identifications and individual and collective pleasures, staff regularly referred to sport as a way of bringing together disparate groups of prisoners:

> It improves social skills and breaks down barriers within rival gangs. (Staff, YOI)

> It brings a togetherness amongst offenders. (Staff, Category C)

However, recognising that sport has a power to evoke violence as well as reduce it, staff emphasised the need for sports activities to be carefully managed in order for them to lead to positive rather than negative outcomes, thus highlighting the need for staff with expertise in reducing conflict and managing violent episodes:

> Team sports can challenge individuals, although anger control can be an issue. (Staff, Category C)

> Managing prisoners in an enclosed and innately competitive arena will always present some problems but we as a department pride ourselves on the general air of respect that is engendered by those using the facilities and enjoying activities.
> We have robust procedures for dealing with breaches but mostly we are able to communicate with our learners on a level that engenders courtesy and respect.
> We operate on a 'college' like ethos and encourage self-discipline and responsibility. (Staff, Category C)

The role of sport in peer support initiatives

Within every prison, 'orderly' positions are available where prisoners work in a range of roles, including in the kitchens, cleaning, maintaining the grounds and providing support for staff where needed. One of the most popular of these positions is that of gym orderly, where prisoners assist PE staff in the running of the prison gym and the organisation of physical activities. The national survey of prison gym managers established that gyms had between one and 23 orderlies at the time of response, with an average of seven in each prison. Gym orderlies also represented over a quarter of the prisoner interviewees, enabling the research to benefit from the insights of prisoners who were not only able to reflect on their own use of sport and physical activity, but also their observations of the importance and use of sport and the gym for their fellow prisoners ('I've seen how sport in prison lets others change and grow,' Prisoner, Local). Of particular interest, gym orderlies were able to explain and discuss the ways in which peer support principles can be implemented in prison sport, a widely supported initiative:

> A key strength is the involvement of prisoners in PE delivery, i.e. qualified and suitably motivated peer supporters. (Senior Manager)

As well as offering a valuable means of developing work experience for those seeking a career in the sport and leisure industry, gym orderly roles appeared to be of particular value to those with long sentences, as the following quote from a prisoner serving a life sentence demonstrates:

> Helping other people has helped me with my sentence. I'm now involved in personal training for inmates and staff. Not a lot of people help each other in prison but this is different. (Prisoner, Category B)

In order to contextualise some of these prisoner and staff observations, I will first introduce the concept of and evidence base for peer support (also regularly referred to as peer mentoring) in prison.

Introducing peer mentoring and support in prison

The Mentoring and Befriending Foundation (2011) defines mentoring as 'a one-to-one, nonjudgmental relationship in which an individual voluntarily gives time to support and encourage another'. Although mentoring has been employed in various settings and is of widespread academic interest, disagreement remains as to the ideal age difference between mentor and mentee, the duration of mentoring and degree of emotional intimacy involved in the relationship (Eby, Rhodes & Allen, 2010). There does, however, tend to be a general consensus on the core elements of mentoring – broadly that the mentor is someone who possesses greater experience/wisdom than the mentee, that the mentor offers guidance or instruction that is intended to facilitate the growth and development of the mentee, and that the mentor and mentee experience an emotional bond, chiefly characterised by trust (Dubois & Karcher, 2005). Although peer-support initiatives typically share the same features as other forms of mentoring, they also require that the individuals offering and receiving the support have a common characteristic, background or experience (Boyce, Hunter & Hough, 2009; Finnegan, Whitehurst & Deaton, 2010). The terms *peer support* and *peer mentoring* are often used interchangeably with other similar constructs such as peer counselling, peer helping and peer tutoring, although peer mentoring tends to be less prescriptive, remedial or task focused (Karcher, 2005).

Very little research has focused specifically on the effectiveness of peer support initiatives (peer-led schemes tend to be included in meta-analyses with traditional mentoring programmes) but the few existing studies have tended to look at its effectiveness as an educational, career or health promotion tool. One study which examined peer mentoring in prison settings, a review by Wright et al. (2011), confirmed that peer mentoring can be an effective way of educating prisoners about drugs and safe injecting practice. Boyce et al. (2009) conducted an independent evaluation of the St Giles Trust Peer Advice Project, a scheme training prisoners to become peer advisors, who are able to gain a recognised National Vocational Qualification (in Advice and Guidance) whilst delivering a housing and advice service to fellow inmates. With a secondary aim of advancing the skills and employability of participating prisoners, the project also offers opportunities for related employment experience to those involved in the scheme upon release. The evaluation concluded that as well as being effective in helping ex-prisoners into paid employment, the rewards of being an advisor were valued by those involved, particularly in terms of increased confidence and self-efficacy. In turn, the recipients of the advice service considered the peer delivery model an advantage due to an assumption that the advisors involved in the scheme could empathise with the specific problems they were facing.

One of the most successful and widespread forms of prison-based peer support is the Listener Scheme, a project run by the Samaritans which aims to reduce incidences of suicide and self-harm by training prisoners to provide a confidential listening service to fellow inmates. Magee and Foster's (2011) interviews with trained listeners and recipients of the scheme found that as well as recipients speaking highly of the service they received, peer supporters reported enjoying their role, with the main motivation for taking part being the desire to support their fellow prisoners (although they also acknowledged the nonaltruistic benefits, such as getting a cell to themselves). Despite recognising the emotional burden of taking part in such an initiative, being a trained Listener was found to contribute to prisoners' personal growth, raising self-esteem, increasing empathy, and improving communication skills, and Jaffe's (2012) evaluation has confirmed that listeners also felt valued by prison staff who recognised the contribution they were making to the prison community. Finally, in responding to the identified problem of significant numbers of prisoners having severe literacy support needs, Toe by Toe is a peer mentoring project run by the Shannon Trust which aims to train prisoners who can read to teach those who are unable to do so. Those involved in the scheme as peer supporters as well as learners reported feeling more positive about their own futures, with improved communication skills and self-confidence (CfBT, 2005), and evaluation of the scheme for young offenders has established that it improves a learner's reading age by almost one year for each month of participation (O'Hagan, 2011).

Using sport to promote active citizenship in prison

Active citizenship is defined as when prisoners 'exercise responsibility by making positive contributions to prison life or the wider community' (Edgar, Jacobson & Biggar, 2011, p. 5). Aside from democratic involvement in prison life (typically involving participation in prison councils), the majority of active citizenship programmes currently running in prisons are concerned with community work schemes and peer support programmes. Arguably, sport can have a prominent role in both these types of citizenship, in participating in unpaid work placements in community sports settings, but also in engaging in sports-led peer support initiatives. It is evident that such programmes offer offenders an opportunity to make a valid and valued contribution to their prison communities and to do something positive and meaningful with their time. The gym orderly role in particular may offer prisoners the opportunity to develop peer support practices, with the following quote illustrating the diversity of their involvement in encouraging fellow prisoners to participate in physical activity:

> I'm taking someone with a heart condition through a cardiovascular programme. I devise the programme and write it up and then help others go through the programme. It's nice to help people out, like those with weight problems. This morning I was supporting someone who self-harms to do work on the cross trainer because they can't do weights from cutting their arms. I also help people with literacy problems talking them through it and helping them fill in forms. (Prisoner, Category B)

Prisoners in orderly roles also referred to the numerous advantages of holding such a challenging and varied position, not just in the development and demonstration of relevant capabilities ('You get skills and qualifications. Through sport here I did the peer mentoring qualification,' Juvenile Prisoner) but in terms of the intrinsic rewards of having something positive to concentrate on ('Being an orderly has given me a focus, something I want to carry on with, something I can achieve,' Female Prisoner), the satisfaction of being entrusted with a position of responsibility ('It's a position of trust, it gives me confidence,' Female Prisoner) and the resulting confidence and self-esteem ('It feels good people coming to you asking for advice, it gives you confidence,' Prisoner, Local).

Most gym orderlies who were interviewed had gained or were in the process of gaining industry-recognised qualifications, and many spoke with enthusiasm about how their experiences in the gym had inspired them to seek further opportunities after release, either in voluntary roles, paid employment or in the case of this interviewee, both:

> This has given me the confidence and impetus to make changes in my own life, which in turn, I hope will allow me to find work upon release. I have already gained several qualifications which will be useful in my endeavours to find work in the voluntary sector initially and eventually into a sustainable career. (Prisoner, Category C)

Innovative practice case study: Civic action in and from the prison gym

Apart from the opportunities offered in every prison to support fellow prisoners in a gym orderly role, and the less common instances of community voluntary placements for those who are successful in applications for RoTL, prison gyms represent what for some may be surprisingly high levels of civic activity. The research revealed a broad range of activities related to the hosting of visiting community groups, with a number of different prisons accommodating and engaging with local groups including those representing children, disabled adults, the elderly (for example in one establishment prisoners organised and participated in a regular bowls tournament with a local group), and those with learning difficulties. Prisoners were encouraged to prepare and deliver specialist sessions and clearly valued the opportunity to interact with members of the public and to 'give back' something to the local community. Staff reported that such initiatives led to more positive attitudes from members of the public and noticeable improvements to the communication skills and confidence of those prisoners involved.

Although opportunities for direct involvement with community groups may not be possible for all prisoners, the research identified examples of civic engagement in the form of regular fundraising activities organised across the prison estate, including in high-security establishments. Several prisons were found to hold regular fundraising events for local and national charities, organising sponsored runs (for example where half marathon distances were calculated around the prison grounds), football tournaments and other sporting challenges, raising sponsorship from members of staff, prisoners and their families. The Soccer Schools organised by the gym at HMP and YOI Portland involved gym staff taking skilled and qualified prisoners who were eligible for RoTL into the local community during school holidays in order to deliver daily football coaching sessions for children between the ages of 5 and 14 years. Although parents were initially reluctant, the initiative proved very popular and as well as promoting engagement with the local community and enabling prisoners to gain experience in preparing and delivering coaching sessions; funds raised through donations from parents were donated to local charities.

Finally, one aspect of the coalition government's Big Society agenda was the implementation of the National Citizen Service (www.ncsyes.co.uk), a voluntary programme for 16 and 17 year-olds in England which commences with a two-week residential programme. Extending the initiative to those in custody, gym staff at Ashfield YOI have arranged for RoTL-eligible juvenile prisoners to take part in the National Citizen Service.

Principles of best practice

Providing direct support for and contact with the community through the hosting of regular events at the prison gym, and through external delivery, with prisoners working alongside staff to organise and deliver activities.

Organising prison-wide fundraising activities through sponsored sporting challenges.

Enabling young prisoners to take part in national citizenship initiatives.

Note

1   And yet these are still considered underestimates, with studies drawing on self-report data indicating that actual figures of assaults and fights may be up to three times higher than those given by official data (Cooley, 1993; Dyson, Power & Wozniak, 1997).

12 Considering the risks and challenges associated with sport and physical activity in prison

Despite the incontrovertible benefits associated with sport and physical education in prisons, it would be at best naïve and at worst dangerous to assume that such activities will inevitably confer only positive outcomes or that physical activity can be utilised as the entirely positive activity which an uncritical review of the research literature might assume. With any sports-based intervention, but especially prison-based ones, just as an overall effect or impact can result from a whole range of factors, negative as well as positive outcomes can come about as a result of participation. Some of these will be explored here, starting with the most complex and controversial – the idea that promoting some activities may actually contribute to an increase in offending.

The relationship between sporting participation and offending

Whilst there is a rationale and plenty of evidence that sport within prison can promote desistance from crime (by, for example, improving skills, instilling values, increasing employability, promoting positive peer networks and providing a more constructive use of leisure time), empirical evidence concerning the relationship between sporting involvement and subsequent criminality does not wholeheartedly support the notion that sport alone is a protective factor from later offending (Begg et al., 1996; Crosnoe, 2002; Eitle, Turner & Eitle, 2002). In community settings, where the bulk of such research has taken place, the relationship between involvement in sport and subsequent offending behaviour has been found to be especially complex and indirect. For example, Hartmann and Massogolia's (2007) longitudinal analysis of 750 individuals from high school through to 30 years of age revealed that high-intensity sports participation during school years decreased self-reported criminality in terms of shoplifting but increased the likelihood of drink driving at age 30, despite being unrelated to composite indices of adult deviance. Furthermore while some studies have concluded that there are few, if any, gender distinctions in the relationship between sport participation and delinquency (Miller et al., 2007), others have indicated that sport can have a stronger negative effect on girls' delinquency (Begg et al., 1996) or indeed a minimal effect (Gardner, Roth & Brooks-Gunn, 2009; Melnick, Vanfossen & Sabo, 1988). Such inconsistent results may reflect methodological discrepancies in the measurement of physical activity and delinquency, but they also serve to demonstrate the complexity of the relationship between sport and criminality and highlight the need for a more sophisticated approach to the use and evaluation of sport within prisons in order to promote positive outcomes.

When exploring the unintended consequences of different types of sport, it is hardly surprising that different sporting activities in diverse contexts will inevitably have differing effects on delinquency which may not always be positive (see Conroy et al., 2001; Hartmann & Massoglia, 2007; Hughes & Coakley, 1991; Kavussanu & Ntoumanis, 2003; Kleiber & Roberts, 1981; Kohn, 1986; Rutten et al., 2007; Shields & Bredemeier, 1995; Vallerand, Deshaies & Cuerrier, 1997). For example, Begg et al.'s (1996) longitudinal study showed that high involvement in individual sports (but not in team sports) was actually associated with increased delinquency, and others have found associations between participation in contact sports and an increased perceived legitimacy of aggressive behaviour (Conroy et al., 2001) and lower levels of moral functioning (Kavussanu & Ntoumanis, 2003) in comparison with noncontact sports. Indeed, despite research suggesting that sport can have a cathartic effect in reducing aggressive behaviours in prison (Wagner et al., 1999) and in promoting social control (Johnsen, 2001; Murtaza & Uddin, 2011), interviews with prisoners participating in team sports in prison also reveal occasional instances where levels of aggression might be elevated.

Psychological literature has established that the 'rules' that individuals use to determine whether or not violence is an acceptable response to a given situation can be used to explain and predict instances of violence. Walker (2005) suggests that violence can be broadly explained by two factors: 'machismo' (for example the justification of violence in response to a threat or attack as a demonstration of strength and masculinity or as a way of avoiding being considered weak or fearful) and 'acceptance of violence' (an explicit enjoyment or tolerance of violence). These typologies have successfully been used to predict violence among general populations as well as mentally disordered offenders and young offenders (see Walker & Gudjonsson, 2006; Warnock-Parkes, Gudjonsson & Walker, 2008; Young, Misch, Collins & Gudjonsson, 2011). What appears to be of most significance when considering violence in prison sport is the way in which members of delivery staff manage and respond to aggressive outbursts and are able to use sport as a way of challenging (rather than reinforcing) justifications of violence. However, although lessons learnt on the pitch have been shown to be especially effective in reducing violence and improving attitudes towards aggression more specifically and offending more generally (see Chapter 8) there are inevitably occasions when violence escalates within prisons, and the gym or sports pitch is no exception. As one interviewee testified, 'People with anger problems sometimes don't know how to manage it and that can result in violence' (Prisoner, Local).

Of course, successfully averting violence can be largely down to how activities are set up, the skills of staff and the philosophical emphasis with which they are delivered. Supporting this view, Trulson (1986) found that young offenders who regularly participated in a form of traditional Tae Kwan Do which emphasises the psychological and philosophical elements of the sport showed reduced tendencies towards delinquency and aggressiveness. On the other hand, those who participated in a modern version of the martial art focusing only on the physical elements actually showed *increased* tendencies towards delinquency and aggressiveness. It seems clear that the context and process of programmes may well be more important than the actual sporting activity itself (Coalter, 1996). Indeed, competitive and performance-orientated social contexts have been linked to increased antisocial behaviour (Anderson & Morrow, 1995; Kohn, 1986; Stephens & Bredemeier, 1996) and decreased prosocial behaviours (Kleiber & Roberts, 1981), suggesting that structuring prison-based activities so as to decrease competitive emphasis and focus instead on alternative goals, such as skills development, may prove most effective. However, to date there is scant evaluative evidence to support the identification of common processes within prison-based sport which are effective, and further evaluations of diverse programmes across populations are required.

Are we at risk of eroding ethical norms through sport?

Despite the rhetoric of sport for moral good (Jones & McNamee, 2003), commentators have also presented a counterargument that the competitive nature of sport can in fact create a context for moral release, suspension of responsibility, and a level of self-interest which could serve to promote antisocial behaviour (Francis, 2012; Shields & Bredemeier, 1995). Formalising this notion, Hughes and Coakley (1991) propose an over commitment to the 'sport ethic', characterised by dedication, goal setting and perusal, defying adversity, and making sacrifices. Although emphasising essentially positive norms, this can also result in deviant behaviours – referred to as *positive deviance* – manifested in excessive drinking, substance misuse and other health risk behaviours. Importantly, Hughes and Coakley hypothesise that such positive deviance may be more likely among men who have low self-esteem, see sport as their exclusive identity and mobility route, are low-income minority athletes in revenue producing sports, and whose interpersonal relationships are primarily based on involvement or successes in sport. This is worth considering when looking to sport to engage marginalised individuals with minimal social networks, since it suggests that wholeheartedly endorsing the sport ethic may leave participants susceptible to alternative deviant behaviours if not managed effectively. Indeed, for some athletes it has been suggested that the extreme sense of belonging within sporting groups can lead to a lack of respect for people outside the immediate community, coupled with the naïve perception that they are above the law (Hartmann & Massoglia, 2007; Hughes & Coakley, 1991). Moreover, Miller et al. (2007) go so far as to suggest that adulation of successful sports celebrities can result in the perception that normal rules do not apply and that deviations will not be penalised, which of course has particular resonance when considering criminal justice implications.

According to Crabbe (2000) crime has increasingly become a prominent feature of sport, and there are no shortages of contemporary examples of elite sports people's skirmishes with the law, for example the England Rugby player Danny Care's drink driving charge (BBC News, 2012), cyclist Lance Amstrong's drug use (Gibson, 2013), and sprinter Dwain Chambers' suspension from competitive sports for the use of anabolic steroids (BBC Sport, 2004), serving to contradict the prevailing argument that sports participation among offenders offers the opportunity to develop positive role models both within custody and after release (Audit Commission, 1996; Carmichael, 2008; Nichols, 1997). With these contrasting hypotheses in mind, in-depth explorations of the how and why of prison sports projects become especially crucial in disentangling the positive and negative effects, either actual or potential, of prison-based sporting initiatives.

Physical risks, public perceptions and the risk of cultivating criminality

In addition to the social and psychological impacts, and in spite of the well documented health benefits of prison-based sport (Buckaloo et al., 2009; Elger, 2009; Nelson et al., 2006) physical activity will inevitably increase the chance of incurring sporting injuries. Since 2004 the prison Ombudsman (the independent body responsible for investigating prisoner complaints and deaths in custody) has considered at least 20 deaths occurring during or shortly following exercise sessions in prisons (Prisons and Probation Ombudsman, 2011). The men who died varied in age and although most were known to have exercised regularly several had significant medical conditions or exercised infrequently. These incidents and the identified inadequate emergency response in some instances has led the Ombudsman to recommend the need for appropriate medical equipment (e.g. defibrillation machines) and training in its use, staff training in symptom recognition (particularly for circulatory conditions) and efficient emergency procedures within prison gyms and throughout prisons more widely. Positive examples of decreasing the risk of injuries have been identified in several establishments, for example specialist training for PE staff to work with people with cardiac problems, and targeted programmes for prisoners with health problems which would normally prevent participation.

In addition to the potential negative impact of sport on prisoner health (although as confirmed in Chapter 10, the physical and mental health benefits overwhelmingly outweigh the drawbacks) it could also be argued that providing opportunities for prisoners to improve their physical fitness could increase an individual's ability to carry out criminal acts. Although there is very little evidence of this, it is certainly worth exploring for there is no denying that sports may reinforce certain images of masculinity or femininity which it is not necessarily desirable to promote (Nichols, 2007). Whilst physical education can be effectively used as part of a structured regime and a way of managing prisoners, paradoxically it also potentially allows for the development of excessive body image and masculinity concerns. Motivations to participate in sport given by participants included a wish to enhance strength and promote muscle development, verified by Nelson et al. (2006) who reported on an intensive exercise programme with 120 inmates in a maximum security prison in the United States which led to increased energy, muscle tone, strength, and stamina. Prisoner motivations to engage in physical activity may not necessarily align with a prison's objective of participation in sport for social and educational purposes (Frey & Delaney, 1996; Johnsen, 2001) and gym staff interviews revealed some trepidation about exercise being used solely to increase body mass ('They'll have a session of weights and then off with their shirts, straight to the mirror'). Although there was evidence, particularly among some of the more traditional prison managers, of concerns that improving the fitness of prisoners might lead to increased levels of violence or that prison staff would be intimidated by an increased physical presence, little evidence of this happening was found. While recognising the concerns that others had about the risks of promoting exercise – particularly weight training – in prisons, gym staff were clear about the benefits prevailing over any drawbacks:

> Certain govs believe that weight training makes people bigger and stronger, but that is greatly outweighed by the health benefits, NHS savings, the impact on families and healthier lifestyles. (Prison Gym Staff)

The paradox between promoting health, well-being and resettlement whilst enabling prisoners to improve their physicality for potentially criminal endeavours may not represent much of an operational concern but it certainly presents a potential challenge in terms of public perceptions of prison sport. This is especially salient for the high-secure estate where offering very high risk and violent prisoners the opportunities for enjoyment through sport may publicly be deemed as inappropriate and unsavoury. Likewise, sports interventions with lower risk prisoners offering the opportunity to participate in activities in the community (for example placements at sports clubs or gyms, or the Duke of Edinburgh Award) can expose prisoners to stigma and hostility from members of the public. Furthermore, prison sport activities can be perceived by the public (and even staff) to be contravening the implied *principle of less eligibility*, a residue of the Poor Law Amendment Act of 1834 which proposed that prison should not raise an inmate's standard of living above that of the lowest paid worker in society.

Self-presentation, steroid use and exercise dependency

Physical activity is widely recognised to confer psychological benefits; however certain sporting activities can have detrimental effects on psychological well-being among some populations. For example, Hughes and Coakley (1991) hypothesise that the previously discussed positive deviance may be more likely among men who have low self-esteem and that there is a risk that competitive sporting environments can foster social comparison concerns in individuals already predisposed to high levels of such anxieties (Andrews & Andrews, 2003; Slater & Tiggemann, 2011). Research focusing on the relationship between anxiety and performance has demonstrated that competitive sport can indeed provoke anxiety which can either facilitate or inhibit performance. Performance anxiety can also cause cognitive intrusions (Jones, 1991; Swain & Jones, 1993) and can serve to impair working memory (Jones, 1995) which could be particularly detrimental among offenders who often already experience deficits in thinking skills (Ross & Fabiano, 1985). Additional negative effects of anxiety have been linked to low self-confidence, poor perceived support from team mates and coaches (Hardy & Jones, 1994) and low expectations around coping and goal attainment (Caver & Scheier, 1986). This suggests that involvement in competitive sports in particular can have a negative psychological impact upon those with low self-confidence/coping strategies and negative perceptions of peer and institutional support, thus leading to poor sporting performance and consequently reaffirming negative self-perceptions.

The risk of sport creating and replicating societal divisions

In spite of efforts to achieve equitable access, there is no doubt that participation in sport is influenced by a range of social and demographic factors such as class, ethnicity, and age (DCMS, 2002; Mahoney, 1997; Stoot, 2002) which can result in lower levels of participation among some groups and conversely excessive participation among others. For example, among a large longitudinal school sample of White and Black teenage males in the United States, lower cultural capital and academic achievement has been found to predict greater involvement in the popular sports of football and basketball, particularly for young Black males. In particular, social disadvantage prompted greater participation, which in turn had a negative impact on academic achievement (Eitle & Eitle, 2002). However, contrary to these findings, other research has suggested that no relationship exists between participation in sport and academic achievement among American high school students (Crosnoe, 2002).

Thinking specifically about offending populations, there is concern that conventional sports can replicate the institutional settings in mainstream society from which many offenders are already alienated (Andrew & Andrews, 2003) and consequently, some argue that sport has little potential value as an alternative to a delinquent subculture (Sugden & Yiannakis, 1982). Within custodial contexts in particular, sport may serve to maintain and promote inequality and division between groups of offenders, with the risk that those who have the greatest social capital and highest status will dominate activities and discourage others from participating. Responding to this, careful attention to the selection of prisoners and promotion of activities across prison populations is evidently important, as is a focus on the circumstances in which sport can best be delivered in light of the psychological and social processes underpinning both the institutional culture and the activities themselves.

In terms of the power of sport to create social inequalities and conflict, rather than reducing them, research in community contexts has found sporting activities to be a catalyst for bullying (Slater & Tiggemann, 2011), which is already recognised as being elevated in custodial contexts where resources are limited and strivings for dominance and power are high (Ireland, 1999). If bullying is allowed to flourish in prisons it can cause numerous difficulties and disruptions, not only to those directly involved but also to the wider regime in undermining safety and security (for example, concerns that bullying can lead to the development of a criminal subculture which risks subverting prison rules have been raised by HM Prison Service, 1993). Sport in prison can of course introduce new power dynamics between prisoners, and according to Johnsen (2001) there is a prevalent fear of failure among prisoners which may prevent participation, particularly among those with lower physical ability.

In response to these concerns, research with young offenders in the community has demonstrated that principles of good practice include: well-trained enthusiastic staff; voluntary participation; reduced competition/minimal rules; challenging activities; leadership and empowerment opportunities; multi-agency working; and the application of sporting activities to other areas of life (Carmichael, 2008; Crompton & Witt, 1997; Gatz, Messner, & Ball-Rokeach, 2002; Morris et al., 2003; Nichols & Taylor, 1996; Taylor et al., 1999). These practices obviously translate into prison environments but further research is evidently required within custodial contexts to establish where the same principles can be applied to reduce the potentially negative impact of sport upon those who are most vulnerable. There is already good evidence of appropriate steps being taken within some prison establishments to ensure that such prisoners still have the opportunity to participate in and gain from physical activity whilst in custody, for example by curtailing the risk of bullying and intimidation by providing separate sessions for vulnerable prisoners. For example HMP Leeds offers low impact activity sessions focusing on stretching and gentle ball exercises for vulnerable prisoners, which has proved highly popular:

> I used to go in the week but I stopped going as I found all the young guys intimidating. It's more supervised with our class, lots of older people do want to go but you don't because the youngsters are all pumping iron and you can't move round. We do lots of stretches at the beginning and I can move more now, touch my toes and everything. It's good just taking part in anything, I look forward to it – I'd go three times a week if there were more of our sessions. (Prisoner, Category B)

Despite evidence of good practice, specialist sessions may focus on those on vulnerable prisoner wings (typically sex offenders), but will not necessarily cater for the high numbers of prisoners who aren't institutionally defined as vulnerable but who still suffer from psychological problems which could render them at heightened risk of the adverse effects of sport. For example, although primary exercise dependency disorders are extremely rare, secondary exercise dependence more commonly occurs alongside eating and image disorders such as body dysmorphia (Matrie, 2002), with time spent on aesthetic physical activity having been related to disordered eating in men as well as women (Slater & Tiggemann,

2011). Indeed, interviews with male and female gym users in custody indicated that excessive exercising could be a concern:

> Over-exercising can be a problem but the officers watch out for this. Some girls come in skin and bone and I don't know how they have the energy. (Prisoner, Female)

For some, exercise served as a new addiction in custody, one that could replace existing addictions to substances:

> You can get obsessed, if you are trying really hard and not seeing the result you want in the mirror. You can give up one drug, and get addicted to another. (Male, Local)

Longitudinal research in the community has suggested that athletic involvement can create a risk of future substance misuse (Crosnoe, 2002) and interestingly some prisoners were evidently concerned that a lack of continuity in opportunities to continue exercising to the same degree once released might result in a return to substance misuse:

> When you get out you don't have the gym anymore and you just pick up drugs again. (Prisoner, Local)

The relationship between sport and drug use is certainly complex in both community and prison settings. Considering that self-reported eating disorders appear to be more prevalent among female prisoners compared to the general population (O'Brien, Mortimer, Singleton & Meltzer, 2001), and that among males it has been suggested that poor body image, body dysmorphia and low self-esteem can also contribute to anabolic steroid use (Wroblewska, 1997) careful consideration needs to be given to the design of sports-based interventions for vulnerable prisoners and those with a history, or risk of drug use.

The prevalence of steroids in prison

To date no systematic association has been made between participation in sport in prison and steroid use, but it is certainly possible that emphasising sport among vulnerable populations with high body consciousness and low self-esteem could increase risk of the misuse of performance enhancing substances such as anabolic steroids, where primary motivations are typically to improve physical appearance or gain muscular strength (Klotz, Petersson, Hoffman & Thiblin, 2010). The use of anabolic steroids is known to have negative health implications in terms of increased risk of heart disease, liver toxicity and tumours, infertility and cosmetic changes such as hair loss, as well as indirect risks such as the transmission of blood-borne viruses through unsafe injection practices (Yesalis, 2000). There is also some evidence of negative psychological and behavioural effects of steroid use, such as mania and aggression in some individuals (Haug, Morland, Olaisen & Myhre, 2004), which raises particular concerns in relation to violent offenders. Importantly, research has demonstrated that steroid use is up to 10 times higher in prison populations compared to the general population, with the highest levels of use being among younger prisoners, for whom the negative effects of steroids are also considered to be most pervasive. Indeed, although rates of steroid use have remained constant in the general population (Home Office, 2012) a number of recent Independent Monitoring and Inspectorate reports have identified steroid use as a growing concern in British prisons (HM Chief Inspector of Prisons, 2011; Independent Monitoring Board, 2010, 2011) and interviews with gym users suggest that steroids are easily and comparatively cheaply available within custody:

> I've been offered steroids, tablets, they are easy to get, but I've never wanted to take them. For small guys who want to get big, they might take steroids. (Prisoner, Category B)

> It does happen [people taking steroids]. I've been offered them, they go for like two or three pounds, cheap. (Prisoner, Local)

Steroid use in prisons is not only problematic in terms of health implications for prisoners, but also presents a threat in terms of security whereby, as is the case with all contraband, illicit supply can encourage debt accumulation and violence. Testing for steroid use as part of drug testing procedures is more costly than for other drugs and is therefore rarely done routinely, resulting in the perception that risk of being caught is low. It is obviously important that steroid awareness training, incorporating ways to recognise misuse and methods of production, continues to be offered to prison staff within gym departments and beyond. There is also a clear need for educational initiatives for prisoners (and staff) concerning the side effects of steroid use and sources of support, with the prison gym being the obvious place to deliver such programmes. Evidence of good practice identified in a small number of establishments includes the implementation of specific steroid policies restricting those suspected of misusing steroids from weight training and the development of innovative programmes linking steroid misusing prisoners to tailored educational sessions and drug support services.

Security concerns arising from the provision of exercise facilities

Despite sport and physical exercise being an integral element of the prison regime, exercise facilities and sporting equipment in prisons represent a real or potential security threat. An extreme example is that in 1987 two dangerous prisoners escaped from a high-security prison by a helicopter which landed within the prison grounds whilst they were taking their daily exercise (Hansard, 1988) and in 1995, three Category A prisoners orchestrated an escape by breaking into the prison gym and making a metal ladder out of goal posts in order to scale the perimeter (Bennetto, Cusick & Davies, 1995). Sports clothing and equipment has been used, including an escape from a Chicago prison in the United States in 2012 when two men were initially undetected after escape because they had changed from their distinctive orange jumpsuits into less conspicuous gym clothes (MSN News, 2012). As well as being directly used in escape attempts, sports equipment may also pose a hazard in the movement and exchange of drugs and in the crafting of weapons. Although clearly there is a need to monitor and manage the procurement and use of sports equipment in custodial settings, this should not be used as a reason to restrict physical activities since, as with other areas within the prison (such as kitchens and industrial workshops) risks can be managed with appropriate assessment procedures and the alertness and expertise of staff.

In terms of prison design, the location of gyms and sports facilities may themselves pose a security risk, since they are not continuously staffed and may be sited on the periphery of the establishment. In 2012 a male prisoner escaped from a London jail by hiding in the gym and subsequently scaling the prison wall (Marsden, 2012). In response to the rare but serious security concerns that have developed in prison gyms, substantial measures have been taken to prevent the recurrence of such events, thus demonstrating the importance of carefully designed facilities as well as the need to prioritise security, implemented, for example, by ensuring that high-risk prisoners cannot consistently predict when and where sports activities will take place.

A final security issue is the concern that the relational dynamics between gym staff and prisoners (a relationship which has typically been characterised as more informal in comparison to relationships with other prison staff) also have the potential to undermine security. Whilst a more informal approach between staff and prisoners may promote good rapport and more trusting relationships in the prison, there is also a risk that it may result in staff becoming complacent. Furthermore, a prisoner could potentially take advantage of the knowledge of a member of staff's physical capabilities, acquired through training alongside them. An example of this can be seen in the escape of four inmates from a prison in the Netherlands in 1992 which started in the gym when prisoners overpowered three officers (Resodihardjo, 2009). Such examples serve to demonstrate that whilst sport confers multiple benefits in custody, activities must be delivered alongside stringent security procedures and clear policies in order to prevent such activities undermining the effective running of a prison.

The risk of the promotion of sport leading to unrealistic expectations

It has already been established that promoting resettlement and desistance through sports-based initiatives is a key potential benefit of sport in prison, and that the vast majority of prisoners applying to undertake sporting qualifications cite future employment within the fitness and leisure industry as a motivation of doing so. It could therefore be argued that equipping prisoners with sports-based qualifications and encouraging the perusal of sports-based employment upon release does though raise the question however of whether such aspirations are realistic, particularly in an economic climate with high rates of unemployment, even for those without criminal convictions. Employers in the sports and leisure industry frequently require Criminal Record Bureau checks, and for some offenders their previous convictions will render them unsuitable to work in certain settings, but apart from the careful consideration needed to be paid to the type of offender being offered, the opportunity to complete sports-based qualifications, or initiatives aimed at promoting employability, even those ex-offenders who do not have previous convictions for offences which would exclude them from employment in the industry are likely to face significant barriers, including employer discrimination (Metcalf, Anderson & Rolfe, 2001). That does not mean that ex-offenders should be discouraged from aspiring to establish a career in sport, but delivery staff should also be aware of the fact that high aspirations followed by disappointment upon release are likely to be extremely demotivating, particularly during the immediate post-release period which is known to be a significant risk period for reoffending. Indeed, this concern was picked up by prison interviewees:

> There needs to be something so you can keep it up, like free gym membership and support like with CRBs. It can be damaging if you get out and then you can't get in anywhere. (Prisoner, Local)

As explained in Chapter 9, in order to increase the chances of prisoners being able to gain employment upon release, some prison gym departments have developed innovative partnerships with local and national employers and voluntary organisations. However we also now know that this type of good practice is not consistent across the prison estate in England and Wales, and is particularly limited within establishments detaining adults. Moreover, prisoners themselves identified the need for post-release support in achieving sporting aspirations, without which attempts to utilise newly gained qualifications and experience in seeking employment were recognised as being very frustrating:

> People constantly try to go down avenues but there is a lack of support on the outside, it just shows with all the guys going back to prison. (Prisoner, Category B)

> Staff in prison really want to help people but there is no one to carry it on once you're out. (Prisoner, Local)

Such concerns highlight how further attention needs to be paid to the extent to which the sporting aspirations that may be nurtured in prison are consistent with the opportunities available, both within prisons (for example in peer support roles, RoTL placements, and the types of activities that are accessible) and in the communities that prisoners will return to after release. A lack of sufficient support, both within prison and after release, will increase the risk that offenders develop unrealistic expectations about the ease with which they will be able to embark on a sports-based career, for example to become a professional footballer or establish a coaching career. A lack of concrete strategies to attain such goals after release, be they sporting or not (Abrams & Aguilar, 2005) can impair the utility of sports-based initiatives in fulfilling resettlement agendas. Furthermore, a failure to set attainable goals has been linked to poor psychological health, in particular an increased likelihood of depression and anxiety (Kasser, 1996) thus highlighting the importance of managing realistic aspirations in sporting domains.

13 The importance of sport and physical activity for prison staff

A discussion of physical activity and fitness in prisons would not be complete without further consideration of the needs and experiences of prison staff – not only those who facilitate, implement and orchestrate sport in prisons but those with responsibilities in other parts of the prison beyond the gym. Residential wing staff will typically spend the most time with prisoners; not only are they responsible for the daily locking and unlocking of cell doors but they also escort prisoners within the prison, manage day-to-day issues and respond to situations when required. One of the direct implications of the National Offender Management Service (NOMS) being established in 2004 is that each prison now has an Offender Management Unit which is staffed by Offender Supervisors and Offender Managers, roles which are mainly fulfilled by prison officers (and a smaller number of seconded probation staff). These are responsible for assessing the needs of individual prisoners, developing sentence plans, arranging offending behaviour programmes and maintaining electronic case records, and although they may spend a considerable amount of time engaging with prisoners, their direct involvement will vary according to the identified need or risk of harm and likelihood of reoffending of an individual. As with gym staff, Offender Managers may be allocated to other operational duties when the need arises (Criminal Justice Joint Inspection, 2012). Apart from those who have no direct contact with prisoners and whose role solely involves administrative duties, staff from across the prison obviously need to be physically fit to carry out their duties, especially if these include responding to conflicts and disturbances, restraining prisoners or reacting rapidly to calls for assistance from elsewhere within the establishment.

Basic training for officers originally included a fairly gruelling level of mandatory fitness training which was considered to be on a par with military training (Crawley, 2004). Although initial training may no longer be so physically demanding, the need for a certain level of fitness among all prison officers is still formally and informally acknowledged – not just in responding to the physical demands of the role as the Justice Committee states:

> Prison Officers need a level of fitness that allows them to cope with the physical demands of the job. (House of Commons Justice Committee, 2009)

Physical fitness is also considered necessary because of a perceived importance of the resulting status it affords:

> Officers need to be physically able to deal with situations. They also need to be able to present themselves in a way to prisoners that commands respect, and being physically fit is an important part of that. (Senior Manager)

The prison workforce may be an increasingly ageing one,[1] but in recognition of the need for a certain level of fitness, annual mandatory testing has been introduced for all prison staff in England and Wales apart from those at governor grade. One result of this is that the prison gym appears to have taken on a more significant role for staff throughout the service, providing a site for fitness testing as well as the facilities and support to help staff pass such tests. In addition to making gym facilities available solely for staff use during specific time periods (typically early mornings, lunchtimes and evenings), many establishments also hold team-building activities and annual staff well-being days, often delivered by trained prisoner orderlies alongside gym staff, which aim to contribute to the physical and mental well-being of members of staff through assessment and testing (for instance blood pressure) and advice and guidance (for example in nutrition or stopping smoking).

Interviews with staff and stakeholders suggest that an unexpected result of the increased involvement of members of prison-wide staff in the gym is that there is evidence of this becoming an increasingly contested space within the prison community, with reports of some tensions arising in the perceived competition for the use of the facilities:

> There is sometimes a conflict between governors wanting prisoners out of their cells, and staff wanting to use the facilities too. (Senior Manager)

Although managed through timetabling of provision by the gym staff, this perceived tension serves to highlight further the gym as a cornerstone of the prison environment and one of the few spaces used and valued by prisoners and prison staff alike.

Staffing of the prison gym: Operational and organisational issues

The current economic climate, austerity measures and changes to the structure of the Prison Service and individual institutions mean that prison staff from across the estate are increasingly experiencing and responding to significant changes in their roles and threats to their longer term prospects in the service. Indeed, during the course of carrying out the research for this book one of the case study sites was 'reroled' (a process where the government decides a particular establishment should hold a different category or type of prisoner) and another was announced to be closing entirely. Members of PE staff reported being aware of imminent funding cuts while not yet knowing the full impact of such cuts, which resulted in anxiety and poor morale. As an explanatory backdrop to this, in 2011 and as a result of organisational restructuring, NOMS introduced a transformation programme to deliver wholesale organisational redesign, and 'Fair and Sustainable' pay and workforce reforms in order to deliver efficiency savings. In 2012–2013 public service prisons were expected to undergo restructuring work, including the mapping of staff onto new structures and closed and open competition for new roles. This is an ongoing process and not only are individual roles (including those of gym staff) changing through this process, there is also a strong awareness of the likelihood that, in an effort to cut costs, aspects of custodial services, including gym provision, could and may well be outsourced to external providers. Within the delivery of sports and physical activities, these operational and establishment threats are accompanied by a widespread concern that members of PE staff are receiving less support at an organisational level:

> Clearly NOMS sees little value in PE and I think that short term gain may prove to be long term pain. They may well regret dismantling what was once a very dynamic and productive asset. (Gym Staff)

It has previously been established that, along with those with responsibilities for teaching and programme delivery, Physical Education Instructors (PEIs) typically have comparably more positive and supportive attitudes towards all forms of education than those in other roles (Bayliss & Hughes, 2008). However, interviews have also confirmed that, although PEIs have long been seen as a strong asset of the Prison Service, their roles and the quality of their work are increasingly being perceived as under threat, partly due to PE training courses having been reduced from 23 weeks in duration in 1997 to 13 weeks in 2011:

> I have been a PE Officer in HM Prisons for over 35 years so I can speak with some experience. Unfortunately we are a service in decline . . . The NOMS hierarchy are attempting to quantify PE in a way that is fatally flawed. I was running integrated key skills, learning through physical education over 20 years ago which we called 'teaching by stealth' as we integrated basic literacy and numeracy and communication skills into PE. It is a very simple and straightforward process, but not one that is taught at the PE College any longer as the course has been diluted and further diluted over the years to the point that a Prison Service PEI is little more qualified than a Level 3 Gym Instructor. (Gym Staff)

Interviewees suggested that, although the robust PEI training was something which members of the prison service were especially proud of, there were suggestions of resentment of gym staff by some wing officers, exacerbated by a perception that working within the gym may be a more enjoyable or less demanding role than elsewhere in the prison ('Certain staff resent PEIs. They think we just do press-ups all day,' Gym Staff). This may be partially attributed to the fact that PEIs are paid slightly more than wing staff or the widely recognised fact that gym staff have a better quality of relationship with prisoners than other staff might: 'Prisoners see gym staff as a friend, but other staff see them as enemies' (Senior Manager).

These perceptions reflect previous research observations that clear divisions and pecking orders exist within the uniformed workforce, with those in segregation units, security and physical education accorded more value (Crewe, 2008). However, in recognising and responding to this potential rift, suggestions of integrating the gym with other departments were also made, strengthening the existing argument of the need to promote more effective interdepartmental working using sport and physical activity:

> In-fighting between gym and wing staff may be reduced and relationships improved if stronger links are made between the gym and health or resettlement. (Senior Manager)

The role of the prison gym in meeting the psychological needs of staff

Just as exercise and fitness have been established as a critical feature of the promotion of the physical and mental health of those detained in prisons, physical activity also clearly plays an important role for prison staff. As well as a recognised need for those working in prisons to be sufficiently fit and healthy in order to carry out their duties, stress and burnout is a significant concern among prison staff, predicted in part by job pressures, heavy workloads and a lack of job rewards (Keinan & Malach-Pines, 2007; Webster, Porritt & Brennan, 2010). Staff absence through stress and health-related problems remains a major challenge for prison administrators and the most recent official management figures from the Ministry of Justice (2012d) have confirmed that an annual average of 9.8 working days per member of staff were lost due to staff sickness (a total of 462,284 days across the 47,097 staff in public prisons in England and Wales) in the year 2011–2012. There is little doubt that staff well-being is a direct predictor of individual and organisational performance, and recognising this there is evidence of many prisons increasingly investing in initiatives to promote the physical and mental health of their workforce, including a commitment to staff well-being days organised and hosted by prison gyms, as well as regular instructor-led gym classes, for example yoga sessions.

In their work on the benefits of physical exercise as a way of combating occupational stress among prison staff, Kielyl and Hodgson (1990) established the positive impact of a designated staff exercise programme, with physical exercise and general fitness identified as stress preventers as well as a means of overcoming the harmful effects of stress. These findings echo those of broader studies into the benefits of promoting exercise at an organisational level, where it has been found that barriers to participation, such as time constraints, can be more easily removed (Tezenas du Montcel, 2013) and that regular moderate participation in suitable physical activity in the workplace leads to reduced absenteeism and improved productivity (see for example Gebhardt & Crump, 1990).

Staff involvement in sport and physical fitness: The role of the PSSA

The Prison Service Sports Association (PSSA) was established to promote and support sport, leisure and recreation for its members, who are made up of Prison Service staff and their families. Funds are raised through subscription fees (there are currently approximately 5,000 members), the Prison Service College licensed bar, and the Prison Service recreational lottery. The published aims of the PSSA include promoting a broad awareness of sport and leisure activities and facilities, developing links with other sporting agencies and bodies, encouraging and supporting participation, promoting a diverse range of activities and providing an enabling and advisory service to sport bodies and establishment representatives of the PSSA.

Members of staff can represent the Prison Service in a wide range of team and individual sports (although participating members were previously awarded special leave for participating in PSSA national teams, this is now granted at the discretion of the governor of the establishment where a member of staff is based).

Recognising the need to promote staff well-being, a member of the PSSA at high-security establishment HMP Frankland applied for and secured £6000 in Millennium Grant funding to develop an external facility, complete with full gym, sauna and pool, specifically for members of staff and their families.

Developing constructive staff-prisoner relationships from the gym

> Officers are officers but when you go over to the gym you don't see a uniform, you don't see an officer. They're friendly and it causes relaxation. (Prisoner, Category C)

Prison officers may see their role primarily as one concerning security and discipline but they can also find involvement in educational and rehabilitative efforts a rewarding experience, particularly if they experience and see first hand the positive impact these activities can have on individual prisoners and the wider prison. As Crewe (2008, p. 426) observes, 'Officers often come into their own when given ownership of projects' and staff interviews revealed numerous examples of prison staff enthused by their involvement in sports-related projects. Beyond seeing sport and physical activities solely as a way of managing offenders, staff evidently found the relations they were able to develop with prisoners through their roles both positive and rewarding, and when asked to reflect on what they saw as the primary benefits of sport and physical activity in prison, members of staff regularly referred to the opportunities that sport afforded in developing such relationships:

> The 'college' environment makes for a positive experience, and small changes in the usual prison relationship, such as using first name terms between staff

and learners, differentiate our department from other parts of the establishment. (Staff, Category C)

As a result of having established more positive relationships with prisoners, staff even reported being called upon to de-escalate situations elsewhere in the prison:

> At times if there are problems on the wings they ring us as they know they are gym users. (Staff, High Security)

Stakeholder interviewees also confirmed the particular expertise of gym staff as bringing added value to the prison staff base:

> PE staff have the ability and enthusiasm to motivate difficult to engage prisoners. They tend to be more amenable to trying new things and taking risks on new projects that others might not in a risk averse culture. (Senior Manager).

In considering the importance of facilitating positive and constructive relationships between staff and prisoners, despite reducing the time available for informal staff-prisoner interaction, NOMS have publicly re-affirmed that the relationship between offender and supervisor is important in reducing reoffending, stating that:

> Purposeful, structured and more effective face-to-face contact can be a powerful way of changing behaviour . . . improving the quality of front line practice in strengthening offender motivation, increasing compliance, reducing reoffending and cutting crime. (National Offender Management Service, 2012a, p. 16)

Despite this awareness of the importance of good interactions between prison staff and those in their care, previous research has established that prisoners do not feel able to use officers as sources of support (Hobbs & Dear, 2000) although subsequent work from Harvey (2007) has found that the quality of trusting relationships varies dramatically. What may be of particular relevance in establishing trust between gym staff and prisoners is the legitimacy of the relationship, not in terms of authority but in terms of the authenticity of such affiliations. As Tyler (1990) argues, professional or mentoring relationships that emulate familial or friendship relationships are more likely to be characterised by a legitimacy that may be lacking in other types of worker-client relationships (particularly in prison settings). Sport may therefore be an important way in which to replicate 'normal' interactions in an environment where it is inevitable that prisoner-staff relationships are typically characterised by hierarchy and power. Reflecting this, as members of gym staff were evidently aware, one result of being responsible for one of the most popular activities within prison is that PEIs are able to enjoy comparably easier relationships with those in their care:

> There is rarely trouble in the gym as people want to be here, the gym and visits are the few things that people actually want to do in prison. It's the best job

in the jail, this blue track suit makes my life so much easier, it's hard on the wings as people don't listen to wing staff but if we ask them to do something they will as they want to be able to come to the gym. (Staff, Local)

It's a different relationship because they come down because they want to and there is that sporting atmosphere. (Staff, Category C)

As well as benefitting from a more positive environment than experienced elsewhere in the prison, gym staff frequently cited the increased potential for establishing positive prisoner-staff relationships from the gym (as a member of gym staff from a high-security prison explained, 'PE is an excellent way of breaking down barriers between staff and prisoners.' Of significance here is the concept of Motivational Interviewing (Rollnick & Miller, 2002), widely recognised as the gold standard of counselling style for eliciting behaviour change, based on dynamics of compassion, acceptance and collaboration. As a technique, motivational interviewing places particular emphasis on the importance of client engagement at the start of the therapeutic encounter in facilitating change, thus demonstrating the importance of establishing trusting relationships between prisoners and staff. Halsey's (2008) depiction of respect (or lack of it) shown to young men by custodial staff in Australian prisons, and his suggestion that the emphasis in training programmes on taking responsibility and acting respectfully are undermined by such disrespectful interactions, are especially pertinent here. The importance of trust was discussed by gym staff in the context of sport's contribution to the development of a supportive environment able to facilitate therapeutic relationships and impact upon other aspects of the prison regime.

However, the finding that gym staff are in a position to establish particularly trusting and mutually respectful relationships with those in their care serves as a partial contradiction to Harvey's (2007) quantitative study of prisoners' willingness to seek support from different staff members, which found that prisoners reported a high willingness to seek practical support from PEI officers but a low willingness to seek support for an emotional problem from PEI officers.

Further research is evidently required to isolate the specific aspects of the prison-staff (or in more therapeutic terms, client-practitioner) interaction which best contribute to transformation and desistance in sporting settings, but some caution should also be exercised to avoid the exploitation of trust. For example, given the opportunities for more positive relationships to develop between prisoners and gym staff, senior manager interviewees expressed a concern that PE staff may be at particular risk of becoming complacent in their role, which can subsequently undermine security concerns (see Chapter 12 for a more in-depth discussion of the risks associated with prison sport). However, rather than problematising the positive relationships which may be more easily nurtured between prisoners and gym staff, others have suggested that gym staff could play a more active role in contributing to through-the-gate support, given that a significant challenge identified in previous literature (Caplan, 1996) and interviews with prison staff and other stakeholders has been that of supporting ex-prisoners to continue engaging in positive sporting activities after release:

> There is plenty of potential for encouraging post-release participation, but they need the right gear and emotional support. They often need someone to take them to the first training session, and as long as the relationship remains professional there's no reason why that shouldn't be a member of gym staff. (Senior Manager)

Aside from ongoing debates about the changing role of gym staff, in a role where employees are expected to exercise authority and contribute to an orderly, safe and secure environment while promoting prosocial behaviour and inspiring positive change, there is no doubt that staff across the prison carry out their duties in an especially demanding environment which is characterised by unique challenges. Indeed, just as sport has been recognised as serving an important function in boosting morale in other professional settings, such as in the military (see Mason & Riedi, 2010), it has become clear that sport and physical activity may be just as significant for prison staff as it is for those in their care.

Note

1   Over a third of all members of prison staff are now aged 50 or over (National Offender Management Service, 2012b).

14 Conclusions, implications and future research directions

To an outsider prisons are extraordinary places – 'total institutions', punitive establishments holding people against their will, characterised by special and particular routines which structure and sustain the institution. But they are also geographical locales with their own histories and culture, serving a particular purpose for those held within and those for whom prisons are their place of work. And there is no doubt that physical activity has the capacity to impact upon the institutional climate of a prison. In the course of researching this book, several prison governors and senior managers have spontaneously spoken of the role of the gym, along with food and communication with the outside world through phone calls and visits, as being of most significance to the smooth running of a prison. Such is the value placed on physical activity that within prison culture it can be regarded as being as important as nutrition and contact with loved ones.

It is hoped that the preceding chapters have succeeded in broadening the understanding of the use of sport and physical activity in the custodial settings, which has, until now, been largely overlooked in discussions of the social and moral uses of sport. Having gathered quantitative data and first-hand accounts from prisoners, prison staff and other stakeholders and witnessed examples of creative, innovative, and imaginative practice in prisons throughout England and Wales, the findings should serve to foster further academic insight and debate, as well as to contribute directly to the promotion and exchange of ideas, responses to challenges, and examples of good practice.

So where does this leave us? As with music and the arts – potentially even more so – sport and physical activity can undoubtedly be used as a 'hook' with which to engage and motivate prisoners, particularly those who typically respond better as a result of active participation methods of delivery. But beyond this, academics have a responsibility to disentangle the meanings of sport, not just in prison settings but elsewhere too, in order to explore whether it has intrinsic value or whether it should solely be utilised as a way of engaging people and under what circumstances it can best be used as a way of facilitating change. Meanwhile, although crime reduction, health promotion, skills development and identity transformations may not be an offender's primary goal when undertaking sports-based programmes during their time in prison, it is evident that these activities can be invaluable in meeting rehabilitative objectives. It would, of course, be naïve and unrealistic to assume that sport and physical activity can be used as a panacea for the complex, deep-rooted and challenging issues often associated with those in prison, but it is also clear that sport and physical activities have great potential to engage, inspire, motivate, and empower. Reflecting this growing recognition at European level, 2014 has been designated the year of sport in prison by the Enlarged Partial Agreement on Sport established by the Council of Europe.

The importance of sport as a way of maintaining order in the prison was emphasised by staff ('PE in essence stops people jumping off roofs') as well as prisoners ('I'd go off my trolley if I didn't have the gym'), serving as a reminder of a primary perceived purpose of sport and physical activity in the survival and management of prison. The key message which I hope has emerged from this book though is that sport in prison can and does offer numerous possibilities and opportunities but that there are also complexities associated with developing, implementing and evaluating sports-based programmes in prison settings and that these activities may have most use if characterised as a vehicle by which to implement social, psychological and physical change, rather than as a solution in themselves. The most effective and inspiring examples drawn from across the prison estate have often come about as initiatives implemented by knowledgeable, enthusiastic members of staff, who in turn are enabled by supportive senior managers who can see the benefit of creating innovative approaches to working with offenders. However, as with any developing areas of practice, particularly those directly involving offenders, there will always be lessons to be learnt and challenges to be overcome, and the following summary will present some of the key messages which have arisen from this programme of research, questions which have been resolved as well as those that remain unanswered.

There is no denying that education can be crucial in the acquisition of new outlooks and perspectives on life, which in turn can support transformations of lifestyles and identities and ultimately promote turning points away from crime. However, many of those in prison have had extremely negative and disrupted experiences of education and are often reluctant to engage or remain motivated in learning. The research uncovered some innovative and successful collaborations between the gym and education departments, with staff recognising in interviews that 'Prisons have got to be more imaginative in how they deliver [education]. Sometimes you've got to change the learning environment.' On occasions when gym staff had successfully collaborated with their colleagues in education they were rewarded with a vibrant learning environment with many gym users becoming intrinsically motivated to return to education.

As well as the challenge of promoting education there is a need to enhance the employability aspect of the prison regime and the programmes and opportunities offered within it. One way in which prison staff have responded to the need to align prison experiences with the skills required in the community, whilst enabling prisoners to get as much relevant experience as possible, is through the development of industry partnerships and recreating a community gym environment in the prison.[1]

In prison gyms, prisoner orderly positions are evidently crucial, not just in enhancing the function and effectiveness of the gym and associated activities by providing peer support but in benefiting those holding such positions. In line with Maruna's (2001) concept of *generativity*, interviewees reported aspirations to participate in sports-based mentoring activities as an opportunity to make amends or to do something constructive and useful, as a way of 'giving back' after being a recipient of a scheme themselves and of enabling them to develop a more positive identity to that of 'prisoner' or 'offender' while establishing feelings of pride and increased self-worth. Gym orderlies reported that their roles helped them to appreciate other people's needs and to develop empathy, and aside from the direct rewards for those prisoners contributing to and benefiting from such schemes, gym-based peer-led initiatives clearly also offer additional potential benefits in terms of freeing up staff time, improving services, and contributing to the overall smooth running of a prison.

One of the recurring messages from the desistance literature is that practice should be individualised, and although sport may not capture the attention of every prisoner, the research findings make a strong case for it to be recognised – alongside other innovative approaches – as playing a role in the promotion of desistance by motivating, engaging and inspiring individuals, and well as in promoting meaningful and constructive therapeutic relationships and opportunities for peer support. Likewise, there is evidently potential for sport to be utilised as a platform for facilitating other innovative prison-based practices, such as victim-offender mediation (Baker, 1994), restorative justice (Edgar & Newell, 2006), and varied forms of civic engagement.

As well as the more obvious contributions of prison sport and physical activity to the promotion of health and well-being of prisons, recognising the importance of health and fitness in the context of staff well-being (particularly among an ageing workforce), prison gyms are also serving an increasingly prominent role in initiatives to promote the physical and mental health of staff. Further research is evidently required to identify the specific features of gym-based activities which can best contribute to better staff well-being and resulting performances of individual prisons, but in the meantime the gym clearly remains an especially significant feature of the modern prison, arguably almost as much for prison staff as it is for those in their care.

Policy and practice implications

Managing change in the prison service

In reflecting upon the role of sport in prisons, a primary concern voiced by prison staff interviewees was the threat (both perceived and actual) to good quality service provision as a result of direct cuts to resources and reductions in the staffing of prison gyms. Changes to the prison regime as a result of moves towards 'working prison' status were seen by some as a threat to their delivery, although there were also positive examples of gyms effectively modifying their programming to accommodate such changes – for example by integrating gym sessions with education and healthcare and increasing availability of resources in evenings and at weekends. Clearly, any changes need to be considered carefully but it is important that senior management remain committed to and supportive of physical activity as part of the core activities of their establishments, and to recognise the significance of the gym – and the expertise and experience of gym staff – in coordinating and contributing to allied activities, even if this means making investments in the upskilling of PE staff (for example so that they can deliver educational courses up to Level 3 or develop particular skills to extend their current duties). In acknowledgement of the importance physical activity within prisons there are also implications for the actual design and architecture of newly built prisons, where sport and physical activity can be integrated into the built environment, just as it has been in community settings (Handy, Boarnet, Ewing & Killingsworth, 2002).

Consultation with prisoners

In terms of developing good practices for the use of sport and physical activities across the prison estate, the findings have suggested that prisons may need to be more receptive to and active in pursuing prisoner consultations. Not only will this enable prisons to target specific groups (for example vulnerable prisoners or those not engaging in physical activity) but it will also enable managers to establish which activities would best promote participation and motivation and consequently be most effective in meeting prison targets. Offering taster sessions for sporting activities has already been identified as an effective way promoting participation in sporting activities; however such promotion should be done with an awareness that academic research has demonstrated that activities primarily focusing on the physical and individual aspects of sport (as opposed to the wider associated psychological processes) can result in negative outcomes such as increased aggression, thus highlighting again the importance of embedding non-sporting activities and objectives in programmes and the role of staff expertise in delivering programmes most effectively.

Chapter 4 explored ways in which sport and physical activity could be tailored for those with diverse needs and presented examples of establishments which had been able to respond to the specific and varied needs of those in their care by engaging in regular consultation regarding existing and requested provision. Not only do consultation processes contribute to feelings of empowerment, trust and responsibility, but they also ensure that resources that remain are being allocated in the most useful way in order to maximise impact. And lastly, and perhaps most importantly, as explored in the qualitative aspects of Chapter 8, ongoing consultation with those taking part in and contributing to prison sport activities is especially critical in identifying and unpacking some of the complexities associated with experiencing prison sport. If we fail to make best use of such consultations, interventions and initiatives that ensue will inevitably be poorer as a result.

Prisons supporting and being supported by external organisations

As has previously been established, organisations external to the prison service are increasingly recognised by offenders (Meek et al., in press), prison staff (Mills, Meek & Gojkovic, 2012) and other criminal justice and voluntary sector stakeholders (Meek et al., 2010) as playing a valuable role, not just as advocates for prisoners but in service provision and direct work with those in custody and after release. The criminal justice system has an established history of working with such voluntary and community-based organisations, but potential for involvement has increased in recent years[2] and community organisations currently provide a range of prison-based services, encompassing education and training, mentoring and advice and the provision of core rehabilitative and resettlement services.

Although direct support from community organisations to prisoners has tended in the past to be most prominent in the areas of housing, financial advice and drug and alcohol treatment, given the perceived strengths of community organisations in diversity of provision, their relative independence from the criminal justice system, and responsiveness to needs (as well as the crucial aspect of being able to provide a bridge between prison and the community), there is clearly plenty of potential for sporting organisations to develop similar partnerships with prisons in meeting the specific needs of offenders and promoting involvement in sport. Initial responsibility for establishing these partnerships should lie jointly with the Prison Service and sporting bodies, and will require commitment from both in order to develop meaningful and productive relationships.

It is well recognised that the transition from custody to community represents a period where ex-prisoners can be particularly vulnerable and even the most determined attempts at re-establishing oneself can be undermined by stigma, practical and psychological barriers and a raft of challenges exacerbated by a period of incarceration. Establishing statutory and voluntary sector supportive networks while still in custody, which that can remain in place through-the-gate in promoting attainable and realistic opportunities after release, may contribute to overcoming such difficulties. Formal partnerships between prisons and organisations would ensure that good practice becomes more widespread and coherent and is robust enough to contribute to longer term initiatives which can sustain ongoing support for ex-prisoners as required.

Positive partnerships between different prison departments were recognised as being an area requiring further improvement in order to make best use of sport. For example, initiatives appeared to be most effective and efficient in establishments where gym staff worked effectively with resettlement, healthcare or psychology services. The impact of programmes will inevitably be undermined when communication between different departments is poor, as illustrated in this typical response from a member of staff when reflecting on interdepartmental work:

> Everyone complains about prison's communication. Whether it happens on purpose or because groups are protecting their little areas or don't want to give up their work to other groups I'm not quite sure. (Gym Staff)

A commitment from local, regional and national clubs and sporting bodies is also required, in facilitating innovative partnerships between prisons and these groups, but also in bringing the expertise of organisations and individuals into prisons in order to contribute to and enhance existing provision. These relationships need to be carefully managed; it can be intimidating as well as practically difficult for external organisations to come into prison, particularly if they have no experience of doing so, and there are time and resource implications for enabling prison staff to develop such partnerships. An illustrative example of a modest partnership project between prisons and a sporting body was developed by the RFU, the governing body of English rugby, in the form of the Prison to Pitch initiative which encouraged prisoners to maintain their involvement in sport after release. However, although being applauded as an example of promising practice, the scheme did not develop into a widespread initiative and feedback from prison staff indicated that more resourcing would be required if it were to be effective in supporting ex-prisoners to maintain their involvement in recreational sport after release:

> It is intimidating for a lad to turn up to a new club for the first time. Support with that will make all the difference. (Prison Staff)

Related to this observation, and recognising that the lack of support for many of those leaving prison was directly contributing to an increased risk of reoffending, in 2012 the British government announced plans to provide ex-prisoners with a mentor to support them in managing the transition from custody to community. In line with these developments, seeking out sporting activities to participate in and local clubs to join could be an important aspect of such a role and, in light of the findings presented here, should be integrated into the resourcing and training of mentors. Likewise, the research suggests an appetite among ex-offenders for engaging in sports-based volunteering opportunities after release as a way of gaining skills as well as remaining motivated and gaining a sense of active citizenship. Given that the overall rate of volunteering among young people has been declining, with those from minority groups being particularly under-represented, while at the same time voluntary sports clubs have on-going difficulties recruiting and retaining volunteers (Deane et al., 2010), rehabilitation-focused sports-based prison interventions may be ideally placed to link offenders with such voluntary organisations, for example as volunteer coaches and referees, as well as recipients of such support.

Supporting innovation and the exchange of good practice

Gyms and their associated facilities are evidently a valuable resource within a prison, but they need to be managed well in order to generate optimum impact for prisoners and for staff. Highlighting the importance of developing and maintaining good relationships between prison gyms and other prison departments as well as external organisations, the research findings highlight the need to consider more innovative and creative uses of sport and physical activity. Just as prison restaurants have been successfully established as social enterprises which engage with the community while raising funds and providing skills and experience to prisoners, a suitably located prison could become home to the first community gym, staffed by serving prisoners and established as a social enterprise.

Any new developments or initiatives in criminal justice require expertise, resources and careful planning; the consequences of making a mistake in the context of prison-based work can be especially grave, but that should not necessarily mean that innovation is inhibited. One of the unintended consequences of the prison weighted scorecard system[3] may well have been the inevitable introduction of an element of competition between establishments, potentially rendering the exchange of knowledge and good practice ideas between prisons less likely. However, just as community-based sporting organisations benefit from networking and mutual support,[4] one way in which progress in prison sport can be supported is though the central funding and development of national umbrella networks, with the primary goal of bringing together and facilitating the growing numbers of organisations and individuals involved in developing and delivering sport and physical activity in prison. Not only would such networks serve to promote the exchange of ideas, resources, informal support and examples of good practice, but they could also monitor the varied activities and initiatives taking place across the prison estate or the criminal justice system more widely.

Although there are currently no umbrella organisations representing sport in prisons, a relevant model to inspire progress in this area may be that of the Arts Alliance (www.artsalliance.org.uk), a membership organisation which is partially funded by the Ministry of Justice. In the same way that the Arts Alliance seeks to form a link between government, policy makers and practitioners, while commissioning and promoting research, influencing policy and sharing good practice relating to the arts in criminal justice, a similar organisation representing sport in prisons and other criminal justice settings would be valuable in supporting and promoting progress and innovation in the use of sport in penal practices. As demonstrated in the case studies presented throughout this text, there are many examples of the innovative, creative, and effective use of sport in prisons. But as a senior manager summarised, 'There is a lot of good practice in pockets, but there is a problem relating to sharing best practice across the estate.' An umbrella organisation or forum that can disseminate good examples of emerging and established practice may help foster a more widespread and effective use of sport and physical activity in prisons.

Developing partnerships between prisons and sporting organisations

Prisons have historically tended to be reluctant to facilitate the involvement of community organisations in their work (a reluctance partly explained by concerns about security and safety), but prison managers and their staff are increasingly recognising the value of bringing external organisations, including sporting organisations, into their establishments. Staff interviews confirmed that if a sporting group or body has the capacity to bring specialist coaches and equipment, motivational speakers or simply an opposing team into a prison this can represent a significant achievement and create a genuine improvement in the prison atmosphere. As well as having a positive impact on prisoners themselves, staff benefit from receiving training and support, visitors have the opportunity to learn more about the criminal justice system, and the prison can establish a community link which may lead to additional opportunities, for example RoTL placements.

Interviews also confirmed, however, that external organisations should be careful not to underestimate the impact of their involvement in a prison, as they have a responsibility to be consistent, reliable and professional in their conduct. Alongside the need for visiting organisations to be alert to the risks as well as the benefits of delivering sporting activities in prisons, a striking finding from prisoner interviews, and one substantiated by staff, was the detrimental effect of being let down by organisations, the cancellation of games which had been organised against visiting teams or promises of visits from sports representatives not being realised. Such disappointment was disproportionate to that experienced in a non-prison setting, usually because such community involvement was typically very rare.

In taking some of these practical, professional and ethical issues into account, training and guidance should be made available for organisations unfamiliar with working directly with prisons and prisoners in order to make best use of such partnerships, while ensuring safety of those concerned. As related examples, *Navigating the Criminal Justice System* and *Developing a Criminal Justice Network* are publications funded by the Ministry of Justice and produced by Clinks, an umbrella organisation supporting voluntary and community sector organisations working with offenders. These guides are designed to provide easily accessible introductory level information on key aspects of the Criminal Justice System for the voluntary and community sector and would be especially suitable for sporting organisations wishing to expand their work to criminal justice settings. Involving representatives from sports organisations in partnership forums[5] would also help to establish and promote productive collaborations between individual prisons and sporting bodies – as would the establishment/extension of a partnership officer[6] whose remit would include working in collaboration with gym staff in order to strengthen links with sports organisations.

Despite requiring some investment to develop, once relationships between prisons and sporting bodies are established the resources and expertise of such organisations could be invaluable in signposting and developing links to other services and clubs, providing support and training in attaining higher level qualifications and in opportunities for post-release support, voluntary and paid opportunities. For example, in the same way that elite athletes and sports personalities contribute their time as United Nations Champions for Sport in promoting the values of physical education and sport, similar initiatives could be developed with individual prisons being partnered with a Champion for Sport, a role which could include encouraging participation and raising the profile of sport as a rehabilitative tool.

Diverse populations and varied penal settings

Previous explorations of the role of sport in pursuing social good have focussed almost entirely on youth settings, and whereas the particular importance of sport for children and young people was discussed in Chapter 6, with the specific findings of a quantitative and qualitative evaluation developed for young adult males presented in Chapter 8, the remaining chapters sought to identify and explore the more varied aspects of prison-based sport, recognising the actual and potential function of sport and physical activity (and barriers to participation) for the varied populations of those in prison custody and the varied risk and support needs reflecting this diversity.

The importance of sporting masculinities in prison settings was introduced in Chapter 2, whilst the significance of sport and physical activity for women prisoners, the role it plays in contributing to psychological well-being and its importance in promoting education and employment opportunities were explored in Chapter 9. Just as the desistance needs of women warrants further research attention, so too do sporting masculinities and femininities and their importance in broader discussions of incarceration and processes of desistance. Despite being beyond the remit of this text, the research has established that the dynamics of, tensions between and performances of gender-based sporting and criminal identities is an area of investigation which deserves academic focus. Likewise, further exploration of the impact of different types of sport is required, not just in the context of masculinities (see, for example, Spandler & McKeown, 2012, for a theoretical exploration of football practices as a way of engaging men in various health and welfare programmes) but more broadly in relation to the influence of different sports and physical activities and the components of specific activities which contribute to such an impact.

Investment in research and establishing a coherent evidence base

Although it draws together a wide range of material demonstrating the powerful impact of engaging in a sports-based resettlement initiative for young men in prison, the evaluation data presented in Chapter 8 raises as many questions as it answers, stressing the particular importance and identified need for future research to separate out the precise successes of particular programmes, since only then can the exact relationship between sport and reductions in reoffending be established. Echoing Kelly's (2012) concern that targeted youth projects are at risk of overstating their ability to prevent crime, the importance of robust evaluation is a theme returned to regularly throughout the book, not just in relation to interventions targeting children and young people. A major challenge is to respond to specific questions about the evidence of a direct relationship between participation in physical activity and reducing reoffending. To this end, identifying meaningful outcome and intermediate measures which can be used to gauge the impact of a programme is especially important.

As has been reflected throughout this book, despite a growing interest in the role of sport and physical activity in prison there remains a dearth of reliable intervention evaluations, experimental studies or vigorous research in this domain. In responding to this shortage of robust evidence, a commitment is required, not just from academics and the research funding bodies which support them, but also from providers of sports-based interventions and those commissioning such services to factor research and evaluation into any contracts and delivery arrangements, while making sure that the necessary time and resources are made available to undertake and support academic investigations. Until robust research findings can establish what aspects of sport-based programmes are most effective, in what ways, and with whom, policy makers, providers and commissioners will lack the insights to target resources most appropriately. Relevant research needs to be prioritised and supported in order to nurture a meaningful evidence base on which to draw in developing future practice. In seeking to enhance our theoretical and practical understandings of the role of sport in prison settings, the present research has identified a number of future avenues of investigation, some of which I will summarise here.

Exploring the plurality of prison sport

While policy makers and prison staff advocate the potential role of sport to fulfil broader objectives, prisoners may not necessarily participate in sporting activities in order to fulfil wider goals but rather for reasons associated with prison life itself. In order to do start recognising and responding to the different ways in which prison sport and physical activity can be used, not only do we need to clarify what we are referring to as outcomes (which in turn rely on well-defined aims of specific programmes and interventions) but we also need to start acknowledging a plurality, not just of prison sport but of 'sport for good' more broadly. Portraying sport or even physical activity as singular concepts denies the complexity of factors at play in sporting interventions and subsequently restricts a more intelligent assessment of how sport can best be utilised in prisons. A potentially useful way in which to identify distinct types of sport and physical activity can be drawn from Passmore and French's (2001) work on leisure activities, which uses a three-factor typology to distinguish between achievement leisure (activities competitive in nature and providing a personal challenge) social leisure (activities undertaken primarily to engage in social interaction) and time-out leisure (activities which are typically solitary or for relaxation purposes). Developing and testing a similar typology for physical activity in prison may help to explain and predict how participation in prison sports can contribute to particular issues, concerns and priorities within the criminal justice system.

Identifying which types of sport are most effective in meeting particular outcomes

Alongside a recognised need to avoid regarding prison sport as a homogenous entity, a primary implication of these research findings has been the need to acknowledge the diverse impact of sport and physical activity in different contexts of incarceration, with those of different demographics, backgrounds and needs, and in targeting different criminogenic requirements. A direct research implication of the recognition of the varied uses and different effects of sport and physical activity across the secure estate is the need to make greater efforts to determine which types of sport are most effective in meeting specific aims, be they physical, psychological or social. These challenges are not necessarily exclusive to prison settings, and similar questions about capturing the specific impact of sports remain valid in community and school settings, particularly in light of renewed investment in school sports.[7] Of particular use in designing prison-based interventions, however, will be the development of a better understanding of how sport and physical activity can be used most effectively to engage with different populations of prisoners or in identifying which aspects of programmes are most effective in targeting specific types of offending behaviour. As well as different offence categories being a statistical predictor of the likelihood of reoffending (for example, those serving sentences for burglary: Ministry of Justice, 2011e), previous research evidence has suggested that the relationship between sports participation and deviance varies depending on the type of offending behaviour examined (Hartmann & Massoglia, 2007), so future research should explore the benefit of targeting specific types of offenders, expanding interventions sufficiently to enable statistical comparison across offence type.

Defining and responding to the negative aspects of prison sport

Whilst recognising that sport *can be* (rather than automatically *is*) used as a catalyst for social (and potentially moral) development, there is also a need to explore whether promoting involvement in particular sports can also lead to increases in problematic behaviours, not only concerning offending directly but in terms of impacting upon violence, attitudes or other factors which may increase the likelihood of offending. One potential area for future investigation concerns narcissism, which is associated with antisocial characteristics such as low empathy (Watson & Morris, 1991), exploitativeness (Campbell, Bush, Brunell & Shelton, 2005) and aggressive reactions to threat (Bushman & Baumeister, 1998). Given the potentially serious implications of increasing narcissism in some offending populations, further research is evidently required to identify whether particular types of sport or physical activities are more or less likely to lead to problematic levels of narcissism among particular groups of offenders.

Extending the research focus to prison staff

Prison gym staff remain an under-researched population, with further exploration required to unpack the processes and dynamics which may explain the enhanced interactions between staff with responsibilities for PE and those in their care. Furthermore, recognising the potential contribution to staff well-being of sport and physical activity, and the relationship between well-being and individual and organisational performance, experimental and longitudinal research is also required to isolate the specific features of gym-based activities which may best contribute to greater staff well-being and the resulting improved performance of individual prisons. Likewise, using research to isolate the specific aspects of prison-staff interactions which best contribute to transformation and desistance in sporting settings will in turn inform professional development and potentially enable prison managers to replicate some of the positive interactions between prisoners and staff in the gym elsewhere in the prison.

In conducting the research which informs this book the enthusiastic of prison gym staff, prisoners and stakeholders to participate in the research process was apparent, with many reporting that it was the first time that they had been consulted on the issues important to them concerning sport, fitness and physical activity. Drawing on this, when pursuing these future areas of investigation, the use of more participatory research methods should also be considered. In seeking to enhance prisoner consultation processes and engage in meaningful action research, data-gathering techniques should seek to utilise better the expertise and enthusiasm of prisoner gym orderlies in research processes, for example by supporting them to carry out peer-led and participatory research into prison sport.

Developing a meaningful and realistic evaluation resource to enable practitioners to assess the impact of their work

Now more than ever, practitioners, providers and commissioners are acutely aware of the need to demonstrate the impact of any criminal justice initiatives and sports-based projects are no exception. Research should play a key role in contributing to developments within the field, identifying priorities and shaping the future direction of programming. Given the extent to which the preceding chapters have established the importance of sport and physical education in contributing to prisoner education, physical health, mental health and rehabilitation, the subject must remain sufficiently high profile for policy makers, commissioners and senior management figures to continue being committed to physical activity in prison in order to avoid it being seen as expendable within an increasingly constrained prison regime. One anxiety revealed in interviews with prison gym staff was that their gym-based services were at risk of being outsourced as a cost-cutting exercise. These concerns are grounded in a reality arising from a context of external providers increasingly being given the opportunity to bid for and win contracts for a range of prison and community based rehabilitative services.

Despite the Prison Service having a long history of specialist staffing in physical education, there was evidence of a widespread fear among staff that gym provision would be jeopardised as a result of evolving changes to the operational regime. Perhaps reflecting these fears, prison staff as well as community sporting organisations were particularly receptive to exploring ways of demonstrating the impact of their work, and interviews with senior managers, operational staff and delivery partners confirmed a need to be able to demonstrate the impact of sport-based programmes in prison settings. To this end, and in line with other initiatives seeking to improve measurement of the impact of, for example, mentoring and arts-based initiatives or interventions which seek to improve family relationships,[8] further resources and research should be committed to developing and refining measurement tools which are accessible and reliable while also being realistic to the context of prison-based initiatives.

Just as evaluations which solely consider reconviction rates[9] may fail to explain how or why a particular initiative is or is not effective, there is a need to define clearly a programme's specific aims (which may include reductions in offending or may focus more specifically on intermediate measures such as more instantaneous changes to attitudes and behaviour) in order to be able to assess such impact. From a research and evaluation perspective the development of a sports-specific 'toolkit' – an evaluation resource which can be adapted to take into account a broad range of measures reflecting the particular aims of a given programme – coupled with specialist academic input in research design and data analysis would make a significant contribution to efforts to explore and explain the impact of different aspects of sports-based initiatives, while also identifying directions for future research and theoretical advances. In turn, and in the context of a growing focus on outcomes-based commissioning processes, such evaluation developments would also play an important role in contributing to decisions about the allocation of resources to sports and activity-based initiatives in criminal justice settings. While recognising the value of qualitative techniques – and the rich data they can generate – in providing in-depth accounts, illustrative case studies and a phenomenological focus (for example on an individual's experiences of participating in a given programme), table 14.1 represents an initial attempt to establish a set of potential individual and institutional indicators for use in capturing the short term and longitudinal impact of a given activity-based intervention.

Table 14.1 Effective measurement of the impact of sports-based initiatives: Illustrative examples of suggested indicators

Indicator	*Possible form(s) of measurement*
Reoffending	• Reoffending within one/two years of release from prison: official (Ministry of Justice) or self report data
Attitude, cognitive and behavioural change	• Attitudes towards offending and perceived life problems (Frude et al., 2009)
	• Motivation for change (Prochaska & DiClemente, 1986)
	• Self-efficacy (Sherer & Adams, 1983)
	• Perceived stress (Cohen, Kamarck & Mermelstein, 1983)
Disruption in prison	• Governor adjudications
	• Positive/negative entries logged on individual files
	• Incentives and Earned Privileges status
Attitudes towards aggression, conflict resolution and impulsivity	• Maudsley Violence Questionnaire (Walker, 2005)
	• Beliefs about Aggression (Farrell et al., 2001)
	• Use of Non Violent Strategies (Farrell et al., 2001)
	• Impulsivity (Bosworth & Espelage, 1995)
	• Conflict Resolution, Impulsivity and Aggression among Violent Offenders (Honess et al., 2001)
Aggression in sport	• Bredemeier Athletic Aggression Inventory (Bredemeier, 1975)
	• Sport Aggression Questionnaire (Thompson, 1990)
	• Competitive Aggressiveness and Anger Scale (Maxwell & Moores, 2007)
Anxiety in sport	• Sport Competition Anxiety Test (Martens, Vealey & Burton, 1990)
Physical health	• General Health Questionnaire (GHQ-12) (Goldberg & Williams, 1988)
	• Bleep / step test

Indicator	Possible form(s) of measurement
Self-esteem / self-concept	• Body Mass Index • VO2 Max test • Rosenberg's Self Esteem scale (Rosenberg, 1989) • Self Esteem (Weinberger & Schwartz, 1990) • Self Concept (Phillips & Springer, 1992)
Volunteering behaviour	• Prevalence of volunteering in custody • Prevalence of volunteering in the community
Progression to other programmes	• Successful completion of established programmes
Quality of relationship with staff	• Prison Social Support and Outside Social Support (Harvey, 2007) • Existing Quality of Prison Life Measures (i.e. perceptions of staff fairness and relationships with staff) (Liebling assisted by Arnold, 2004)
Adjustment to prison	Prison Locus of Control (Pugh, 1994) Psychological Distress, Perceived Adaptability, Perceived Safety (Harvey, 2007) Leisure Coping Belief Scale (Iwasaki & Mannell, 2000) Leisure Coping Strategies Scale (Iwasaki & Mannell, 2000)
Participation in sport during incarceration (individual)	• Leisure Questionnaire (achievement leisure, social leisure and time-out leisure) (Passmore & French, 2001) • Existing HMIP Prisoner Questionnaire measures, for example Q10.6-7: Regularity of attending the gym and going outside for exercise each week. • Health Survey Questionnaire (Garratt et al., 1993) • Physical Activity Questionnaire (Kriska & Caspersen, 1997) • Number and type of sports-based qualifications gained
Participation and provision during incarceration (institutional)	• Prison's PPL figures • Number of sporting external organisations that prisons have formal partnerships with • Number and type of sports-based qualifications offered / gained • Numbers of gym orderly places • Number and quality of sports-based RoTL opportunities
Participation in sport after release from custody	• Paffenbarger Physical Activity Questionnaire (Paffenbarger, Blair, Lee & Hyde, 1993) • Perceived benefits and barriers to exercise (Sechrist, Walker & Pender, 1987) • Health Survey Questionnaire (Garratt et al., 1993) • Physical Activity Questionnaire (Kriska & Caspersen, 1997) • Whether a member of a sporting organisation • Participation in paid / voluntary sports-related activities (coaching, fitness instructor, etc.)
Attitudes towards exercise	• Perceived benefits and barriers to exercise (Sechrist et al., 1987)
Attitudes towards exercise in prison	• Existing HMIP measure concerning perceived safety during exercise: prevalence of responses at the gym, in an exercise yard and in gym showers in response to Q7.3: In which areas of the prison have you felt unsafe?
Staff participation in sport	• Self reported frequency of gym use • Fitness test outcomes • Employee Engagement Index (Cabinet Office, 2013) • Established Quality of Prison Life Measures, such as: job satisfaction dimensions; recognition and personal efficacy dimensions, and prisoner orientation dimensions (Liebling assisted by Arnold, 2004)

Final conclusions

I have already emphasised the need to invest in programmes of research and good quality and rigorously conducted evaluations which take into account pre-existing involvement in sport in order to evaluate the impact of specific programmes. As well as seeking to align the principles of sports-based transformations with other phenomena (such as psychological programming, arts or faith-based interventions) and in other contexts (such as community and school settings), further research also needs to concentrate on establishing which sports are more or most useful in prison and in meeting specific needs, be that to reduce violence, promote health, enhance self-esteem, to facilitate constructive working relationships between prisoners and staff or simply to contribute to the overall quality and decency of a prison.

Sport can offer a unique means of enabling transformation and adaptation, promoting education and desistance and addressing mental and physical health problems in prisoner populations who may be harder to engage and motivate through traditional means, but further work is still required to identify and disseminate principles of best practice in order to inform policy, improve the evidence base and encourage a move away from a universally uncritical acceptance of the positive value of all sports provision in current policy and practice. A naïve tendency in some discussions of sport to construct it as inherently good or as an unquestionable and morally correct activity represents an assumption which is not only flawed but which also fails to take into account and celebrate the complexity of sport.

Just as sport can encompass an enormous range of individual or team activities requiring different levels of exertion, skills or physical capabilities, so too can outcomes of sport be separated into those concerned with sport as an end in itself (for example in eliciting positive health outcomes and individual dispositions developed directly through participation) or its role as a development tool, a hook with which to promote engagement or as a way of enabling social support through participation. The previous chapters have highlighted the validity of sport in each of these functions, which I hope can serve not only as a reminder of its potential uses, but also as a caution of its potential misuses. As academics we appear to have a particular responsibility, not solely to act as 'critical friends' to those criminal justice practitioners seeking to integrate sport in their work and those sporting practitioners wishing to extend their reach to criminal justice settings, but also to evidence good practice while remaining sufficiently curious about the *how* and *why* of sport in order to continue developing a robust evidence base of 'what works' in prison sport.

Notes

1   This may inevitably be easier in some establishments than others, for example those prisons located in remote rural areas may simply not have local sporting organisations with whom to develop partnerships. The amount of space afforded to the prison gym also varies considerably.

2   The Offender Management Act 2007 empowered private and third-sector organisations to take a more direct role in work with offenders, and various government consultation papers, strategies and action plans have promoted working in partnership with voluntary and community sector organisations (Ministry of Justice, 2008), particularly in relation to through-the-gate provision and efforts to reduce reoffending (Ministry of Justice/National Offender Management Service, 2008).

3   First introduced in 2001, the Prison Weighted Scorecard (subsequently replaced by the Prison Rating System) measures the relative performance of individual prisons based on an accumulated set of key performance targets concerning the standards and regime of a prison and staff/resource inputs.

4   See, for example, global organisations such as Beyond Sport (www.beyondsport.org) and national organisations such as the Youth Sport Trust (www.youthsporttrust.org) which promote the use of sport to create positive social change, and the European Women and Sport Network (www.ews-online.org), a European-wide initiative which promotes gender equality in sport.

5   Partnership forums typically involve external organisations being invited into prisons to share information, publicise their service and raise concerns with each other and prison staff. Frequency of such provision across the prison estate varies.

6   Some prisons have a member of prison staff with specific responsibilities for developing and maintaining community links.

7   In March 2013, the British government announced a £150 million overhaul of primary school sport.

8   In 2012 NOMS awarded funding to a range of research and community organisations in order to develop a framework for outcome measurement which can be used by organisations delivering (a) mentoring and arts and (b) family and relationship interventions to offenders.

9   Reconviction rates are recognised as being one of, if not the, most important measure of an intervention's success, despite the methodological challenges associated with attributing participation in a given intervention directly to reduced reconviction rates. Reliable reconviction data have historically been difficult to capture, although the Ministry of Justice's (2013c) Data Lab initiative now allows organisations to request proven one-year reoffending figures for programme participants in comparison with a matched (on propensity score matching) cohort of nonparticipants.

References

Abrams, L. and Aguilar, J. (2005). Negative trends, possible selves and behaviour change. *Qualitative Social Work*, 42, 2, 175–196.

Active Sussex. (2013). *Sports Scheme Goes Behind Bars at Lewes Prison*. Retrieved from: http://www.activesussex.org/news-and-events/latest-news/view/24463-sports-scheme-goes-behind-bars-at-lewes-prison

Ajzen, I. (1985). From intentions to actions: A theory of planned behaviour. In J. Kuhl and J. Beckmann (Eds.), *Action Control: From Cognition to Behaviour* (pp. 11–39). Berlin: Springer.

Allender, S., Cowburn, G. and Foster, C. (2006). Understanding participation in sport and physical activity among children and adults: a review of qualitative studies. *Health Education Research*, 21, 6, 826–835.

Amtmann, J. (2001). Physical activity and inmate health. *Corrections Compendium*, 26, 11, 6–7.

Anderson, C. and Morrow, M. (1995). Competitive aggression without interaction: effects of competitive versus cooperative instructions on aggressive behaviour in video games. *Personality and Social Psychology Bulletin*, 21, 1020–1030.

Anderson, S. with Carins, C. (2011). *The Social Care Needs of Short Sentenced Prisoners*. London: Revolving Doors.

Andrews, D., Bonta, J. and Hoge, R. (1990). Classification for effective rehabilitation: rediscovering psychology. *Criminal Justice and Behavior*, 17, 19–52.

Andrews, D., Zinger, I., Hoge, R., Bonta, J., Gendreau, P. and Cullen, F. (1990). Does correctional treatment work? a psychologically informed meta-analysis. *Criminology*, 28, 369–404.

Andrews, J. and Andrews, G. (2003). Life in a secure unit: the rehabilitation of young people through the use of sport. *Sport Science and Medicine*, 56, 531–550.

Audit Commission. (1996). *Misspent Youth – Young People and Crime*. Oxford: Audit Commission.

Baker, N. (1994). Mediation, reparation and justice. In J. Brunside and N. Backer (Eds.), *Relational Justice: Repairing the Breach*. Winchester: Waterside Press.

Bandura, A. (1977). *Social Learning Theory*. Englewood Cliffs, NJ: Prentice Hall.

Basca, B. (2002). *Literature Review of Youth Development/Asset Tools*. The EMT Group, Inc. Retrieved from: http://www.emt.org/userfiles/YouthLit_Final.pdf

Bayliss, P. and Hughes, S. (2008). Teachers and instructors in prisons. In J. Bennett, B. Crewe and A. Wahidin (Eds.), *Understanding Prison Staff*. Cullompton: Willan.

BBC News. (2012). Danny Care guilty of drink-driving on New Year's Day. 16th January. Retrieved from: http://www.bbc.co.uk/news/uk-england-hampshire-16578054

BBC Sport. (2004). Chambers gets two-year ban. Retrieved from: http://news.bbc.co.uk/sport1/hi/athletics/3492427.stm

Beebe, L., Tian, L., Morriss, N., Goodwin, A., Allen, S. and Kuldau, J. (2005). Effects of exercise on mental and physical health parameters of persons with schizophrenia. *Issues in Mental Health Nursing*, 26, 661–676.

Beesley, F. and McGuire, J. (2009). Gender role identity and hypermasculinity in violent offending. *Psychology, Crime and Law*, 15, 2, 241–268.

Begg, D.J., Langley, J.D., Moffitt, T. and Marshall, S.W. (1996). Sport and delinquency: an examination of the deterrence hypothesis in a longitudinal study. *British Journal of Sports Medicine*, 30, 335–341.

Belknap, J. (1996). Access to programmes and health care for incarcerated women. *Federal Probation*, 34, 40, 34–39.

Bennetto, J., Cusick, J. and Davies, P. (1995). Prison escape key is found near postbox. *The Independent*, 6th January.

Berman, G. (2012). *Prison Population Statistics*. SN/SG/4334 House of Commons Library. Retrieved from: http://www.parliament.uk/briefing-papers/SN04334.pdf

Berry, V., Little, M., Axford, N. and Cusick, G.R. (2009). An evaluation of Youth at Risk's Coaching for Communities programme. *The Howard Journal of Criminal Justice*, 48, 1, 60–75.

Bevins, V. (2012). Brazil prisoners ride bikes toward prison reform. *Los Angeles Times*, September 5th.

Big Lottery Fund. (2009). *New Opportunities for PE and Sport: Final Evaluation Summary*. Retrieved from: http://www.biglotteryfund.org.uk/er_eval_nopes_final_eval_summary.pdf

Bloyce, D. and Smith, A. (2010). *Sport Policy and Development: An Introduction*. Abingdon: Routledge.

Bosworth, K. and Espelage, D. (1995). *Teen Conflict Survey*. Bloomington, IN: Centre for Adolescent Studies, Indiana University.

Bottoms, A. (1999). Interpersonal violence and social order in prison. In M. Tonry and J. Petersilia (Eds.), *Crime and Justice: A Review of Research* (pp. 205–282). Chicago: University of Chicago.

Bourdieu, P. (1978). Sport and social class. *Social Science Information*, 17, 819–840.

Bourdieu, P. (1998). *Practical Reason: On the Theory of Action*. Stanford, CA: Stanford.

Bourdieu, P. (1999). The state, economics and sport. In H. Dauncey and G. Hare (Eds.), *France and the 1998 World Cup: The National Impact of a World Sporting Event* (pp. 15–21). London: Frank Cass.

Boyce, I., Hunter, G. and Hough, M. (2009). *St. Giles Trust Peer Advice Project: An Evaluation*. Retrieved from: http://www.stgilestrust.org.uk/stats-and-info/p518-evaluation-reports-on-st-giles-trust-services.html

Bradley, K. (2009). *The Bradley Report. Lord Bradley's Review of People with Mental Health Problems or Learning Disabilities in the Criminal Justice System*. London: Department of Health.

Bradshaw, R. (2008). *Common Themes from Analysis of 120 Prisons and Probation Ombudsman (PPO) Reports*. London: Department of Health.

Bredemeier, B.J. (1975). The assessment of reactive and instrumental athletic aggression. *Psychology of Sport and Motor Behaviour*, 71–83.

Brown, D. (2005). An economy of gendered practices? Learning to teach physical education from the perspective of Pierre Bourdieu's embodied sociology. *Sport, Education
and Society,* 10, 3–23.

Buckaloo, B., Krug, K. and Nelson, K. (2009). Exercise and the low-security inmate:
changes in depression, stress, and anxiety. *The Prison Journal,* 89, 3, 328–343.

Burdsal, C., and Buel, C. (1980). A short term community-based early stage intervention
program for behavior problem youth. *Journal of Clinical Psychology,* 36, 226, 241.

Burnett, R. and Maruna, S. (2006). The kindness of prisoners: strengths-based resettlement
in theory and in action. *Criminology and Criminal Justice,* 6, 1, 83–106.

Bushman, B. and Baumeister, R. (1998). Threatened egotism, narcissism, self-esteem, and
direct and displaced aggression: does self-love or self-hate lead to violence? *Journal of
Personality and Social Psychology,* 75, 219–229.

Bushman, B., Baumeister, R. and Stack, A. (1999). Catharsis, aggression, and persuasive
influence: Self-fulfilling or self-defeating prophecies? *Journal of Personality and Social
Psychology,* 76, 367–376.

Busseri, M., Costain, K., Campbell, K., Rose-Krasnor, L. and Evans, J. (2011). Brief
report: engagement in sport and identity status. Journal of Adolescence, 34, 1087–1091.

Byrne, C. and Trew, K. (2008). Pathways through crime: the development of crime and
desistance in the accounts of men and women. *The Howard Journal,* 47, 3, 238–258.

Cabinet Office. (2013). *Civil Service People Survey 2012: Summary of Findings.* London:
Cabinet Office.

Caldwell, L. (2005). Leisure and health: why is leisure therapeutic? *British Journal of
Guidance and Counselling,* 33, 1, 7–26.

Cameron, M. and MacDougall, C. (2000). Crime prevention through sport and physical
activity. *Trends and Issues in Crime and Criminal Justice,* 165, 1–6.

Campbell, W., Bush, C., Brunell, A. and Shelton, J. (2005). Understanding the social costs
of narcissism: the case of tragedy of the commons. *Personality and Social Psychology
Bulletin,* 31, 1358–1368.

Cann, J., Falshaw, L., Nugent, F. and Friendship, C. (2003). *Understanding What Works:
Cognitive Accredited Skills Programmes for Adult Men and Young Offenders,* Research
Findings 226. London: Home Office.

Caplan, A. (1996). *The Role of Recreational Sports in the Federal Prison System.* Unpublished doctoral dissertation, Acadia University.

Carmichael, D. (2008). *Youth Sport vs. Youth Crime: Evidence that Youth Engaged in
Organised Sport Are Not Likely to Participate in Criminal Activities.* Ontario: Active
Healthy Links Inc.

Cashin, A., Potter, E. and Butler, T. (2008). The relationship between exercise and hopelessness in prison. *Journal of Psychiatric and Mental Health Nursing,* 15, 1, 66–71.

Catton, S. (2007). Fit for inclusion: working with overweight and obese men with disabilities. In A. White and M. Pettifer (Eds.), *Hazardous Waist: Tackling Male Weight
Problems* (pp. 135–159). New York: Radcliffe Publishing.

Cauffman, E., Piquero, A., Brodidy, L., Espelage, D. and Mazerolle, P. (2008). Hetero-
geneity in the association between social-emotional adjustment profiles and deviant
behavior among male and female serious juvenile offenders. *International Journal of
Offender Therapy and Comparative Criminology,* 48, 235–252.

Caver, C. and Scheier, M. (1986). Functional and dysfunctional responses to anxiety: the
interaction between expectancies and responses to anxiety. In R. Schwarzer (Ed.), *Self
Related Cognitions in Anxiety and Motivation.* Hillsdale, NJ: Erlbaum.

CfBT. (2005). *Report on Toe by Toe: The Shannon Trust Reading Scheme in the Secure Estate*. London: DfES Offenders' Learning and Skills Unit.

Chalat, A. (2012). Hope behind bars. *The Junket*, 18th October.

Charity Commission (2013). *Search for Charities by their Registered Details*. Retrieved from: www.charitycommission.gov.uk/find-charities

Clement, J. (1995). Contributions of the sociology of Pierre Bourdieu to the sociology of sport. *Sociology of Sport Journal*, 12, 147–157.

Coakley, J. (1998). *Sport in Society: Issues and Controversies*. Boston: McGraw Hill.

Coalter, F. (1989). *Sport and Anti-Social Behaviour: A Literature Review*. Edinburgh: Scottish Sports Council.

Coalter, F. (1996). *Sport and Anti-Social Behaviour: A Policy Analysis*. Research Digest, 41. Edinburgh: Scottish Sports Council.

Coalter, F. (2002). *Community Sports Development Manual*. Edinburgh: Sports Scotland.

Coalter, F. (2005). Sport, social inclusion and crime reduction. In G. Faulkner and A. Taylor (Eds.), *Exercise Health and Mental Health*. Abingdon: Routledge.

Coalter, F. (2009). *The Value of Sport: Crime Reduction and Community Safety*. London: Sport England / UK Sport.

Coalter, F., Allison, M. and Taylor, J. (2000). *The Role of Sport in Regenerating Deprived Areas*. Edinburgh: SECRU.

Cohen, S. (1972). *Folk Devils and Moral Panics: The Creation of the Mods and Rockers*. London: MacGibbon and Kee.

Cohen, S., Kamarck, T. and Mermelstein, R. (1983). A global measure of perceived stress. *Journal of Health and Social Behavior*, 24, 385–396.

Colledge, M., Collier, P. and Brand, S. (1999). Crime reduction programme and constructive regimes in prison. Programmes for offenders: Guidance for evaluators. *Crime Reduction Programme Guidance*. Research, Development and Statistics Directorate. London: Home Office.

Collingwood, T., Sunderlin, J. and Kohl, H. (1994). The use of a staff training model for implementing fitness programming to prevent substance abuse with at risk youth. *American Journal of Health Promotion*, 9, 20–32.

Collingwood, T., Sunderlin, J., Reynolds, R. and Kohl, H. (2000). Physical training as a substance abuse prevention intervention for youth. *Journal of Drug Education*, 30, 435–451.

Collins, M. (Ed.) (2009). *Examining Sports Development*. Abingdon: Routledge.

Condon, L., Hek, G. and Harris, F. (2008). Choosing health in prison: prisoners' views on making healthy choices in English prisons. *Health Education Journal*, 67, 155–166.

Conroy, D., Silva, J., Newcomer, R., Walker, B. and Johnson, M. (2001). Personal and participatory socializers of the perceived legitimacy of aggressive behaviour in sport. *Aggressive Behaviour*, 27, 405–418.

Conservative Party. (2009). *Extending Opportunities: A Conservative Policy Paper on Sport*. London: The Conservative Party.

Conservative Party. (2010). *Conservative Sports Manifesto*. London: The Conservative Party.

Conservative Party. (2011). *Prisons with a Purpose. Our Sentencing and Rehabilitation Revolution to Break the Cycle of Crime. Security Agenda*. Policy Green Paper No. 4. London: The Conservative Party.

Cooley, D. (1993). Criminal victimization in male federal prisons. *Canadian Journal of Criminology*, 479–495.

Cooney, F. and Braggins, J. (2010). *Good Practice with Older People in Prison: The Views of Prison Staff*. London: Prison Reform Trust.

Cooper, C. (2011). Disability – the next equality challenge. *Prison Service Journal*, 195, 16–21.

Corey, F. (1996). Personal narratives and young men in prison: labelling the outside inside. *Western Journal of Communication*, 60, 1, 57–75.

Crabbe, T. (2000). A sporting chance? using sport to tackle drug use and crime. *Drugs: Education, Prevention and Policy*, 7, 4, 381–391.

Crawley, E. (2004). *Doing Prison Work: The Public and Private Lives of Prison Officers*. Cullompton: Devon.

Crewe, B. (2008). Concluding comments on the social world of prison staff. In J. Bennett, B. Crewe and A. Wahidin (Eds.), *Understanding Prison Staff*. Cullompton: Willan.

Crighton, D. and Towl, G. (1995). Evaluation issues in groupwork. In G. Towl (Ed.), *Group Work in Prisons: Issues in Criminological and Legal Psychology* (pp. 9–14). Leicester: The British Psychological Society.

Criminal Justice Joint Inspection. (2012). *Second Aggregate Report on Offender Management in Prisons: Findings from a Series of Joint Inspections by HM Inspectorate of Probation and HM Inspectorate of Prisons*. London: Criminal Justice Joint Inspection.

Cripps, H. (2010). *Children and Young People in Custody 2009–2010: An Analysis of the Experiences of 15–18 year olds in Prison*. HM Inspectorate of Prisons/Youth Justice Board. London: The Stationary Office.

Crompton, J. and Witt, P. (1997). Programs that work: the Roving Leader program in San Antonio. *Journal of Park and Recreation Administration*, 15, 84–92.

Crosnoe, R. (2002). Academic and health-related trajectories in adolescence: the intersection of gender and athletics. *Health and Social Behavior*, 43, 317–335.

Cunniffe, C., Van de Kerckhove, R., Williams, K. and Hopkins, K. (2012). *Estimating the Prevalence of Disability Amongst Prisoners: Results from the Surveying Prisoners Crime Reduction (SPCR) Survey*. London: Ministry of Justice.

Czajkowska, B., Golemba, M. and Popieluch, W. (1967). The importance of physical education in the medical-educative process of mentally disturbed inmates and the attitude of these inmates toward physical education. *Przeglad Psychologiczny*, 5, 3, 90–94.

Dale, M. (1976). Barriers to the rehabilitation of ex-offenders. *Crime and Delinquency*, 22, 3, 322–337.

Davies, K., Lewis, J., Byatt, J., Purvis, E. and Cole, B. (2004). *An Evaluation of the Literary Demands of General Offending Behaviour Programmes*. London: Home Office.

DCMS. (2004). Bringing communities together through sport and physical activity. London: DCMS.

Deane, J., Mawson, H., Crone, A., Parker, A. and James, D. (2010). Where are the future sports volunteers? *LSA Newsletter*, 80, 29–32.

Deem, R and Gilroy, S. (1998). Physical activity, lifelong learning and empowerment: situating sport in women's leisure time. *Sport, Education and Society*, 7, 3, 206–216.

Deges, F. (2010). Scaling the wall. *Rugby World*, May: 116–119.

Department for Business, Innovation and Skills / Ministry of Justice. (2011). *Making Prisons Work: Skills for Rehabilitation. Review of Offender Learning*. London: BIS.

Department for Education and Skills (2003). Every Child Matters. Presented to Parliament by the Chief Secretary to the Treasury by Command of Her Majesty, September 2003. Cm 5860. London: Stationery Office.

Department of Health. (2002). *Health Promoting Prisons: A Shared Approach*. London: Department of Health.

Department of Health. (2004). *At Least Five a Week: Evidence on the Impact of Physical Activity and its Relationship to Health*. London: Department of Health.

Department of Health. (2006). *Choosing Health and Supporting the Physical Health Needs of People with Severe Mental Illness*. London: Department of Health.

Department of Health. (2009a). *Improving Health, Supporting Justice: The National Delivery Plan of the Health and Criminal Justice Programme Board*. London: Department of Health.

Department of Health. (2009b). *The Bradley Report: Lord Bradley's Review of People with Mental Health Problems or Learning Disabilities in the Criminal Justice System*. London: Department of Health.

Devis-Devis, J., Peiro-Velart, C. and Martos-Garcia, D. (2012). *Sport and Physical Activity in European Prisons: A Perspective from Sport Personnel*. Prisoners on the Move. Retrieved from: http://www.prisonersonthemove.eu

Digennaro, S. (2010). Playing in the jail: sport as a psychosocial tool for inmates. *International Review on Sports and Violence*, 2, 4–24.

Dubberley, S. (2010). *Young Offenders, Imprisonment and the Duke of Edinburgh Award*. Unpublished doctoral dissertation, University of Wales.

Dubberley, S., Parry, O. and Baker, S. (2011). Mending fences: reparation and the reorientation of young people in the secure estate. *Criminal Justice Studies*, 24, 4, 337–350.

Dubois, D. and Karcher, M. (2005). Youth mentoring: theory, research and practice. In D. Dubois and M. Karcher (Eds.), *Handbook of Youth Mentoring*. New York: Sage.

Dulmen, M. and Ong, A. (2006). New methodological directions for the study of adolescent competence and adaptation. *Journal of Adolescence*, 29, 6, 851–856.

Durcan, G. (2008). *From the Inside: Experiences of Prison Mental Health Care*. London: Sainsbury Centre for Mental Health.

Dyson, G., Power, K. and Wozniak, E. (1997). Problems with using official records from Young Offender Institutions as indices of bullying. *International Journal of Offender Therapy and Comparative Criminology*, 41, 2, 121–138.

Ebaugh, H. (1988). *Becoming an Ex: The Process of Role Exit*. Chicago: University of Chicago Press.

Eby, L., Rhodes, J. and Allen, T. (2010). Definition and evolution of mentoring. In T. Allen and L. Eby (Eds.), *The Blackwell Handbook of Mentoring*. Chichester: Blackwell.

Edgar, K. (2007). Black and minority ethnic prisoners. In Y. Jewkes (Ed.), *Handbook on Prisons*. Cullumpton: Willan.

Edgar, K., Jacobson, J. and Biggar, K. (2011). *Time Well Spent: A Practical Guide to Active Citizenship and Volunteering in Prison*. London: Prison Reform Trust.

Edgar, K. and Newell, T. (2006). *Restorative Justice in Prisons: A Guide to Making it Happen*. Winchester: Waterside Press.

Edgar, K., O'Donnell, I. and Martin, C. (2012) *Prison Violence: The Dynamics of Conflict, Fear and Power*. Abingdon: Routledge.

Edge, D. (2006). *A Scoping Review of Policy and Provision*. London: The Prisoner Health Research Network / Department of Health.

Eitle, T and Eitle, D. (2002). Just don't do it: high school sports participation and young female adult sexual behaviour. *Sociology of Sport Journal*, 19, 403–418.

Eitle, D., Turner, R. and Eitle, T. (2003). The deterrence hypothesis reexamined: sports participation and substance use among young adults. *Journal of Drug Issues*, 33, 1, 193–221.

Eitzen, D. (2000). Social control and sports. In J. Coakley and E. Dunning (Eds.), *Handbook of Sports* (pp. 370–381). London: Sage.

Eitzen, D. (2006). *Fair and Foul: Beyond the Myths and Paradoxes of Sport*. Oxford: Rayman and Littlefield.

Ekeland, E., Heian, F. and Hagen, K. (2005). Can exercise improve self esteem in children and young people? A systematic review of randomised controlled trials. *British Journal of Sports Medicine*, 39, 792–798.

Elger, B. (2009). Prison life: television, sports, work, stress and insomnia in a remand prison. *International Journal of Law and Psychiatry*, 32, 74–83.

Ellis, N., Crone, D., Davey, R. and Grogan, S. (2007). Exercise interventions as an adjunct therapy for psychosis: a critical review. *British Journal of Clinical Psychology*, 46, 95–111.

European Committee for the Prevention of Torture and Inhuman or Degrading Treatment or Punishment. (2006). *European Prison Rules*. Strasbourg: Council of Europe.

European Union Agency for Fundamental Rights. (2010). *Racism, Ethnic Discrimination and Exclusion of Migrants and Minorities in Sport: A Comparative Overview of the Situation in the European Union*. Belgium: Union Agency for Fundamental Rights.

Evans, K. (2011). Big society in the UK: a policy review. *Children and Society*, 25, 164–171.

Evans, R. and Fraser, E. (2009). The views and experiences of Aboriginal and Torres Strait Islander young people on Queensland youth detention centres. *Indigenous Law Bulletin*, 7, 9–13.

Falshaw, L., Friendship, C., Travers, R. and Nugent, F. (2003). *Searching for What Works: An Evaluation of Cognitive Skills Programmes*. Home Office Research Study 206. London: Home Office.

Farooq, S., Moreland, B., Parker, A. and Pitchford, A. (2013). Sport, volunteering and marginalised youth. In A. Parker and D. Vinson (Eds.), *Youth Sport, Physical Activity and Play*. Abingdon: Routledge.

Farrall, S. (2002). *Rethinking What Works With Offenders*. Cullompton: Willan.

Farrall, S. and Calverley, A. (2006). *Understanding Desistance from Crime*. London: Open University Press.

Farrell, A., Meyer, A. and White, K. (2001). Evaluation of responding in peaceful and positive ways (RIPP): A school based prevention programme for reducing violence among urban adolescents. *Journal of Clinical Child Psychology*, 301, 4, 451–463.

Farrell, W., Johnson, R., Sapp, M., Pumphrey, R. and Freeman, S. (1996). Redirecting the lives of urban black males: an assessment of Milwaukee's Midnight Basketball League. *Journal of Community Practice*, 2, 91–107.

Farrington, D. (1983). Randomized experiments in crime and justice. In M. Tonry and N. Morris (Eds.), *Crime and Justice a Review of Research* (pp. 257–307). Chicago: University of Chicago.

Farrington, D., Ditchfield, J., Hancock, G., Howard, P., Joliffe, D., Livingston, M. and Painter, K. (2002). *Evaluation of Two Intensive Regimes for Young Offenders*. London: Home Office Research, Development and Statistics Publications.

Fawcett Society. (2007). *Justice and Equality. Second Annual Review of the Commission on Women and the Criminal Justice System*. London: Fawcett Society.

Fazel, S., Bains, P. and Doll, H. (2006). Substance abuse and dependence in prisoners: a systematic review. *Addiction*, 101, 181–191.

Fazel, S. and Danesh, J. (2002). Serious mental disorder in 23000 prisoners: a systematic review of 62 surveys. *The Lancet*, 359, 9306, 545–550.

Feldman, S. and Weinberger, D. (1994). Self restraint as a mediator of family influences on boys delinquent behaviour: a longitudinal study. *Child Development*, 65, 1, 195–211.

Felson, R. (1997). Routine activities and involvement in violence as actor, witness, or target. *Violence and Victims*, 12, 3, 209–221.

Fiji Corrections Service. (2011). *Budding Rugby Coaches and Referees*. Retrieved from: http://www.corrections.org.fj/pages.cfm/rehabilitation-progrmaes/sport.html

Finnegan, L., Whitehurst, D. and Deaton, S. (2010). *Models of Mentoring for Inclusion and Employment: Thematic Review of Existing Evidence on Mentoring and Peer Mentoring*. London: Centre for Economic and Social Inclusion.

Fischer, J., Butt, C., Dawes, H., Foster, C., Neale, J., Plugge, E. and Wright, N. (2012). Fitness levels and physical activity among class A drug users entering prison. *British Journal of Sports Medicine*, published online April 20, doi: 10.1136/bjsports–2011–090724

Folkins, C. and Sime, W. (1981). Physical fitness training and mental health. *American Psychologist*, 36, 4, 373–389.

Francis, P. (2012). Sport and harm. *Criminal Justice Matters*, 88, 1, 14–15.

Frank, P. and Dahn, J. (2005). Exercise and wellbeing: a review of mental and physical health benefits associated with physical activity. *Current Opinion in Psychiatry*, 18, 2, 189–192.

Franklin, T., Franklin, C. and Pratt, T. (2006). Examining the empirical relationship between prison crowding and inmate misconduct: a meta-analysis of conflicting research results. *Journal of Criminal Justice*, 34, 4, 401–412.

French, D. and Hainsworth, J. (2001). 'There aren't any buses and the swimming pool is always cold': obstacles and opportunities in the provision of sport for disabled people. *Managing Leisure*, 6, 1, 35–49.

Frey, E. and Epkins, C. (2002). Examining cognitive models of externalizing and internalizing problems in subgroups of juvenile delinquents. *Journal of Clinical Child and Adolescent Psychology*, 31, 4, 556–566.

Frey, J. and Delaney, T. (1996). The role of leisure participation in prison: a report from consumers. *Journal of Offender Rehabilitation*, 23, 1–2, 79–89.

Friendship, C., Beech, A. and Browne, K. (2002). Reconviction as an outcome measure in research: a methodological note. *British Journal of Criminology*, 42, 442–222.

Friendship, C., Blud, L., Erikson, M. and Travers, R. (2002). *An Evaluation of Cognitive Behavioural Treatment for Prisoners*. Findings 161. London: Home Office.

Frude, N., Honess, T. and Maguire, M. (2009). *CRIME-PICS II*. Cardiff: M&A Research.

Gabriel, R. (1994). *Self Enhancement, Inc Violence Prevention Programme, Grades 7,8, 9: Year 1 Evaluation Report*. Portland: RMC Research Corporation.

Gaes, G. and McGuire, W. (1985). Prison violence: the contribution of crowding versus other determinants of prison assault rates. *Journal of Research in Crime and Delinquency*, 22, 1, 41–65.

Gardner, M., Roth, J. and Brooks-Gunn, J. (2009). Sports participation and juvenile delinquency: the role of the peer context among adolescents boys and girls with varied histories of problem behaviour. *Developmental Psychology*, 45, 2, 341–353.

Garratt, A., Ruta, D., Abdalla, M., Buckingham, J. and Russell, I. (1993). The SF-36 Health Survey Questionnaire: an outcome measure suitable for routine use within the NHS? *British Medical Journal*, 306, 1440–1444.

Gatz, M., Messner, M. and Ball-Rokeach, S. (Eds.) (2002). *Paradoxes of Youth and Sport*. New York: State University of New York Press.

Gebhardt, D. and Crump, C. (1990). Employee fitness and wellbeing programs in the workplace. *American Psychologist*, 45, 2, 262–272.

Gelsthorpe, L. and Sharpe, G. (2007). Women and resettlement. In A. Hucklesby and L. Hagley-Dickinson (Eds.), *Prisoner Resettlement: Policy and Practice* (pp. 199–223). Cullompton: Willan.

Gentleman, A. (2012). Inside Halden, the most humane prison in the world. *The Guardian*, 19th May.

Gibson, D. (2013). Lance Armstrong 'comes clean' over doping in Oprah Winfrey interview. *The Guardian*, 15th January.

Giordano, P., Cernkovich, S. and Rudolph, J. (2002). Gender, crime and desistance: toward a theory of cognitive transformation. *American Journal of Sociology*, 107, 990–1064.

Goetting, A. and Howsen, R. (1983). Women in prison: a profile. *Prison Journal*, 63, 2, 27–46.

Goldberg D. and Williams, P. (1988). A user's guide to the General Health Questionnaire. Windsor: NFER-Nelson.

Gould, D. and Larson, S. (2008). Life skills development through sport: current status and future directions. *International Review of Sport and Exercise Psychology*, 1, 1, 58–78.

Gras, L. (2005). Inmates on sports-related leaves: a decisive experience. *Champ Pénal*, Vol II. doi: 10.4000/champpenal.2302

Griffin, P. (1992). Changing the game: homophobia, sexism and lesbians in sport. *Quest*, 44, 2, 251–265.

Hagan, J. (1989). Role and significance of sport/recreation in the penal system. *Prison Service Journal*, 75, 9–11.

Halsey, M. (2008). Risking desistance: respect and responsibility in custodial and post-release contexts. In P. Carlen (Ed.), *Imaginary Penalities*. Cullompton: Willan.

Hamlyn, B. and Lewis, D. (2000). *Women Prisoners: A Survey of Their Work and Training Experiences in Custody and on Release*. Home Office Research Study 208. London: Home Office.

Handy, S., Boarnet, M., Ewing, R. and Killingsworth, R. (2002). How the built environment affects physical activity: views from urban planning. *American Journal of Preventive Medicine*, 23, 2S, 64–73.

Hansard HC, 21 January 1988, 125 cc785–6W.

Hansard HC, 2 November 2009, c746W.

Hansard HC, 9 January 2013, c326.

Hardwick, N. (2012). *Women in Prison: Corston Five Years On*. University of Sussex Lecture, 29th February.

Hardy, L. and Jones, G. (1994). Future directions for performance related research in sport psychology. *Journal of Sport Sciences*, 12, 327–334.

Harner, H. and Riley, S. (2012). The impact of incarceration on women's mental health: responses from women in a maximum-security prison. *Qualitative Health Research*, 23, 1, 26–42.

Harris, F., Hek, G. and Condon, L. (2006). Health needs of prisoners in England and Wales: the implications for prison healthcare of gender, age and ethnicity. *Health and Social Care in the Community*, 15, 1, 56–66.

Harter, S. (1990). Adolescent self and identity development. In S. Feldman and G. Elliot (Eds.), *At the Threshold: The Developing Adolescent*. Cambridge, MA: Harvard University Press.

Hartmann, D. (2001). Notes on midnight basketball and the cultural politics of recreation, race and at-risk urban youth, *Journal of Sport and Social Issues*, 25, 4, 339–71.

Hartmann, D. and Depro, B. (2006). Rethinking sports-based community crime prevention: a preliminary analysis of the relationship between midnight basketball and urban crime rates. *Journal of Sport and Social Issues*, 30, 2, 180–196.

Hartmann, D. and Massaglia, M. (2007). Reassessing the relationship between high school sports participation and deviance: evidence of enduring bifurcated effects. *The Sociological Quarterly*, 48, 485–505.

Hartwig, C., Stöver, H. and Weilandt, C. (2008). *Report on Tobacco Smoking in Prison: Final Report Work Package 7*. Directorate General for Health and Consumer Affairs (DG SANCO). DG SANCO/2006/C4/02.

Harvey, J. (2005). Crossing the boundary: the transition of young adults into prison. In A. Liebling and S. Maruna (Eds.), *The Effects of Imprisonment*. Cullompton: Willan.

Harvey, J. (2007). *Young Men in Prison: Surviving and Adapting to Life Inside*. Abingdon: Routledge.

Haug, E., Morland, J., Olaisen, B. and Myhre, K. (2004). *Androgenic Anabolic Steroids (AAS) and Violent Behavior*. Report from NOKC. Retrieved from: http://www.kunnskapssenteret.no/Publikasjoner

Hawkins, B. (1998). Evening basketball leagues: The use of sport to reduce African American youth criminal activity. *International Sports Journal*, 2, 2, 68–77.

Health Development Agency and ASH. (2003). *Smoking and Health Inequalities*. Retrieved from: http://www.nice.org.uk/nicemedia/documents/smoking_and_health_inequalities.pdf

Heaven, P. (2001). *The Social Psychology of Adolescence*. Basingstoke: Macmillan.

Henderson, C., Dakof, G., Schwartz, S. and Liddle, H. (2006). Family functioning, self concept and severity of adolescents' externalizing problems. *Journal of Child and Family Studies*, 15, 721–731.

Herbert, K., Plugge, E., Foster, C. and Doll, H. (2012). Prevalence and risk factors for non-communicable diseases in prison populations worldwide. *The Lancet*, 397, 1975–1982.

Hirschi, T. (1969). *Causes of Delinquency*. Berkeley: University of California Press.

HM Chief Inspector of Prisons. (1999). *Inspection of Close Supervision Centres: A Thematic Review by HM Chief Inspector of Prisons for England and Wales*. London: HM Inspectorate of Prisons.

HM Chief Inspector of Prisons. (2009). *Disabled Prisoners: A Short Thematic Review on the Care and Support of Prisoners with a Disability*. London: HM Inspectorate of Prisons.

HM Chief Inspector of Prisons. (2011). *Report on an Unannounced Short Follow Up Inspection of HMP Erlestoke*. London: HM Inspectorate of Prisons.

HM Inspectorate of Prisons. (2008). *Older Prisoners in England and Wales: A Follow-up to the 2004 Thematic Review by HM Chief Inspector of Prisons*. London: HM Inspectorate of Prisons.

HM Inspectorate of Prisons. (2010). *Chief Inspector of Prisons for England and Wales Annual Report 2008–09*. London: HM Inspectorate of Prisons.

HM Inspectorate of Prisons. (2012). *Chief Inspector of Prisons for England and Wales Annual Report 2011–12*. London: HM Inspectorate of Prisons.

HM Prison Service. (1993). *Bullying in Prison: A Strategy to Beat It*. London: HMSO.

HM Prison Service. (2000). *Clinical Services for Substance Misusers*. PSO 3550.

HM Prison Service. (2002). *Effective Regime Interventions*. PSO 4350.

HM Prison Service. (2003). *Health Promotion*. PSO 3200.

HM Prison Service. (2004). *Regimes for Juveniles*. PSO 4950.

HM Prison Service. (2008). *Women Prisoners*. PSO 4800.

HM Prison Service. (2009). *Physical Education*. PSO 4250.

Hobbs, G. and Dear, G. (2000). Prisoners' perceptions of prison officers as sources of support. *Journal of Offender Rehabilitation*, 31, 1/2, 127–142.

Hodge, R. (2009). Advances in the assessment and treatment of juvenile offenders. *Kriminologija I Socijalna Integracija*, 17, 2, 49–69.

Home Affairs Select Committee. (2004). *The Committees Prison Diaries Project*. Retrieved from: http://www.publications.parliament.uk/pa/cm200405/cmselect/cmhaff/193/19325.htm

Home Office. (1988). *Criminal Statistics England and Wales, 1988*. CM825. London: HMSO.

Home Office. (1991). *Prison Disturbances April 1990: Report of an Inquiry by the Rt Hon. Lord Justice Woolf (Parts I and II) and His Honour Judge Stephen Tumin (Part II)* (Cm 1456). London: HMSO.

Home Office. (2004). *The Reducing Reoffending National Action Plan*. London: HMSO.

Home Office. (2007). *A Report by Baroness Jean Corston of a Review of Women with Particular Vulnerabilities in the Criminal Justice System*. London: Home Office.

Home Office. (2011). *Counting Rules for Recorded Crime*. London: Home Office.

Home Office. (2012). *Drug Misuse Declared: Findings from the 2011/12 Crime Survey for England and Wales (2nd Edition)*. London: Home Office.

Honess, T., Maguire, M. and Vanstone, M. (2001). *CRIAQ*. M&A Research.

Hopkins, K. (2012). *The Pre-Custody Employment, Training and Education Status of Newly Sentenced Prisoners. Results from the Surveying Prisoner Crime Reduction (SPCR) Longitudinal Cohort Study of Prisoners*. Research summary 3/12. London: Ministry of Justice.

Horne, J., Tomlinson, A., Whannel, G. and Woodward, K. (2012). *Understanding Sport: A Socio-Cultural Analysis*. Abingdon: Routledge.

House of Commons Home Affairs Committee. (2007a). *Young Black People and the Criminal Justice System. Second Report of Session 2006–07 Volume I*. London: The Stationary Office.

House of Commons Home Affairs Committee. (2007b). *Young Black People and the Criminal Justice System. Second Report of Session 2006–07 Volume II*. London: The Stationary Office.

House of Commons Justice Committee. (2009). *Role of the Prison Officer*. London: The Stationary Office.

House of Commons Treasury Committee. (2007). *The 2007 Comprehensive Spending Review*. London: The Stationary Office.

Hucklesby, A. and Hagley-Dickinson, L. (2007). Conclusion: opportunities, barriers and threats. In A. Hucklesby and L. Hagley-Dickinson (Eds.), *Prisoner Resettlement: Policy and Practice*. Cullompton: Willan.

Hudson, K. and Meek, R. (2007). *Evaluation of the 'Going Straight Contract' Pilot Project. Final Report*. Cardiff: Cardiff University.

Hughes, E. (2009). Thinking inside the box: prisoner education, learning identities, and the possibilities for change. In B. Veysey, J. Christian and D. Martinez (Eds.), *How Offenders Transform Their Lives*. Abingdon: Routledge.

Hughes, R. and Coakley, J. (1991). Positive deviance among athletes: The implications of over conformity to the sport ethic. *Sociology of Sport Journal*, 8, 307–325.

Humberstone, B. (1990). Gender, change and adventure education. *Gender and Education* 2, 2, 199–215.

Independent Monitoring Board. (2010). *HMP Grendon Annual Report of the Independent Monitoring Board*. London: Independent Monitoring Board.

Independent Monitoring Board. (2011). *HMP Ford Annual Report of the Independent Monitoring Board*. London: Independent Monitoring Board.

Independent Monitoring Board. (2012a). *Annual Report of the Independent Monitoring Board of Brook House Immigration Removal Center 2012*. London: Independent Monitoring Board.

Independent Monitoring Board. (2012b). *Annual Report of the Independent Monitoring Board of Tinsley House Immigration Removal Center 2012*. London: Independent Monitoring Board.

Inter-American Commission on Human Rights. (2008). *Principles and Best Practices on the Protection of Persons Deprived of Liberty in the Americas*. Washington, DC: IACHR.

International Working Group on Women and Sport. (1994). *The Brighton Declaration on Women and Sport*. Helsinki, Finland: IWG.

Ireland, J. (1999). Bullying amongst prisoners: a study of adults and young offenders. *Aggressive Behavior,* 25, 162–178.

Iwasaki, Y. and Mannell, R. (2000). Hierarchical dimensions of leisure stress coping. *Leisure Sciences*, 22, 163–181.

Jaffe, M. (2012). *Peer Support and Seeking Help in Prison: A Study of the Listener Scheme in Four Prisons in England*. Unpublished doctoral dissertation, Keele University.

James, C., Stams, G., Asscher, J., De Roo, A. and van der Laan, P. (2013). Aftercare programs for reducing recidivism among juvenile and young adult offenders: a meta-analytic review. *Clinical Psychology Review*, 33, 263–274.

Jebb, S. and Moore, M. (1999). Contribution of a sedentary lifestyle and inactivity to the etiology of overweight and obesity: current evidence and research issues. *Medicine and Science in Sports and Exercise,* 31, 11, S534–S541.

Jetten, J., Postmes, T. and McAuliffe, B. (2002). 'We're *all* individuals': group norms of individualism and collectivism, levels of identification and identity threat. *European Journal of Social Psychology*, 32, 189–207.

Jewkes, Y. (2002). *Captive Audience: Media, Masculinity and Power in Prisons*. Cullompton: Willan.

Jewkes, Y. (2005). Loss, liminality and the life sentence: managing identity through a disrupted lifecourse. In A. Liebling and S. Maruna (Eds.), *The Effects of Imprisonment*. Cullompton: Willan.

Johnsen, B. (2001). *Sport, Masculinities and Power Relations in Prison*. Unpublished doctoral dissertation, Norwegian University of Sport and Physical Education, Oslo.

Jones, C. and McNamee, M. (2003). Moral development and sport: character and cognitive development contrasted. In J. Boxill (Ed.), Sports Ethics (pp. 40–52). Oxford: Blackwell.

Jones, G. (1991). Recent developments and current issues in competitive state anxiety research. *The Psychologist*, 4, 152–155.

Jones, G. (1995). More than just a game: research developments and issues in competitive anxiety in sport. *British Journal of Psychology*, 86, 4, 449–478.

Jones, R. (2002). The black experience within English semi professional soccer. *Journal of Sport and Social Issues*, 26, 1, 47–65.

Joseph Rowntree Foundation. (2007). *Social Cohesion in Diverse Communities*. New York: Joseph Rowntree Foundation.

Karcher, M. (2005). Cross-age peer mentoring. In D. Dubois and M. Karcher (Eds.), *Handbook of Youth Mentoring*. New York: Sage.

Kasser, T. (1996). Aspirations and well being in a prison setting. *Journal of Applied Social Psychology,* 26, 15, 1367–1377.

Kavussanu, M. and Ntoumanis, N. (2003). Participation in sport and moral functioning: does ego-orientation mediate their relationship? *Journal of Sport and Exercise Psychology*, 25, 501–518.

Kay, J. and Laberge, S. (2002). The 'new' corporate habitus in adventure racing. *International Review for the Sociology of Sport*, 37, 17–36.

Kay, T. (2003). Gender, sport and social exclusion. In M. Collins and Kay, T. (Eds.), *Sport and Social Exclusion*. Abingdon: Routledge.

Kehily, M. (2007). Playing. In M. Kehily (Ed.), *Understanding Youth: Perspectives, Identities and Practices* (pp. 249–282). London: Sage Publications.

Keinan, G. and Malach-Pines, A. (2007). Stress and burnout among prison personnel: sources, outcomes and intervention strategies. *Criminal Justice and Behavior*, 34, 3, 380–398.

Kelly, B. (2011). *Leisure Participation and Mental Health in Tasmania: A Lifecycle Approach*. Unpublished doctoral dissertation, University of Tasmania.

Kelly, L. (2012). Representing and preventing youth crime and disorder: intended and unintended consequences of targeted youth programmes in England. *Youth Justice*, 12, 2, 101–117.

Kenyon, J. and Rockwood, J. (2010). 'One eye in Toxteth, one eye in Croxteth'- examining youth perspectives of racist and anti-social behaviour, identity and the value of sport as a integrative enclave in Liverpool. *International Journal of Arts and Sciences*, 3, 5, 496–519.

Kershaw, C. (1997). *Interpreting Reconviction Rates*. Proceedings from the Criminology Conferences Volume 2. Belfast: Queens University.

Kielyl, J. and Hodgson, G. (1990). Stress in the prison service: the benefits of exercise programs. *Human Relations*, 43, 6, 551–571.

Kleiber, D. and Roberts, G. (1981). The effects of sport experience in the development of social character: a preliminary investigation. *Journal of Sport and Exercise Psychology*, 3, 114–122.

Klotz, F., Petersson, A., Hoffman, O. and Thiblin, I. (2010). The significance of anabolic androgenic steroids in a Swedish prison population. *Comprehensive Psychiatry*, 51, 312–315.

Knight, M. and Plugge, E. (2005). The outcomes of pregnancy among imprisoned women: a systematic review. *BJOG: An International Journal of Obstetrics and Gynaecology*. 112, 11, 1467–1474.

Kohn, A. (1986). *No Contest: The Case Against Competition*. Boston: Houghton Mifflin.

Kremner, J., Trew, K. and Ogle, S. (1997). *Young People's Involvement in Sport*. Abingdon: Routledge.

Kriska, A. and Caspersen, C. (1997). A collection of physical activity questionnaires for health-related research. *Medicine and Science in Sports and Exercise,* 29, S1–S205.

Krouwel, A., Boonstra, N., Duyvendak, J. and Veldboer, L. (2006). A good sport? Research into the capacity of recreational sport to integrate ethnic Dutch minorities. *International Review for the Sociology of Sport*, 41, 2, 165–180.

Labour Party. (1997). *Labour's Sporting Nation*. London: The Labour Party.

Lawson, H. (2005). Empowering people, facilitating community development, and contributing to sustainable development: the social work of sport, exercise, and physical education programs. *Sport, Education and Society*, 10, 1, 135–160.

Leberman, S. (2007). Voices behind the walls: female offenders and experiential learning. *Journal of Adventure Education and Outdoor Learning*, 7, 3, 113–130.

Lester, C., Hamilton-Kirkwood, L. and Jones, N. (2003). Health indicators in a prison population: asking prisoners. *Health Education Journal*, 62, 4, 341–349.

Lester, S. and Russell, W. (2008). *Play for a Change: Play, Policy and Practice: A Review of Contemporary Perspectives*. London: Play England.

Levinson, M. and Sparkes, A. (2003). Gypsy masculinities and the school-home interface: exploring contradictions and tensions. *British Journal of Sociology of Education*, 24, 5, 587–603.

Lewis, E. and Heer, B. (2008). *Child Matters in Secure Settings: A Practical Toolkit for Improving the Health and Well-Being of Young People*. London: National Children's Bureau.

Lewis, G. and Meek, R. (2012). Sport and physical education across the secure estate: an exploration of policy and practice. *Criminal Justice Matters*, 90, 32–4.

Libbus, M., Genovese, J. and Poole, M. (1994). Organised aerobic exercise and depression in male county jail inmates. *Journal of Correctional Health Care*, 1, 5–16.

Liebling, A. assisted by Arnold, G. (2004). *Prisons and their Moral Performance: A Study of Values, Quality and Prison Life*. Oxford: Clarendon Press.

Liebling, A., Arnold, H. and Straub, C. (2011). *An Exploration of Staff-Prisoner Relationships at HMP Whitemoor: 12 Years On*. London: Cambridge Institute of Criminology/ Ministry of Justice.

Light, R. and Kirk, D. (2000). High school rugby, the body and the reproduction of hegemonic masculinity. *Sport, Education and Society*, 5, 163–176.

Little, M. (1990). *Young Men in Prison: The Criminal Identity Explored Through the Rules of Behaviour*. Aldershot: Dartmouth.

Lloyd, C., Mair, G. and Hough, M. (1994). *Explaining Reconviction Rates: A Critical Analysis*. London: Home Office.

Lochman, J. and Dodge, K. (1994). Social cognitive processes of severely violent, moderately aggressive and non-aggressive boys. *Journal of Consulting and Clinical Psychology*, 62, 2, 366–374.

Long, J., Hylton, K., Spracklen, K., Ratna, A. and Bailey, S. (2009). *Systematic Review of the Literature on Black and Minority Ethnic Communities in Sport and Physical Recreation*. Birmingham: Sporting Equals.

Lovell, G., El Ansari, W. and Parker, J. (2010). Perceived exercise benefits and barriers of non-exercising female university students in the United Kingdom. *International Journal of Environmental Research and Public Health*, 7, 3, 784–798.

Luthar, S. (Ed.) (2003). *Resilience and Vulnerability*. Cambridge: Cambridge University Press.

MacClancy, J. (Ed.) (1996). *Sport, Identity and Ethnicity*. Oxford: Berg.

Magee, H. and Foster, J. (2011). *Peer Support in Prison Health Care: An Investigation into the Listening Scheme in one Adult Male Prison*. London: University of Greenwich/ The Samaritans.

Maguire, M. and Raynor, P. (2006). How the resettlement of prisoners promotes desistance from crime: or does it? *Criminology and Criminal Justice*, 6, 19–38.

Mahoney, C. (1997). Age and sport participation. In J. Kermer, K. Trew and S. Ogle, (Eds.) *Young People's Involvement in Sport* (pp. 98–113). Abingdon: Routledge.

Mair, G. and May, C. (1997). *Offenders on Probation: A Research and Statistics Department Report*. London: Home Office.

Major, B. and O'Brien, L. (2005). The social psychology of stigma. *Annual Review of Psychology*, 56, 393–421.

Majors, R. (2001). Understanding the current educational status of Black children. In R. Majors (Ed.), *Educating our Black Children: New Directions and Radical Approaches*. Abingdon: Routledge.

Marsden, S. (2012). Guards 'may have helped' bedsheet escape prisoner. *The Telegraph*, 29th June.

Martens, R., Vealey, R. and Burton, D. (1990). *Competitive Anxiety in Sport*. Champaign, IL: Human Kinetics.

Martos-Garcia, D., Devis-Devis, J, and Sparkes, A. (2009a). Sport and physical activity in a high security Spanish prison: An ethnographic study of multiple meanings. *Sport, Education and Society*, 14, 1, 77–96.

Martos-Garcia, D., Devis-Devis, J. and Sparkes, A. (2009b). Sport behind bars: anything beyond social control? *Revista Internacional de Sociologia*, 67, 2, 391–412.

Maruna, S. (2001). *Making Good: How Ex Convicts Reform and Rebuild their Lives*. Washington: American Psychological Association.

Mason, G. and Wilson, P. (1988). *Sport Recreation and Juvenile Crime*. Canberra: Australian Institute of Criminology. Retrieved from: http://www.aic.gov.au/documents/F/E/A/%7BFEA056F5–6ED8–4932–8CC3-B9D5FFCD8055%7 Dsport.pdf

Mason, T. and Riedi, E. (2010). *Sport and the Military: The British Armed Force 1990–1960*. Cambridge: Cambridge University Press.

Math, S., Murthy, P., Parthasanthy, R., Kumar, C. and Mudhusudhan, S. (2011). *Mental Health and Substance Use Problems in Prisons*. Bangalore: National Institute of Mental Health and Neuro Sciences.

Matrie, N. (2002). Healthy body, healthy mind? *The Psychologist*, 15, 8, 412–413.

Mawson, H. and Parker, A. (2013). The next generation: young people, sport and volunteering. In A. Parker and D. Vinson (Eds.), *Youth Sport, Physical Activity and Play*. Abingdon: Routledge.

Maxwell, J. and Moores, E. (2007). The development of a short scale measuring aggressiveness and anger in competitive athletes. *Psychology of Sport and Exercise*, 8, 179–193.

McDougall, C., Clarbour, J., Perry, A. and Bowels, R. (2009, March). *Evaluation of HM Prison Service Enhanced Thinking Skills Programme: Report on the Implementation of a Randomised Controlled Trial*. London: Ministry of Justice.

McMahon, S. and Washburn, J. (2003). Violence prevention: an evaluation of program effects with urban African American students. *The Journal of Primary Prevention*, 24, 1, 43–62.

McMurran, M. and Cusens, B. (2003). Controlling alcohol-related violence: a treatment programme. *Criminal Behaviour and Mental Health*, 13, 59–76.

McMurran, M., Theodosi, E., Sweeney, A. and Sellen, J. (2008). What do prisoners want? Current concerns of adult male prisoners. *Psychology, Crime and Law*, 14, 3, 267–274.

McNeill, F. (2006). A desistance paradigm for offender management. *Criminology & Criminal Justice*, 6, 1, 39–62.

McSweeney, T. and Hough, M. (2006). Supporting offenders with multiple needs: Lessons for the 'missed economy' model of service provision. *Criminology and Criminal Justice*, 6, 1, 107–125.

Meek, R. (2007). The experiences of a young Gypsy-Traveller in the transition from custody to community: an interpretative phenomenological analysis. Legal and Criminological Psychology, 1, 133–148.

Meek, R. (2010). Can crime be 'cured'? Cognitive behavioural programmes. In M. Herzog-Evans (Ed.), *Transnational Criminology Manual* (pp. 555–564). Nijmegen, The Netherlands: Wolf Legal.

Meek, R., Champion, N. and Klier, S. (2012). *Fit for Release: How Sports-Based Learning can Help Prisoners Engage in Education, Gain Employment and Desist from Crime*. London: Prisoners Education Trust.

Meek, R., Gojkovic, D. and Mills, A. (2010). *The Role of the Third Sector in Work with Offenders: The Perceptions of Criminal Justice and Third Sector Stakeholders*. Third Sector Research Centre Briefing and Working Paper Series No. 34. Southampton: TSRC.

Meek, R., Gojkovic, D. and Mills, A. (2013). The involvement of nonprofit organizations in prisoner reentry in the UK: prisoner awareness and engagement. *Journal of Offender Rehabilitation*, 52, 5, 338–357.

Mehrabian, A. and Bekken, M. (1986). Temperament characteristics of individuals who participate in strenuous sports. *Research Quarterly for Exercise and Sport*, 57, 2, 160–166.

Melnick, M., Vanfossen, B. and Sabo, D. (1988). Developmental effects of athletic participation among high school girls. *Sociology of Sport Journal*, 5, 1, 22–36.

Mentoring and Befriending Foundation. (2011). *Glossary*. Retrieved from: http://www.mandbf.org/guidance-and-support/what-is-mentoring-and-befriending/glossary

Messent, P. and Cooke, C. (1998). Physical activity, exercise and health of adult with mild and moderate learning disabilities. *British Journal of Learning Disabilities*, 26, 1, 17–22.

Messerschmidt, J. (1993). *Masculinities and Crime*. Lanham: Rowman and Littlefield.

Metcalf, H., Anderson, T. and Rolfe, H. (2001). *Barriers to Employment for Ex Offenders*. Research Report No 155. London: Her Majesty's Stationary Office.

Miller, K., Melnick, M., Barnes, G., Sabo, D. and Farrell, M. (2007). Athletic involvement and adolescent delinquency. *Journal of Youth and Adolescence*, 36, 711–723.

Mills, A., Meek, R. and Gojkovic, D. (2012). Partners, guests or competitors: Relationships between criminal justice and third sector staff in prisons. *Probation Journal*, 59, 4, 391–405.

Ministry of Justice. (2008). *Third Sector Strategy: Improving Policies and Securing Better Public Services through Effective Partnerships 2008–2011*. London: Ministry of Justice.

Ministry of Justice. (2009). *Tackling Drugs through Physical Education*. London: Ministry of Justice.

Ministry of Justice. (2010a). *Breaking the Cycle: Effective Punishment, Rehabilitation and Sentencing of Offenders*. London: Ministry of Justice.

Ministry of Justice. (2010b). *Statistics on Women and the Criminal Justice System*. London: Ministry of Justice.

Ministry of Justice. (2011a). *Ensuring Equality*. PSI 32/2011. London: Ministry of Justice.

Ministry of Justice. (2011b). *Physical Education (PE) for Prisoners*. PSI 58/2011. London: Ministry of Justice.

Ministry of Justice. (2011c). *Statistics on Race and the Criminal Justice System 2010*. London: Ministry of Justice.

Ministry of Justice. (2011d). *Young Adult Remand and Sentenced Population in Prison by Offence Group and Sex, on a Quarterly Basis, September 2009 to December 2010, England and Wales (Young Adults)*. London: Ministry of Justice.

Ministry of Justice. (2011e). *2011 Compendium of Reoffending Statistics and Analysis*. Statistics Bulletin. London: Ministry of Justice.

Ministry of Justice. (2012a). *Business Plan 2012–2015*. London: Ministry of Justice.

Ministry of Justice. (2012b). *Equalities Annual Report 2011–12*. London: Ministry of Justice.

Ministry of Justice. (2012c). *National Offender Management Service Annual Report 2011/12: Management Information Addendum*. London: Ministry of Justice.

Ministry of Justice. (2012d). *Population Bulletin Weekly 30th November 2012*. London: Ministry of Justice.

Ministry of Justice. (2012e). *Proven Reoffending Statistics Quarterly Bulletin January to December 2010, England and Wales*. London: Ministry of Justice.

Ministry of Justice. (2012f). *Proven Reoffending Tables Jan-Dec 2010*. London: Ministry of Justice.

Ministry of Justice. (2013a). *Offender Management Statistics: Quarterly Bulletin July to September 2012, England and Wales*. London: Ministry of Justice.

Ministry of Justice. (2013b). *Offender Management Statistics: Quarterly Bulletin October to December 2012*. London: Ministry of Justice.

Ministry of Justice. (2013c). *Justice Data Lab: Methodology Paper*. London: Ministry of Justice.

Ministry of Justice/National Offender Management Service. (2008). *Working with the Third Sector to Reduce Reoffending: Securing Effective Partnerships 2008–2011*. London: Ministry of Justice/National Offender Management Service.

Morsbach, G. (2011). *A Very Different Alcatraz*. Retrieved from: http://news.bbc.co.uk/1/hi/world/americas/4854506.stm

Morris, L., Sallybanks, J., Willis, K. and Makkai, T. (2003). Sport, physical activity and antisocial behaviour in youth, *Trends and Issues in Crime and Criminal Justice*, 249, 1–6.

MSN News. (2012). Update: Chicago jail escapees hailed a cab to get away. Retrieved from: http://news.msn.com/us/update-chicago-jail-escapees-hailed-a-cabtogetawayinvestigators-say

Multisite Violence Prevention Project. (2004). *Description of Measures: Cohort-Wide Student Survey*. (Unpublished). Atlanta, GA: Centers for Disease Control and Prevention, National Center for Injury Prevention and Control.

Muncie, J. (2004). *Youth and Crime*. London: Sage.

Muncie, J. (2008). The 'punitive turn' in juvenile justice: cultures of control and rights compliance in Western Europe and the USA. *Youth Justice*, 8, 2, 107–121.

Murray, C. (in press). Sport in care: using Freedom of Information requests to elicit data about looked after children's involvement in physical activity. *British Journal of Social Work*.

Murtaza, T. and Uddin, R. (2011). Probing study on facilities of competitive sport in District Jail, Lucknow (India). *European Journal of Business and Management*, 3, 8, 69–79.

National Audit Office. (2006). *Serving Time: Prisoner Diet and Exercise*. London: The Stationary Office.

National Audit Office. (2008). *Promoting Healthier Lifestyles for Prisoners*. London: National Audit Office.

National Audit Office. (2010). *Managing Offenders on Short Custodial Sentences*. London: National Audit Office.

National Audit Office. (2012). *The London 2012 Olympic Games and Paralympic Games: Post-Games Review*. London: National Audit Office.

National Children's Bureau. (2008). *Delivering Every Child Matters in Secure Settings: A Practical Toolkit for Improving the Health and Well-Being of Young People*. London, National Children's Bureau.

National Correctional Recreation Association. (1995). *NCRA Position Statement on Weight Lifting Programs in Correctional Settings*. Retrieved from: http://www.strengthtech.com/correct/ncra/ncra.htm#position

National Offender Management Service. (2005). *Understanding Research Methods and Findings*, 'What Works' Briefing 3/05. London: Ministry of Justice.

National Offender Management Service. (2012a). *Business Plan 2012–2013*. London: NOMS.

National Offender Management Service. (2012b). *Equalities Annual Report 2011/12*. London: NOMS.

National Offender Management Service. (2012c). *NOMS Commissioning Intentions for 2013–14: Negotiation Document*. London: Ministry of Justice.

Nelson, M., Specian, V., Tracy, N., and DeMello, J. (2006). The effects of moderate physical activity on offenders in rehabilitative program. *Journal of Correctional Education*, 57, 4, 276–285.

Newburn, T. and Stanko, E. (Eds.) (1994). *Just Boys Doing Business? Men, Masculinities and Crime.* Abingdon: Routledge.

Newberry, A. and Duncan, R. (2001). Roles of boredom and life goals in juvenile delinquency. *Journal of Applied Social Psychology,* 31, 3, 527–541.

NHS National Treatment Agency for Substance Misuse (2011). *Service Case Study Prison Drug Recovery Wing Bristol: Drug Strategy Outcome: A Reduction in Crime and Reoffending.* Retrieved from: http://www.nta.nhs.uk/uploads/bristolwing.pdf

Nichols, G (1997). A consideration of why active participation in sport and leisure might reduce criminal behaviour. *Sport, Education and Society,* 2, 2, 181–190.

Nichols, G. (2007). *Sport and Crime Reduction: The Role of Sports in Tackling Youth Crime.* Abingdon: Routledge.

Nichols, G. and Crow, I. (2004). Measuring the impact of crime reduction interventions involving sports activities for young people. *The Howard Journal,* 43, 3, 267–283.

Nichols, G. and Taylor, P. (1996). *West Yorkshire Sports Counselling: Final Evaluation Report.* Sheffield: University of Sheffield Management Unit.

Nurse, J., Woodcock, P. and Ormsby, J. (2003). Influence of environmental factors on mental health within prisons: focus group study. *British Medical Journal,* 327, 480–485.

O'Brien, M., Mortimer, L., Singleton, N. and Meltzer, H. (2001). *Psychiatric Morbidity Among Women Prisoners in England and Wales.* London: Office for National Statistics.

Office for National Statistics (2012). *Ethnicity and National Identity in England and Wales 2011.* London: ONS.

O'Donnell, I. and Edgar, K. (1998). *Bullying in Prisons.* Oxford: Centre for Criminological Research, University of Oxford.

O'Hagan, S. (2011). *Shannon Trust, West Midlands Reading Network Pilot 2008–2010 Final Report.* London: Shannon Trust.

Olaitan, S., Shnaila, H., Sikiru, L. and Lawal, I. (2009). Correlates of selected indices of physical fitness and duration of incarceration among inmates in some selected Nigerian prisons. *Ethiopia Journal of Health Science,* 20, 1, 65–69.

Ozano, K.A. (2008). *The Role of Physical Education, Sport and Exercise in a Female Prison.* Unpublished MSc dissertation, University of Chester.

Paffenbarger, R., Blair, S., Lee, I. and Hyde, R. (1993). Measurement of physical activity to assess health effects in free-living populations. *Medicine and Science in Sports and Exercise,* 25, 1, 60–70.

Parke, S. (2009). *Children and Young People in Custody 2006–2008: An Analysis of the Experiences of 15–18-Year-Olds in Prison.* HM Inspectorate of Prisons/Youth Justice Board.

Parker, A. and Meek, R. (2013). Sport, physical activity and youth imprisonment. In A. Parker and D. Vinson (Eds.), *Youth Sport, Physical Activity and Play.* Abingdon: Routledge.

Passmore, A., and French, D. (2001). Development and administration of a measure to assess adolescents' participation in leisure activities. *Adolescence,* 36, 141, 67–75.

Patel, K. (2010). *Reducing Drug-Related Crime and Rehabilitating Offenders, Recovery and Rehabilitation for Drug Users in Prison and on Release: Recommendations for Action.* London: Prison Drug Treatment Strategy Review Group.

Patterson, I. and Coleman, D. (1996). The impact of stress on different leisure dimensions. *Journal of Applied Recreation Research,* 21, 3, 243–263.

Penney, D. (2002). *Gender and Physical Education: Contemporary Issues and Future Directions.* Abingdon: Routledge.

Pfefferbaum, B. and Wood, P. (1994). Self-report study of impulsive and delinquent behavior in college students. *Journal of Adolescent Health,* 15, 295–302.

Phillips, J. and Springer, F. (1992). *Extended National Youth Sports Program 1991–1992 Evaluation Highlights, Part Two: Individual Protective Factors Index (IPFI) and Risk Assessment Study*. Report prepared for the National Collegiate Athletic Association. Sacramento, CA: EMT Associates.

Plugge, E. Douglas, N. and Fizpatrick, R. (2006). *The Health of Women in Prison Study Findings*. Oxford: Department of Public Health, University of Oxford.

Plugge, E., Foster, C., Yudkin, P. and Douglas, N. (2009). Cardiovascular disease risk factors and women prisoners in the UK: the impact of imprisonment. *Health Promotion International*, 24, 4, 334–343.

Plugge, E., Neale, J., Dawes, H., Foster, C. and Wright, N. (2011). Drug using offenders' beliefs and preferences about physical activity: implications for future interventions. *International Journal of Prisoner Health*, 7, 1, 18–27.

Power, C. (2004). *Room to Roam: England's Irish Travellers*. London: The Community Fund.

Prison Reform Trust. (2008). *Doing Time: The Experiences and Needs of Older People in Prison*. London: Prison Reform Trust.

Prison Reform Trust. (2012). *Women in Prison*. London: Prison Reform Trust.

Prisoners on the Move. (2012). *Final Report*. Retrieved from: http://www.prisonerson themove.eu

Prisons and Probation Ombudsman (2011). *Annual Report 2010–2011*. London: COI.

Prochaska, J. and DiClemente, C. (1986). Toward a comprehensive model of change. In W. Heather (Ed.), *Treating Addictive Behaviors: Processes of Change* (pp. 3–27). New York: Plenum.

Pugh, D. (1994). Revision and further assessments of the prison locus of control scale. *Psychological Reports*, 74, 979–986.

Putnam, R. (2000). *Bowling Alone: The Collapse and Revival of American Community*. New York: Simon and Schuster.

Ravizza, D. (2011). We don't play war anymore: sport and the reintegration of former child soldiers in Northern Uganda. In W. Bennett and K. Gibert (Eds.), *Sport for Peace and Development*. Champaign, IL: Common Group Publishers.

Ravizza, D. and Motonak, E. (2011). *Peaceful Play: Guidelines for Conflict in Sport and Strategies for Resolution*. Centre for Conflict Resolution: Salisbury University.

Resnicow, K., Yarah, A., Davis, A., Wong, D., Carter, S., Slaughter, L., Coelman, D. and Baranowski, J. (2000). Go girls!: Results from a nutrition and physical activity programme for low income, overweight African American adolescent females. *Health, Education and Behaviour,* 27, 5, 616–631.

Resodihardjo, S. (2009). *Crisis and Change in the British and Dutch Prison Services: Understanding Crisis-Reform Processes*. Farnham: Ashgate Publishing.

Richman, E. and Shaffer, D. (2000). 'If you let me play sport': How might sport participation influence the self-esteem of adolescent females? *Psychology of Women Quarterly,* 24, 2, 189–199.

Robbins, L., Puder, N. and Kazonis, A. (2003). Barriers to physical activity perceived by adolescent girls. *Journal of Midwifery and Woman's Health* 48, 3, 206–212.

Robins, D. (1990). *Sport as Prevention: The Role of Sport in Crime Prevention Programmes Aimed at Young People*. Centre for Criminological Research occasional paper no. 12. Oxford: University of Oxford.

Rodriguez, J., Keene, J. and Li, X. (2006). The substantial service demands of offenders and frequent offenders. *European Journal of Criminology*, 3, 149.

Rollnick, S. and Miller, W. (2002). *Motivational Interviewing: Preparing People for Change*. New York: Guilford Press.

Rosenberg, M. (1989). *Society and the Adolescent Self-Image*. CT: Wesleyan University Press.

Ross, M. (2013). *Health and Health Promotion in Prisons*. Abingdon: Routledge.

Ross, R. and Fabiano, E. (1985). *Time to Think: A Cognitive Model of Delinquency Prevention and Offender Rehabilitation*. Johnson City, TN: Institute of Social Sciences and Arts.

Russell, G. (2008). *Aggression in the Sports World: A Social Psychological Perspective*. New York: Oxford University Press.

Rutten, A., Abu-Omar, K., Frahsa, A. and Morgan, A. (2009). Assets for policy making in health promotion: overcoming political barriers inhibiting women in difficult life situations to access sports facilities. *Social Science and Medicine*, 69, 667–1673.

Rutten, E., Stams, G., Biesta, G., Schuengel, C., Dirks, E. and Hoeksma, J. (2007). The contribution of organised youth sport in antisocial and prosocial behaviour in adolescent athletes. *Journal of Youth and Adolescence*, 36, 255–264.

Ryder, S. (2013). Why are the labels 'offender' and 'ex-offender' so offensive? *Discovering Desistance: An ESRC Knowledge Exchange Project*. Retrieved from: http://blogs.iriss.org.uk/discoveringdesistance/2013/02/11/820/

Sabo, D. (2001). Doing time, doing masculinity: sports and prison. In D. Sabo, T. Kupers and W. London, (Eds.) *Prison Masculinities* (pp. 61–66). Philadelphia, PA: Temple University Press.

Sadlier, G. (2010). *Evaluation of the Impact of the HM Prison Service Enhanced Thinking Skills Programme on Reoffending. Outcomes of Surveying Prisoner Crime Reduction (SPCR) Sample*. Research Services 19/10. London: Ministry of Justice.

Salisbury, J. and Jackson, D. (1996). *Challenging Macho Values: Practical Ways of Working with Adolescent Boys*. London: Falmer Press.

Sandford, R., Armour, K. and Warmington, P. (2006). Re-engaging disaffected youth through physical activity programmes. *British Educational Research Journal*, 32, 2, 251–271.

Schaenman, P., Davies, E., Jordan, R. and Chakraborty, R. (2013). *Opportunities for Cost Savings in Corrections Without Sacrificing Service Quality: Inmate Health Care*. Washington: The Urban Institute.

Schafer, W. (1969). Participation in interscholastic athletics and delinquency: a preliminary study. *Social Problems*, 17, 1, 40–47.

Sechrist, K., Walker, S. and Pender, N. (1987). Development and psychometric evaluation of the exercise benefits/barriers scale. *Research in Nursing and Health*, 10, 357–365.

Segar, M., Jayaratne, T., Hanlon, J. and Richardson. C. (2002). Fitting fitness into women's lives: effects of a gender-tailored physical activity intervention. *Women's Health Issues*, 12, 6, 338–347.

Sharpe, C., Schagen, I. and Scott, E. (2004). *Playing for Success: The Longer Term Impact*. London: Department for Education and Science / National Foundation for Educational Research.

Sheffield Hallam University. (2012). *Resettlement of Women (Ex) Offenders*. Retrieved from: hyyp://shu.ac.uk/assets/[df/hccj-resettlement.pdf

Shepherd, A. and Whiting, E. (2006). *Reoffending of Adults: Results from the 2003 Cohort*. Home Office Statistical Bulletin 20/06. London: NOMS.

Sherer, M. and Adams, C. (1983). Construct validation of the self-efficacy scale. *Psychological Reports*, 53, 899–902.

Sherry, E. (2010). *Port Phillip Prison Street Soccer Program Research Report*. Centre for Sport and Social Impact: La Trobe University.

Sherry, E. (2012). *The Big Issue Community Street Soccer Program Townsville Women's Correctional Centre Evaluation Report January 2012*. Centre for Sport and Social Impact: La Trobe University.

Shevlin, M., Miles, J., Davies, M. and Walker, S. (1998). Coefficient alpha: a useful indicator of reliability? *Personality and Individual Differences*, 28, 229–237.

Shields, D. and Bredemeier, B. (1995). *Character Development and Physical Activity*. Champaign, IL: Human Kinetics.

Shover, N. (1996). *Great Pretenders: Pursuits and Careers of Persistent Thieves*. Boulder, CO: Westview Press.

Sidney, K. (1987). Attitudinal changes of correctional service officers following an on-site physical exercise programme. *Canadian Journal of Sports Science*, 12, 2, 83–90.

Silverman, S. J. and Hajela, R. (2012). *Briefing: Immigration Detention in the UK*. The Immigration Observatory: University of Oxford.

Sim, J. (1994). Tougher than the rest? Men in prison. In T. Newburn and E. Stanko (Eds.), *Just Boys Doing Business? Men, Masculinities and Crime*. Abingdon: Routledge.

Sim J. (2002). The future of prison health care: A critical analysis. *Critical Social Policy*, 22, 2, 300–323.

Sim, J. (2008). Pain and punishment: the real and the imaginary in penal institutions. In P. Carlen (Ed.), *Imaginary Penalities*. Cullompton: Willan.

Slater, A. and Tiggemann, M. (2011). Gender differences in adolescent sport participation, teasing, self-objectification and body image concerns. *Journal of Adolescence*, 34, 3, 455–463.

Smith, A. and Waddington, I. (2004). Using 'sport in the community schemes' to tackle crime and drug use among young people: some policy issues and problems. *European Physical Education Review*, 10, 3, 279–298.

Social Exclusion Unit. (2002). *Reducing Reoffending by Ex-Prisoners*. London: Cabinet Office.

Spandler, H. and McKeown, M. (2012). A critical exploration of using football in health and welfare programs: gender, masculinities and social relations. *Journal of Sport and Social Issues*, 36, 4, 387–409.

Sport England. (2012). *Sport Participation Factsheet: Summary of Results for England*. London: Sport England.

Sporting Equals. (2010). *BME Sports Participation: Results from the Active People Survey*. Birmingham: Sporting Equals.

Stark, R., Kent, L., Finke, R. (1987). Sports and delinquency. In M. Gottfredson and T. Hirschi (Eds.), *Positive Criminology* (pp. 115–124). Newbury Park: Sage.

Stephens, D. and Bredemeier, B. (1996). Moral atmosphere and judgments about aggression in girls' soccer: relationships among moral and motivational variables. *Journal of Sport and Exercise Psychology*, 18, 158–173.

Stewart, D. (2008a). Drug use and perceived treatment need among newly sentenced prisoners in England and Wales. *Addiction*, 104, 243–247.

Stewart, D. (2008b). *The Problems and Needs of Newly Sentenced Prisoners: Results from a National Survey*, London: Ministry of Justice.

Stidder, G. and Hayes, S. (Eds.) (2012). *Equity and Inclusion in Physical Education and Sport*. Abingdon: Routledge.

Stoot, S. (2002). Socialisation and participation in sport. In A. Laker (Ed.), *The Sociology of Sport and Physical Education* (pp. 129–147). Abingdon: Routledge.

Stöver, H. and Thane, K. (2011). *Towards a Continuum of Care in the EU Criminal Justice System. A Survey of Prisoner Needs in Four Countries (Estonia, Hungary, Lithuania, Poland)* (Vol. 20). Oldenburg: Oldenburg University.

Sugden, J. and Yiannakis, A. (1982). Sport and juvenile delinquency: a theoretical base. *Journal of Sport and Social Issues*, 6, 1, 22–30.

Summerfield, A. (2011). *Children and Young People in Custody 2010–2011. An Analysis of the Experiences of 15–18 Year Olds in Prison*. HM Inspectorate of Prisons/Youth Justice Board. London: The Stationary Office.

Swain, A. and Jones, G. (1993). Intensity and frequency dimensions of competitive state anxiety. *Journal of Sports Sciences*, 11, 533–542.

Swain, J. (2000). 'The money's good, the fame's good, the girls are good': the role of playground football in the construction of young boys' masculinity in junior school. *British Journal of Sociology of Education*, 21, 95–109.

Sykes, G. (1958). *The Society of Captives*. Princeton, NJ: Princeton University Press.

Tacon, R. (2007). Football and social inclusion: evaluating social policy. *Managing Leisure*, 12, 1, 1–23.

Tajfel, H. and Turner, J. (1986). The social identity theory of intergroup behaviour. In S. Worchel and W. Austin (Eds.), *Psychology of Intergroup Relations*. Chicago: Nelson Hall.

Talbot, J. (2008). *Prisoners Voices: Experiences of the Criminal Justice System by Prisoners with Learning Disabilities and Difficulties*. London: Prison Reform Trust.

Talbot, J. (2011). Prisoners with learning disabilities and learning difficulties. *Prison Service Journal*, 195, 29–34.

Talleu, C. (2011). Links between the sports movement and prisons. *Sport and Citizenship*, 17, 20.

Taylor, P., Crow, I., Irvine, D. and Nichols, G. (1999) *Demanding Physical Activity Programmes for Young Offenders Under Probation Supervision*. London: Home Office Research, Development and Statistics Publications.

Taylor Gibbs, J. and Merighi, J. (1994). Young Black males: marginality, masculinity and criminality. In T. Newburn and E. Stanko (Eds.), *Just Boys Doing Business? Men, Masculinities and Crime*. Abingdon: Routledge.

Tesu-Rollier, D. (2008). Sport and therapeutic alliance in prison. *Annales Medico-Psychologiques*, 155, 865–869.

Teufel, T. and Kroger, W. (2011). *Felon Fitness: How to Get a Hard Body Without Doing Hard Time*. Avon, MA: Adams Media.

Tezenas du Montcel, M. (2013). Sport in the workplace. *Sport and Citizenship*, 22, 11. Health and Social Care Information Centre. (2006). *Statistics on Smoking: England 2006*. Retrieved from: www.hscic.gov.uk

Theokas, C., Danish, S., Hodge, K., Heke, I. and Forneris, T. (2007). Enhancing life skills through sport for children and youth. In N. Holt (Ed.), *Positive Youth Development through Sport* (pp. 71–81). Abingdon: Routledge.

Thomas, C. (1977). Theoretical perspectives on prisonization: a comparison of the importation and deprivation models. *Journal of Criminal Law and Criminology*, 68, 135–145.

Thompson, J., Jago, R., Brockman, R., Cartwright, K., Page, A. and Fox, K. (2010). Physically active families – debunking the myth? A qualitative study of family participation in physical activity. *Child: Care, Health and Development*, 36, 2, 265–274.

Thompson, M. (1990). Sport aggression questionnaire (SAQ). In A. Ostrow (Ed.), *Directory of Psychological Tests in the Sport and Exercise Sciences*. West Virginia: Fitness Information Technology.

TNS. (2011). *Encouraging involvement in Big Society: Cultural and Sporting Perspective*. JN219002 November 2011 V2.

Toch, H. (1998). Hypermasculinity and prison violence. In L. Bowker (Ed.), *Masculinities and Violence*. Thousand Oaks, CA: Sage.

Tomlinson, A. (2004). Pierre Bourdieu and the sociological study of sport: habitus, capital and field. In R. Guilanotti (Ed.), *Sport and Modern Social Theorists* (pp. 161–172). London: Palgrave Macmillan.

Townsend, M., Moore, J. and Mahoney, M. (2002). Playing their part: the role of physical activity and sport in sustaining the health and well being of small rural communities. *International Electronic Journal of Rural and Remote Health Research, Education, Practice and Policy*, 2, 1, 1–6.

Trejos-Castillo, E. Vazsonyi, A. and Jenkins, D. (2008). Violent and criminal behaviours in rural and non-rural African American youth: a risk-protective factor approach. *Southern Rural Sociology*, 23, 2, 108–130.

Trulson, E. (1986). Martial arts training: a novel 'cure' for juvenile delinquency. *Human Relations*, 39, 1131–1140.

Tsuchiya, M. (1996). Leisure recreation programmes for young delinquents: the non-custodial option. In M. Collins (Ed.), *Leisure in Industrial and Post-Industrial Societies* (pp. 287–302). Eastbourne: Leisure Studies Association.

Tucker, L. (1983). Weight training: a tool for the improvement of self and body concepts of males. *Journal of Human Movement Studies*, 9, 31–37.

Tye, D. (2009). *Children and Young People in Custody 2008–2009. An Analysis of the Experiences of 15–18 Year Olds in Prison*. HM Inspectorate of Prisons Youth Justice Board.

Tyler, T. (1990). *Why People Obey the Law*. New Haven, CT: Yale University Press.

Uggen, C., Manza, J. and Behrens, A. (2004). Less than the average citizen: stigma, role transition and the civic reintegration of convicted felons. In S. Maruna and R. Immarigeon (Eds.), *After Crime and Punishment: Pathways to Offender Reintegration* (pp. 261–293). Cullompton: Willan.

UNICEF. (2011). *Rugby as a Tool for Rehabilitation and Reintegration*. Retrieved from: www.unicef.org/georgia/media_18249.html

United Nations (1989). *United Nations Convention on the Rights of the Child*. Geneva: United Nations.

United Nations Commission for Human Rights (2006). *Treatment of Prisoners*. Retrieved from: www.unodc.org/pdf/compendium/compendium_2006_part_01_01.pdf

Utting, D. (1996). *Reducing Criminality among Young People: A Sample of Relevant Programmes in the United Kingdom*. London: Home Office Research and Statistics Directorate.

Vallerand, R.J., Deshaies, P., Cuerrier, J.P. (1997). On the effects of the social context on behavioral intentions of sportsmanship. *International Journal of Sport Psychology*, 28, 26–140.

van Zyl, D. and Snacken, S. (2002). *Principals of European Prison Law and Policy. Penology and Human Rights*. Oxford: Oxford University Press.

Verdot, C., Champely, S., Clement, M., and Massarelli, R. (2010). Physical practice as a means to limit the noxious effects of prison confinement: impact of a physical program on prisoners' perceived health and psychological well-being. *Psychologie Du Travail et Des Organisations*, 16, 1, 63–78.

Verhoef, M., Love, E. and Rose, M. (1992). Women's social roles and their exercise participation. Women Health, 19, 14–29.

Wade, P. (2009). *Convict Conditioning*. St. Paul: Dragon Door Publications.

Wagner, M., McBride, R. and Crouse, S. (1999). The effects of weight-training exercise on aggression variables in adult male inmates. *Prison Journal*, 79, 1, 72–89.

Walker, J. (2005). The Maudsley Violence Questionnaire: initial validation and reliability. *Personality and Individual Differences*, 38, 187–201.

Walker, J. and Gudjonsson, G. (2006). The Maudsley Violence Questionnaire: relationship to personality and self-reported offending. *Personality and Individual Differences*, 40, 795–806.

Warnock-Parkes, E., Gudjonsson, G. and Walker, J. (2008). The relationships between the Maudsley Violence Questionnaire and official recordings of violence in mentally disordered offenders. *Personality and Individual Differences, 44, 833–841.*

Waters, G. (2003). Changes in criminal thinking and identity in novice and experienced inmates. *Criminal Justice and Behaviour*, 30, 399–421.

Watson, P. and Morris, R. (1991). Narcissism, empathy and social desirability. *Personality and Individual Differences*, 12, 575–579.

Webster, I., Porritt, D. and Brennan, J. (2010). Reported health, life style and occupational stress in prison officers. *Community Health Studies*, 7, 3, 266–277.

Weeks, J. (1993). Offender typologies: incentivising treatment – relevant personality characteristics. *Research on Offender Programming Issues*, 5, 10–12.

Weinberger, D. (1997). Distress and self-restraint as measures of adjustment across the life span: confirmatory factor analyses in clinical and nonclinical samples. *Psychological Assessment*, 9, 2, 132–135.

Weinberger, D. and Schwartz, G. (1990). Distress and restraint as superordinate dimensions of adjustment: a typological perspective. *Journal of Personality*, 8, 2, 381–417.

Wellard, I. (2002). Men, sport body performance and the maintenance of 'exclusive masculinity'. *Leisure Studies*, 21, 3–4, 235–247.

Wellard, I. (2009). *Sport, Masculinities and the Body*. Abingdon: Routledge.

Werch, C., Moore, M., DiClemente, C., Bledsoe, R. and Jobli, E. (2005). A multi health behaviour intervention integrating physical activity and substance use prevention for adolescents. *Prevention Science*, 6, 3, 213–226.

West, S. and Crompton, J. (2001). A review of the impact of adventure programs on at-risk youth. *Journal of Park and Recreation Administration*, 19, 113–140.

Whitehead, S. and Barrett, F. (Eds.) (2001). *The Masculinities Reader*. Cambridge: Polity Press.

Wichmann, T. (1990). *Interpersonal Problem Solving and Asocial Behavior in a Therapeutic Wilderness Program*. Unpublished doctoral dissertation, Southern Illinois University.

Women's Sport Foundation. (1998). *Reports: Sport and Teen Pregnancy*. New York: Women's Sports Foundation.

World Health Organisation (WHO). (2007). *Health in Prisons: A WHO Guide to the Essentials in Prison Health*. Copenhagen, Denmark: WHO.

Woodall, J. (2010). Working with prisoners and young offenders. In D. Conrad and A. White (Eds.), *Promoting Men's Health* (pp. 195–203). Oxford: Radcliff Publishing.

Woodward, K. (2012). *Planet Sport*. Abingdon: Routledge.

Wright, N., Bleakley, A., Butt, C., Chadwick, O., Mahmood, K., Patel, K. and Salhi, A. (2011). Peer health promotion in prisons: a systematic review. *International Journal of Prisoner Health*, 7, 4, 37–51.

Wroblewska, A-M. (1997). Androgenic-anabolic steroids and body dysmorphia in young men. *Journal of Psychosomatic Research*, 42, 3, 225–234.

Yesalis, C. (2000). *Anabolic Steroids in Sport and Exercise*. Champaign, IL: Human Kinetics.

Young, S., Misch, P., Collins, P. and Gudjonsson, G. (2011). Predictors of institutional behavioural disturbance and offending in the community among young offenders. *Journal of Forensic Psychiatry and Psychology*, 22, 72–86.

Youth Justice Board. (2002). *The National Specification for Learning and Skills for Young People on a Detention or Training Order in Prison Service Accommodation.* London: Youth Justice Board.

Youth Justice Board. (2013). *Youth Custody Data: Monthly Youth Custody Report, Table 2.2 Population.* London: Youth Justice Board.

Zamble, E. and Quinsey, V. (1997). *The Criminal Recidivism Process.* Cambridge: Cambridge University Press.

Zhen, S., Xie, H., Zhang, W., Wang, S. and Li, D. (2011). Exposure to violent computer games and Chinese adolescents' physical aggression, hostile expectations and empathy. *Computers in Human Behaviour*, 27, 5, 1675–1687.

Zuckerman, M. (1991). Sensation seeking: the balance between risk and reward. In L. Lipsitt and L. Mitnick (Eds.), *Self Regulatory Behavior and Risk Taking: Causes and Consequences* (pp. 143–152). Norwood, NJ: Ablex Publishing Corporation.

Index